YALE STUDIES IN POLITICAL SCIENCE, 5

DAVID HORNE, EDITOR

PUBLISHED UNDER THE DIRECTION OF
THE DEPARTMENT OF POLITICAL SCIENCE

GERMAN ADMINISTRATION SINCE BISMARCK

CENTRAL AUTHORITY VERSUS LOCAL AUTONOMY

BY HERBERT JACOB

NEW HAVEN AND LONDON, YALE UNIVERSITY PRESS, 1963

74299

To My Mother and Father

FOREWORD

Professor Jacob has written a book that can stand by itself with no difficulty. It is a lucid and important analysis of the development of German field administration over the past century. The author has engaged himself—and the reader—in a quest for the conditions that promoted or weakened administrative responsiveness under Germany's remarkably varied regimes. The book can be read then as a valuable contribution to the understanding of German history and of the contemporary Germany that is the product of that history.

At the same time Mr. Jacob contributes an important building block to an undertaking of broader scope: a comparative study of field administration in England, France, Germany, Italy, and the United States. A grant to Yale University by the Carnegie Corporation of New York supported the initial phase of the comparative study, and specifically financed Mr. Jacob's field research in Germany, and that in Italy of Robert C. Fried, whose book, *The Italian Prefects,* is being published simultaneously by the Yale University Press.

The present volume illustrates several ways in which the larger project may serve to invite exploration of several new, forgotten, or seldom-trod avenues toward understanding the governing process. Though politics and policy and their social and economic context are never long absent from Mr. Jacob's consciousness, this is primarily a study of administration, and more of how subordinates can (or cannot) be depended on to execute higher-level decisions than of how they may engage in the shaping of broad national policies. Neglect of administration, in favor of focusing on policy and the processes for its formation, has recently characterized the distribution of energies in political science, as it has the technical assistance programs for developing countries. Here, for Germany, is a revealing explanation of how a succession of governments, heirs to a tradition that laid stress on administrative efficiency and order, organized themselves to assure responsiveness by bureaucratic agents in the field.

A second characteristic of the book is that it is a richly informed analysis of institutions on a macroscopic scale. The new enthusiasm for comparative administration as a field of study, several judicious critics have noted, has initially stimulated more construction of research designs and theoretical models than assembly and analysis of empirical data from real countries. And the thrust of the behavioral 'revolution' in political science has perhaps unduly demeaned the role of institutions. Mr. Jacob, while attentive to such model-suggested clues as 'responsiveness'—which is also a behavioral property of human beings—uses these clues in order to organize and interpret his abundant data. Furthermore he makes it apparent that an institution, like a structurally sound house, may survive a succession of tenants whose individual values and idiosyncrasies temporarily invest the structure with a special atmosphere.

A third striking characteristic is that a political scientist is organizing his study along a historical continuum. The fact that at most universities American political science attained status in its own right by detaching itself from the department of history may in part explain our failure to draw on the wealth of man's recorded governmental experience. Mr. Jacob's study admirably reveals the compatibility of historical data with the analytical styles prevalent in modern political science. He displays four national governmental systems—the Second Reich, the Weimar Republic, the Third Reich, and the German Federal Republic. These can be treated separately and comparatively almost as if they were four national governments simultaneously operating in different countries. But an advantage is gained for scientific study in that some of the more troublesome independent variables can be held relatively constant—the people, the geography, the resources, the culture, and the occupational status of such pursuits as public administration. To be sure, changes in these elements are as important as their constancy, but the chances for error in noting variations may be less than in simultaneous comparison of such different polities as, say, the contemporary American, British, French, and German.

More importantly, the historical mode of approach to an analytical problem in political science reintroduces a dynamic concept of organic development at a time when social scientists are finding static models severely limited as instruments for epitomizing the ideal or typical behavior of social institutions. A study of field administration perforce establishes that governments move in space. The present study assumes that governments also move in time.

The specific contribution of German experience to a comparative assessment of field administration systems can be determined only as studies of other countries' experience accumulates. The two most distinctive features of German field administration, however, lend special significance to the present study. The German governmental system has been basically federal or confederal, with the exception of the Nazi period. And field administration for the national government's functions has been for the most part not a responsibility of the national bureaucracy but instead has been in the hands of the constituent states or Laender. How so structurally decentralist a system could be compatible with a national regime like that of Kaiser Wilhelm II, prove a handicap to the liberal regime of the Weimar period, succumb to totalitarianism under Hitler, and then revive under Adenauer is a fascinating problem for the student of field administration. If he did not know the facts he would probably have underestimated their probability. But Mr. Jacob knows the German system, and it is the reader's privilege to have so sure a guide through its intricacies.

JAMES W. FESLER

New Haven, Connecticut

PREFACE

The intellectual debts of a young scholar are always numerous; in my case they are legion. I am indebted to the hundreds of scholars cited in the text; the chapter on the Bonn Republic could not have been written without the cooperation of various German officials who consented to lengthy interviews. Numerous libraries also aided the author. My thanks go particularly to the staffs of the Staatsbibliothek of Munich, and of the libraries of the University of Cologne, Yale University, and Tulane University. I have benefited greatly from the advice of many colleagues, especially Fred I. Greenstein, James D. Barber, Rufus P. Browning, L. V. Howard, and Henry L. Mason. The book is the result of a suggestion by Professor James W. Fesler of Yale University; without the generosity of his advice and encouragement, this study would not have reached fruition.

Finally, I gratefully acknowledge financial assistance from several sources. A Carnegie Foundation grant to Yale University enabled the author and his wife to live nine months in Germany while conducting the research for this book. A fellowship from the Social Science Research Council gave the author a year free from academic obligations in order to write an earlier version which served as a doctoral dissertation submitted to the Graduate School of

Yale University. A grant from the Tulane University Research Council helped defray the expenses of typing the manuscript.

To all those listed and to many more go my heartfelt thanks. The errors of fact and judgment that remain stand witness to the stubbornness of the author.

A word is necessary about the geographic scope of this study and the sources upon which I have drawn. The administrative organization of the Reich and Prussian governments form the basis of our discussion for the period 1871–1945. These two governments not only ruled most areas of Germany but also set the pattern for field administration in the other German Laender. Some of these Laender admittedly had long histories of independent existence; the problems they faced and the solutions they found in some instances differed from the Reich and Prussian experience. Examination of administration in every larger Land, however, would have lengthened this study inordinately. Moreover, so little literature exists about the administrative development of Baden, Wuerttemberg, Saxony, and Bavaria that each of these would have required a research effort equal to that expended for this study.

The sources I have used to examine Reich and Prussian administration from 1871 to 1945 are a combination of all available published monographs on administration, political, economic, and administrative histories, memoirs of leading politicians and administrators, official handbooks, and archival materials. They are fully cited in the extensive notes in each chapter.

The examination of field administration after 1945 is limited to developments in the Western occupation zones and the Federal Republic of Germany. Once more I have examined official documents and the limited other published materials available. However, the primary source of information for the postwar development of German field administration is a series of interviews with field officials conducted by the author in Germany. Because it was not possible to conduct this kind of investigation in Eastern Germany, the study remains limited to developments in the West.

The extensive scope of this study as well as the lack of previous investigations of German field administration forced me to resist many temptations to examine the administrative procedures of particular agencies in greater detail. When appropriate, I have indicated where further intensive study might be particularly fruitful.

The purpose of this study will be fulfilled if it meets two criteria. First, it should clarify a segment of German political development that has been neglected both by Germans and by others. Second, it should demonstrate the nature of the obstacles that hinder the attainment of a responsive field administration when a nation quickly develops into an industrialized, urban society and undergoes the political tensions that often accompany such transformations. Examination of Germany provides exceptionally interesting case materials, for Germany not only went through such a development but also experimented with four different regimes while doing so. The German experience, therefore, furnishes rich and varied materials to begin the analysis of the development of field administration in a changing society.

H. J.

New Orleans, Louisiana
February 1962

ABBREVIATIONS

a.D.	*Ausser Dienst* (retired)
ALVG	*Allgemeines Landesverwaltungsgesetz* (General Code, for Prussia)
BFBl	*Bundesfinanzblatt* (Federal Revenue Code Gazette)
BGBl	*Bundesgesetzblatt* (Federal Legal Gazette)
GBl	*Gesetzblatt* (Legal Gazette, of various Laender)
GS	*Gesetzsammlung* (Legal Gazette, of Prussia)
GVBl	*Gesetz und Verwaltungsblatt* (Legal and Administrative Gazette)
IMT	International Military Tribunal (Nuremberg Trial Documents)
LKO	*Landkreisordnung* (County Charter Law)
RABl	*Reichsarbeitsblatt* (National Labor Law Gazette)
RFBl	*Reichsfinanzblatt* (National Revenue Code Gazette)
RFFSS&CdDP	*Reichsfuehrer SS und Chef der Deutsche Polizei* (Himmler's title as chief of the SS and German police)
RGBl	*Reichsgesetzblatt* (National Legal Gazette)
RMBliV	*Reichsministerialblatt fuer des innere Verwaltung* (Gazette of the National Ministry of Interior)
SA	*Sturmabteilung* (Storm Troopers)
SD	*Sicherheitsdienst* (Nazi party security service)
SS	*Schutzstaffel* (Black Shirts)

CONTENTS

1. THE SOCIAL AND GOVERNMENTAL CONTEXT OF FIELD ADMINISTRATION

Government and politics are often described with the vocabulary of dramatic conflict. The struggle for domination, the clash over issues, the conflict over policy formation rightly attract interest from students of government. Behind these dramatic scenes, however, lesser skirmishes with equally important results are continually waged within factions of political parties, inside legislative halls and lobbies, and within the great complex called the administration.

The administrative process—indeed only one phase of it—is the focus of this essay. Every regime faces the troublesome task of making certain that its policies are translated into action rather than remaining paper mandates. This requires stationing government officials outside the capital, that is, in the "field." Such field officials must be given enough flexibility to carry out programs as they see fit so they can meet the variety of local conditions that exist in all countries. They must also be permitted to initiate local policies to meet the peculiar problems of their locale. At the same time, the central government must retain sufficient control over its field agents to assure full-fledged execution of national programs, for they are removed from direct contact with central officials. Indeed, they often work in environments that promote parochialism or even hostility to the central regime. The central government must also make certain that local programs remain compatible with national policies. These conflicting demands constitute the setting for one of the universal problems of field administration—the quest for responsiveness.

Most previous examinations of this problem study it in terms of the degree of centralization or decentralization present in the administrative system.[1] They seek to determine where decisions are made. When the central government or ministry decides most questions, the system is called centralized; when most problems are left to local decision-makers, it is a decentralized system. The difficulty with this approach is that it assumes that one can locate the decision-maker with relative accuracy. It directs one to look for documentary evidence showing who had the final say on a particular matter. In practice, however, many decisions are not "made"; they happen.[2] Each level of a hierarchy takes tentative actions that may or may not be overruled by a superior. What appears to be a top-level decision often constitutes only the ratification of actions taken by subordinates. Thus we become unable to apply the centralization-decentralization scale with accuracy.

In speaking of responsiveness or lack of responsiveness, we avoid most such problems. Responsiveness is relatively easy to define and measure; it refers simply to the behavior of officials. When the central ministry orders action and it is performed, the field agent is responsive. When he ignores central directives, he is unresponsive. We can *define* responsiveness in terms of the extent to which the field agents execute directives within the time and in the way the central regime desires. We can *measure* the degree of responsiveness by noting the central regime's complaints in official documents, in legislative debates, and in internal correspondence about

1. See especially David B. Truman, *Administrative Decentralization* (Chicago, University of Chicago Press, 1940), and James W. Fesler, "Field Organization," in Fritz Morstein Marx, ed., *Elements of Public Administration* (1st ed. New York, Prentice-Hall, 1946), pp. 246–73. For an interesting definitional discussion see Paul Meyer, *Administrative Organization* (London, Stevens and Sons, 1957), pp. 56–61.

2. The relative nondeterminacy of decision-making is repeatedly illustrated by the cases on public administration published by the Inter-University Case Program. See for instance Harold Stein, ed., *Public Administration and Policy Development* (New York, Harcourt, Brace, 1952).

the performance of its field agents. Where complaints are rare, we assume a responsive field administration; where they are frequent, the regime lacks the degree of responsiveness it demands.

To maintain its power position, every regime requires a responsive administrative system. Sometimes the central government will make few demands on its field agents, for it is satisfied with minimal government action or is founded on a political compromise which leaves localities a high degree of autonomy. Other regimes will seek to control all phases of a country's life; they require a more active corps of field agents and will make more demands on them. To understand why a central government demands responsiveness and how it seeks to obtain it, we must, therefore, examine the nation's social and political structure.

The dimensions of the quest for responsiveness are manifold. A regime may fail to obtain responsive administration because it lacks communication facilities or trained personnel, because local agents are disloyal, or because it is unstable. Each of these problems has legal, political, social, and administrative ramifications that require close analysis.

Facile communications are a first essential for an effective administrative system. Policy-makers must be able to obtain information from their field agents about local conditions and problems in order to formulate their directives. Likewise, they must be able to communicate their orders to local agents quickly and without error if they desire their execution. Modern technology potentially increases man's ability to establish and maintain a broad communication network. The telephone and telegraph speed the communication process while modern transportation makes it possible for central officials to inspect field operations on a moment's notice. However, technical prowess is only of secondary importance, for the usefulness of these modern tools depends on how the administrative organization is structured to facilitate communications. Indeed, we can conceive of organizational structure as constituting principally a communication network.[3] To

3. Herbert Simon, *Administrative Behavior* (2d ed. New York, Macmillan, 1958), pp. 154–57; John Dorsey, "A Communication Model for Administration," *Administrative Science Quarterly*, 2 (1947), 307–24; John M. Pfiffner and Robert V. Presthus, *Public Administration* (4th ed. New York, Ronald Press, 1960), pp. 136–38.

be effective, such a network cannot randomly link one official to another; rather, it must link them in a pattern that promotes the attainment of the organization's goals. In a field administration, each local official must know to whom in the capital information must be sent in order to obtain results; likewise, the central offices must direct their messages to the local official most likely to respond appropriately.[4] Normally, such communications must follow a hierarchical pattern so that higher levels of the organization can know what each subordinate office is doing and can coordinate local actions if necessary.[5] Although simple in the abstract, the construction of a communication network that allows field agents to receive all relevant central directives and that promotes speedy communication between the field and the center is usually quite difficult. Failure to erect such a network is one of the most common barriers to responsive field administration.

Unhindered communication channels, however, do not necessarily insure effective communication, for communication involves not only sending and receiving messages but also understanding them. Where a regime rules over people who speak different languages, the central government has often adopted a special language to communicate with its officials. The most striking modern case is India where Hindi is the language of government and administration although half the people speak other languages exclusively. Likewise, colonial administrations and sometimes their native successors often adopt a single tongue to administer a multilingual nation.

Even in countries where only a single language is spoken, the administrative bureaucracy often develops its own *lingua franca,* its own jargon. Like most career professions, the civil service jargon grows from daily concern with specialized problems. It is largely for this reason that a well-trained civil service is required

4. Simon, pp. 157–62; Herbert A. Simon, Donald W. Smithburg, and Victor A. Thompson, *Public Administration* (New York, Alfred A. Knopf, 1958), pp. 219–22.

5. However, a dual system of supervision may sometimes be employed. The argument for this is best stated by W. W. MacMahon, John D. Millett, and Gladys Ogden, *The Administration of Federal Work Relief* (Chicago, University of Chicago Press, 1940), pp. 265–68; for a contrary view see James W. Fesler, *Area and Administration* (University, Ala., University of Alabama Press, 1949), pp. 73 ff.

to obtain responsive administration.[6] The education of higher civil servants is essentially an orientation into the language and structure of administrative organizations; thus, in many countries, administrative law is considered the most appropriate training for the higher civil service.[7] Such training facilitates meaningful communication between civil servants in the center and in the field, for the officials at both echelons speak the same technical language and can fully understand each other. The absence of such a common jargon will inevitably produce friction and unresponsive execution of central policies, for even if the field agents receive a policy directive through a well-ordered communication network, they may misunderstand it. Such problems occur with particular frequency when the field agents are specialists, trained in a technical skill such as engineering, medicine, or forestry. They speak their own jargon and fail to understand that of their administrative colleagues and superiors.[8] Likewise, the addition of new governmental functions often creates severe communication problems, for the agencies charged with such new duties are usually not integrated in the administrative structure and their officials are often unfamiliar with the language of administration. As such functions lose their novelty and trained civil servants take over their administration, these problems gradually decrease.

Trained civil servants facilitate responsive administration in yet another way. Such officials give a central government command over the necessary technical competence to carry out its programs. Even a century ago when governmental activities were relatively simple, technical competence was desirable. The collection of taxes always required both honesty and expertise, for the government had to be able to outwit merchants, landowners, and other taxpayers. The construction of roads, the supervision of education, the maintenance of public health required then as it does now

6. Simon, *Administrative Behavior*, pp. 169–71; Simon, Smithburg, and Thompson, pp. 229–32; James G. March and Herbert A. Simon, *Organizations* (New York, John Wiley and Sons, 1958), pp. 166–69.

7. See especially the essays in Leonard D. White, ed., *Civil Service Abroad* (New York, McGraw-Hill, 1935).

8. Fesler, *Area and Administration*, pp. 78–85, concerns himself with the problem of specialists communicating and coordinating their actions with other administrators.

both the ability to understand national policy and the technical competence to carry it out. In short, the effectiveness of national policies will always be limited by the technical capabilities of the civil servants who are to execute them. The absence of a competent civil service will hinder the quest for responsiveness.

Competence is not enough; the civil service must also be loyal to the regime.[9] Disloyalty is a particularly vexing problem in field administration, for the field agent typically works far from the capital. He is removed from many of the influences that would reinforce his identification and ties with the central regime. He sees his superiors only infrequently; he cannot participate in the pomp and ceremony of events in the capital. Rather than being one of thousands, he is the only representative of the central government in a village or one of a few score in a district center. Moreover, he is exposed to numerous alienating influences. The region he serves will try to make him *its* representative in administrative affairs; it will seek to localize his perspectives so that he becomes the region's advocate at the capital rather than the government's representative in the region. He may marry into a prominent local family; he will be invited to join local clubs; he may acquire a stake in the local economy. As as result, when local interests clash with national policy, he may seek to minimize the impact of such policies by delaying their execution, by altering their content, and, at the extreme, by disobeying central directives.

The extent to which a field administrator remains loyal often depends on whether he is a member of a career elite.[10] When he is a member of the civil service corps, he has shared educational and appenticeship experiences with the officials who serve in the central ministries. Such a common pool of experiences teaches the field agent to look at problems as a national official rather than as a local patriot. Moreover, his title and uniform set him apart

---

9. On the general problem of loyalty, see Arnold Brecht, "Bureaucratic Sabotage," *Annals of the American Academy of Political and Social Science, 189* (January 1937), 48–57; also Simon, *Administrative Behavior*, pp. 204–19. A brilliant case study of loyalty in a field agency is Herbert Kaufman, *The Forest Ranger* (Baltimore, Johns Hopkins Press, 1960); the problem in a different context is described by Merle Fainsod, *Smolensk under Soviet Rule* (Cambridge, Mass., Harvard University Press, 1958).

10. March and Simon, pp. 70–71, 73–75.

from the local population and constantly remind him of his allegiance to the capital. The leading role he typically plays at local patriotic ceremonies as *the* government representative and as a member of the ruling elite sometimes offsets his isolation and strengthens his loyalty to the regime. Finally, if he is a member of a career group, the central government may transfer him to a new locality where he has no ties to the local population and where he may operate more effectively as the agent of the national government.

Often the civil service corps constitutes not only a career but also a social elite.[11] Entrance to it is limited to sons of the wealthy, the landowners, the army, or the party faithful. Such narrow social foundations may reinforce the corps' loyalty to the regime, for it becomes the government's political ally as well as its servant. When a bureaucracy is drawn from the nobility in a monarchy, for instance, field agents feel bound to the government not only by contract but also by aristocratic tradition. Social pressures may thus be utilized to reinforce administrative measures to insure responsive administration.

Such a political alliance between the central government and a socially elite civil service, however, only benefits an established regime. A country experiencing a series of revolutions will find such a bureaucracy an additional threat to its political stability. A new regime can scarcely dismiss the civil servants; yet from their position of authority and trust, civil servants—especially field agents—may undermine confidence in the new government and hamper its attempts to initiate new domestic programs. As a result, most successful social revolutions eventually eject the old bureaucratic elite and replace it with one more sympathetic to its policy goals.[12]

An adequate communication network, the ability to make central directives understood by field agents, a trained and loyal corps of civil servants, and political stability thus constitute some of the essentials for establishing and maintaining a responsive

11. Cf. J. Donald Kingsley, *Representative Bureaucracy* (Yellow Springs, Ohio, Antioch Press, 1944).

12. For example the Russian revolution; see Merle Fainsod, *How Russia Is Ruled* (Cambridge, Mass., Harvard University Press, 1956), pp. 330–32.

field administration. Our next task is to discover the conditions under which these prerequisites may be established.

The following chapters will examine one administrative system through its tortuous development over nearly a century. Such macrocosmic analysis imposes certain limits which should be made clear at the outset. It is largely explorative; it seeks to discover the grosser relationships and to suggest some of the more subtle ones. Therefore, it cannot allow as detailed an examination of any single institution as we might like; on the other hand, it allows us to examine an administrative system as a whole rather than isolated fragments of it.

Germany is the subject of this examination, for the development of German administration offers the investigator handsome advantages in searching for the conditions that appear to promote an effective administrative system. The German bureaucrat has been a symbol of honesty and devotion; the administrative system was considered a model of efficiency. Thus we are examining what has been regarded by many as one of the world's most developed systems.

More important for our purposes are the circumstances under which German administration developed during the last century. Before 1871 Germany did not exist as a single nation; there were many German states which were loosely allied with each other in a confederation but which developed separate administrative institutions. The most powerful of these states, Prussia, finally managed to unite all except Austria into a federation that was dominated by her but whose structure allowed even the tiniest state considerable administrative autonomy. This result was achieved by establishing a type of federalism that became a controlling influence in Germany's administrative development.

Unlike American federalism, which allows the states to legislate, administer, and adjudicate in their spheres of competence, Germany's federal structure allotted only administrative and adjudicative functions to the states (or *Laender* as they were later called).[13] From the very beginning, legislation was an arena in which the national government (*Reich*) dominated when it so desired. As the

13. Germans referred to their states as *Staate* rather than *Laender* until 1919. To avoid confusion in our discussion, however, we shall use the term *Laender* throughout this study.

Reich matured, more and more activities became subject to Reich legislation; however, until the Second Reich crumbled with Germany's defeat in World War I, the national government's executive branch consisted only of central ministries. It depended almost entirely on the states to execute policies in the field. After World War I, the Reich began to invade the administrative sphere by establishing its own field agencies. The Nazi state extended nationalization of administration to its ultimate conclusion by destroying Germany's federal structure and centralizing control over administration as well as over legislation and adjudication. Since World War II, West Germany has reverted to the old federal structure while East Germany (which will not be discussed in this book) retains the centralized, unitary structure bequeathed it by Hitler.

Germany's federal structure had an enormous impact on the development of field administration. It produced an unusual set of problems, for field agents were responsible not only to the state governments which hired, promoted, or fired them but also to the more remote national government although it often had no direct control over them. To achieve control despite structural obstacles, German governments invented a repertory of administrative and political techniques which gave a peculiar flavor to German administration. As the federal structure made direct controls impossible, German governments resorted to indirect ones which utilized social, cultural, and political channels outside the administrative hierarchy.

Moreover, the short life span of German regimes since 1918 produced acute problems in the administrative structure which in today's unstable world can teach us important lessons. The revolution of 1918 turned German politics topsy-turvy. Kaiser and princes were expelled; the formerly despised Socialists took office in their place. The bureaucracy, however, remained intact and was even guaranteed its rights and privileges by the new constitution. Yet the civil service did not become a completely neutral instrument. Its narrow social base induced some officials to prefer the old regime and led them to ally themselves with rightist opposition to the new one. As a result, not all officials gave their complete loyalty to the Republic.

The next two regimes had to grapple with similar problems.

Hitler's government provoked disloyalty among a few civil servants for it disappointed them by failing to acknowledge the traditional privileges of the civil service and its claim to a special place in German society. Instead, Hitler made a vigorous attempt to change the character of the civil service by filling it with elements that intuitively would support his regime. After World War II, the new West German Republic faced the problem of "denazifying" its bureaucracy. Although denazification failed, other circumstances and controls have allowed the Bonn government to acquire a loyal bureaucracy.

Thus the last half century of German administrative development has taken place during a series of political upheavals. Each successive regime has tried to utilize some of the administrative agencies and operating personnel that existed when it seized power. Each stumbled over the barriers raised by inefficient communications and insufficient loyalty.

These turbulent years of administrative development may serve to illustrate some of the critical problems facing a new regime that seeks to establish or maintain a responsive field administration. Each German government faced the task of repelling threats to the integrity of its administrative system and of imposing its will on field agents who sometimes preferred to neglect their obligations toward the central government. German regimes resorted to the entire spectrum of administrative controls in order to overcome these obstacles; they succeeded without sacrificing Germany's reputation for administrative efficiency, albeit at the cost of gaining an unparalleled reputation for ruthlessness. The following chapters will describe these developments in detail by analyzing the barriers to responsiveness that German governments encountered, the conditions from which these barriers arose, the countermeasures adopted, and the administrative and political consequences of Germany's quest for responsiveness.

2. THE ORIGINS OF MODERN GERMAN FIELD ADMINISTRATION

The roots of modern German administration lie in Prussia. Her energetic monarchs in the first half of the 18th century gave Prussia a much envied administrative apparatus; it made "Prussian" the trademark of administrative efficiency and honesty. Despite her defeat at the hands of Napoleon, Prussia never lost this reputation, for defeat caused reforms that led to a resurgence of power. The Prussia that emerged from the peace talks at Vienna became the leader of North Germany and eventually united all German states except Austria. The constitution of united Germany confirmed Prussia's hegemonical position. As a result, the national government (*Reich*) based its administrative structure on the Prussian model; many of the smaller *Laender* also emulated Prussian administrative practices.[1]

1. French institutions had only a limited influence on the Prussian reforms of the Stein-Hardenberg era despite the fact that the reforms came as a reaction to weaknesses made apparent by the struggle against Napoleonic France. Nowhere was a Prefect established. His parallel, the Landrat, was much lower in the hierarchy and performed local government functions not then assigned to a Prefect. Moreover, the Landrat was often an untrained noble in contrast to the professional Prefect. Finally, the Landrat's office was a continuation of an agency which originated in the 18th century when the Prussian kings first sought to extend their effective authority throughout their realm. Only the

The principal characteristics of Prussian administration during the 19th century were simple; the bureaucracy was established on a hierarchical model and staffed by a socially elite career civil service. During most of the 19th century, it remained unaffected by popular pressures. It was essentially an autocratic apparatus designed to support the Hohenzollern monarchy through administrative efficiency and political loyalty.

The hierarchical structure of the administrative machine developed after Prussia's defeat in battle by Napoleon in 1807 at Jena. The existing structure had required the sort of personal monarchical control that a Frederick William I or Frederick the Great could provide. When Prussia no longer had such rulers, control over the administrative machine had to be institutionalized. This was the task undertaken by two remarkable Prime Ministers—Baron von Stein and Prince von Hardenberg.

Although Stein and Hardenberg based their reforms on different principles, both must be credited with establishing the administrative structure that survived in its essentials for more than a century. Stein placed primary emphasis on appointing laymen to honorific administrative positions in order to nurture Prussian patriotism. His projects remained stillborn except for the City Charter Law (*Staedteordnung*) of 1808, yet his ideas on lay participation (*Selbstverwaltung*) remained influential throughout the 19th century. Hardenberg left his imprint more directly on the administrative structure; his contribution was to emphasize bureaucratic (in contrast to collegial) organization to maximize efficiency.

Stein and Hardenberg reorganized both the central and regional administrative structures. At the center, the reformers established purely functional ministries for foreign affairs, war, interior, finances, and justice. Each ministry was organized on the bureau-

---

Prussian rural police, the Gendarmerie, were patterned on a French model. French influence can also be noted in areas occupied by the French and later returned to Prussia, for the territorial changes were retained by the Prussians. Consolidated townships (*Buergermeistereien*) in the Rhineland and Westphalia were also retained by the Prussians but never extended to other territories. See Ernst von Meier, *Franzoesische Einfluesse auf die Staats- und Rechtsentwicklung Preussens im XIX. Jahrhundert* (Leipzig, Verlag von Duncker und Humblot, 1908), 2, 205 ff., especially 395–96.

cratic model. This meant that the minister became individually responsible for all affairs in his office and no longer had to share his decision-making powers with his colleagues in the collegium. While Stein still planned a ministerial council to set general policies and coordinate the ministries with one another, Hardenberg centralized these responsibilities in the hands of the Prime Minister, a post he created for himself. After Hardenberg's death in 1822, this position once more fell into oblivion; policy direction and coordination came from the King, from a particularly trusted minister, or not at all.[2]

The reformers performed an even more valuable task in remolding the structure of Prussia's field administration. The Peace of Vienna gave Prussia more than 2,000 square miles of new territory; it imposed on her the need for reorganizing her regional administration. Consequently Hardenberg created the post of Provincial Governor (*Oberpraesident*) for each of Prussia's larger regions and established several bureaucratically organized district offices (*Bezirksregierungen*) within each province. Finally, the county offices (*Landratsaemter*) within each district were placed more directly under the hierarchical control of the Berlin government.

The governor's original duty was to represent the King's authority at the provincial level, especially on ceremonial occasions.[3] As early as 1817, however, he gained purely administrative functions, such as ruling on complaints against the district offices in his provinces, auditing provincial charitable institutions, supervising government censorship, commenting on and relaying reports from districts to the ministries, and controlling the award of contracts by the district offices.[4] In addition, the governor

2. The reforms at the center are best summarized by Ernst von Meier, *Die Reform der Verwaltungsorganisation unter Stein und Hardenberg* (Leipzig, Verlag von Duncker und Humblot, 1881), pp. 177 ff.

3. Verordnung, April 30, 1815, GS, 85; Instruktion, Oct. 23, 1817, GS, 248; Instruktion, Dec. 31, 1825, GS 1826, 1. The post was not entirely new, having been established in 1808 and abandoned for lack of use in 1810. See Instruktion, Dec. 23, 1808, GS 1806–10, 373; Cabinet Order, Oct. 27, 1810, GS 1810–11, 3.

4. Instruktion, Dec. 31, 1825, GS 1826, 1, paragraph 2; H. Kube, *Die geschichtliche Entwicklung der Stellung des preussischen Oberpraesidenten* (Ph.D. Dissertation, University of Berlin, 1939), p. 20.

served as chief of the district in which his office was located. These duties immersed the governor in a welter of bureaucratic routine. For example, Governor von Hydebreck of Brandenburg reported that in 1817 his office handled 22,040 pieces of correspondence just in dealing with the district offices of his province (there were two).[5] Moreover, he supervised two specialized agencies which operated within the province: the Provincial Tax Directorate, which collected indirect taxes, and the General Commission for Readjustment of the Status of the Nobility and Peasants, which implemented the policy of emancipating peasants. In both cases the governor exercised administrative supervision but lacked authority to rule on technical matters which the appropriate central ministry in Berlin decided.[6] As a result of all these duties, the Provincial Governor quickly emerged from his position as symbolic representative of the Crown to become an important participant in the administrative process.

Yet the governor's office was only an appendage to the administrative system. The bulk of the supervisory work was the responsibility of the district offices established in each province. The district offices were the successors of the Chambers of War and Finance created by Frederick William I in 1723. However, in contrast to the collegially organized chambers, the new district offices operated as bureaucratic agencies. The chief, the District Officer (*Regierungspraesident*), possessed complete responsibility to direct the work of his subordinates. He won the right to decide all routine matters alone; the only decisions on which a vote of all senior officials was still required were proposals for new laws, general matters of interest to all divisions of the district office, and problems that were to be referred to the Provincial Governor.[7]

Twenty-five districts were established in Prussia, each headed by a District Officer. His office became the focal point for almost all governmental functions performed by field agents. Its scope can be seen by examining the duties of its three divisions. The

---

5. Kube, p. 20. Hartung notes that this governor then had a staff of only one deputy and one secretary! Fritz Hartung, *Der Oberpraesident*, Abhandlungen der preussischen Akademie der Wissenschaften (Berlin, Verlag der Akademie der Wissenschaften, 1943), p. 33 n.

6. Hartung, p. 30.

7. Instruktion, Oct. 23, 1817, GS, 248, paragraph 5.

first (division of interior) handled all police matters, emigration permits, censorship actions, medical and health regulations, control of agriculture, supervision of local governments, and recruitment of soldiers. The second (division of church administration) controlled public education, appointed teachers, supervised Protestant pastors, and regulated financial affairs of the Protestant churches. The third (division for administration of direct taxes, domains, and forests) supervised the collection of direct taxes and controlled the management of all public lands. Thus, the district office administered or supervised almost all domestic functions of the Prussian government. The only agency remaining free from its control was the Provincial Tax Directorate which collected indirect taxes.[8]

While the district office supervised most field programs, it did not act as an operating agency, for its territory was too large. The typical district office in 1817 had jurisdiction over an area of 188 square miles with 500,000 inhabitants;[9] it included on the average two cities and twelve counties.[10] Consequently, in the larger urban areas Prussia delegated administrative operations to city governments. Their municipal agencies then served as field administrators for the central ministries under the supervision of the district office. In rural areas operational duties were assigned to counties (*Landkreise*) and their executive official, the Landrat. The Landrat was a royal official appointed by the King with the advice of the local nobility sitting in the county council (*Kreistag*).[11] He also served as executive official for whatever local government functions the county council assigned him. His principal responsibility, however, was to the central government in Berlin. He became the linchpin of the Prussian system of field administration.

---

8. The functions of the district office are prescribed by ibid. and Instruktion, Dec. 31, 1825, GS 1826, 1. See also Gerhard Sommerfeld, *Das Amt des Regierungspraesidenten* (Ph.D. Dissertation, University of Freiburg, 1934), p. 4.

9. Koeniglichen Statistischen Bureau, *Uebersicht der Bodenflaeche und Bevoelkerung des preussischen Staates* (Berlin, 1819), p. 18.

10. Ibid.

11. Indeed before 1807 the Landrat's office was reserved for noblemen alone. Lysbeth W. Muncy, *The Junker in the Prussian Administration under William II, 1888–1914* (Providence, R.I., Brown University Press, 1944), p. 21.

The Landrat ruled his county with an iron fist. Every piece of state business flowed through his hands. Although some specialists like the county doctor worked in the county, the Landrat executed all general laws. He also supervised the municipal administration of the villages and smaller towns, for only cities with more than 10,000 inhabitants were supervised directly by the district office. Finally, he exercised the police powers in his county; this entailed issuing police regulations to ensure local health and safety and supervising the work of the local police who, east of the Elbe River, inherited their posts with their estates. These police powers gave the Landrat an especially powerful position, for his actions could be revoked only by the District Officer. They were subject neither to legislative approval nor to court review.[12] It was perhaps no exaggeration when in 1845 one of the Landraete described his position in the following terms:[13] "The Landrat still has an authority which often frightens me. When people tell their children that the Pope is not allowed to marry, they ask if the Landrat has forbidden it."

Thus the Stein–Hardenberg reforms established a three-level field organization. It can be characterized as a uniquely integrated hierarchical system. Each of the three levels—the Landrat (or city official), the District Officer, and the Provincial Governor—had distinctive duties. The Landrat was the operating official responsible for carrying out most governmental functions in his county; he remained clearly subordinate to the District Officer. The District Officer controlled or coordinated all activities within the district, supervising the Landraete and mayors of larger cities as well as the few specialized field officials who operated at the Landrat's side. The District Officer was directly responsible to the central ministries in Berlin except for educational and religious matters where the governor interposed a provincial control. The Provincial Governor represented the King at festive

12. Good descriptions of the Landrat's powers during this period are given by Franz Gelpke, *Die geschichtliche Entwicklung des Landrathamtes der preussischen Monarchie* (Berlin, Carl Heymanns Verlag, 1902), pp. 67 ff., and Ernst R. Huber, *Deutsche Verfassungsgeschichte seit 1789* (Stuttgart, W. Kohlhammer Verlag, 1957), *1*, 180–81.

13. Cited by Muncy, p. 180, from Herman von Petersdorff, *Hans v. Kleist-Retzow* (Berlin, 1907), p. 84.

occasions, supervised provincial agencies, and reported the climate of opinion in his province to Berlin. Only the Provincial Tax Directorates, which were organs of the Finance Ministry, operated relatively independently of this general administrative structure although they too were appended to the governor's office and sent liaison agents to the district offices.

This administrative machine provided more than routine efficiency: It furnished political support for Prussia's autocratic government, for it enlisted the Junker nobility and excluded unwanted popular elements from political activity. As a result, the Prussian monarchy maintained a tight control over its domains.

As a matter of policy, the monarchy reserved the government's top civil and military positions for the landholding nobility, the Junkers. They constituted the most powerful social group in early 19th-century Prussia, for political power was still a correlate of landholdings; peasant emancipation, agricultural depressions, and industrialization—all of which undermined the traditional basis of Prussian culture—took their toll very slowly. Consequently, it was a hallmark of the Prussian civil service that it included almost all landowners who were politically ambitious. Dominated by Junker families, the Prussian bureaucracy remained a remarkably homogeneous group. The few talented sons of bourgeois merchants who found their way into the civil service were quickly assimilated into the dominant Junker bureaucratic mold.[14] The army was similarly composed. Thus as officer or official, the Junker held the highest status positions available in 19th-century Prussia. When a Junker dabbled in politics, he usually did it in his role as Landrat or District Officer in support of the King's policies. In this way the administrative machine harnessed the political energy of Prussia's social elite.

Not only did the recruitment of Junkers give the monarchy a loyal civil service; it also established one which by temperament enjoyed autocratic rule. The monarchy used it to suppress political opposition and resist the political importunities of the rising bourgeoisie. Landraete and District Officers operated under the permissively broad provisions of the General Code of 1794 which

14. Muncy, pp. 28–29, and Fritz Morstein Marx, "Civil Service in Germany" in L. D. White, ed., *Civil Service Abroad*, pp. 178 ff.

read: "The necessary measures (*Anstalten*) for the maintenance of public peace, security, and order, and for the prevention of danger to the general public or one of its members is the function (*Amt*) of the police."[15] Under this provision, Prussian field administrators intervened in every aspect of political life. They prohibited opposition meetings, pamphlets, newspapers, and other forms of political agitation. They imposed such restrictions without any interference from the judiciary, for an 1842 law took all matters involving the use of police powers out of the jurisdiction of the courts.[16] Complaints against illegal, unnecessary, or inappropriate police regulations could only be lodged with the next highest administrative official, the Landrat or District Officer, and appealed only as far as the minister. To remove even borderline cases from the courts, another law in 1854 allowed a minister to order the suspension of legal proceedings until a special court staffed by civil servants as well as judges determined whether a court or an administrative agency had jurisdiction.[17] Consequently few legal restrictions hindered field officials in following their group-inspired inclination to support the King's government.

After 1849 when a central legislature (the *Landtag*) was superimposed on Prussia's autocratic government, field officials gained the task of assuring that a docile majority was elected to it. Many Landraete themselves became deputies; in all counties they were under pressure from Berlin to intimidate voters in order to assure favorable election results. Their task was made simple as votes were cast by public, oral statement.[18] Field officials, thus, had political as well as administrative mandates to fulfill.

These measures succeeded in preserving the Prussian autocracy. Even the administrative structure remained remarkably stable for the fifty years after 1817; the few changes that did occur gave field officials still greater authority. In 1831 revisions of the City Char-

---

15. General Code of 1794, 2, 17, paragraph 10.

16. Law of May 11, 1842, GS, 192.

17. Law of Feb. 13, 1854, GS, 86. Composition of the court was specified by the Law of April 8, 1847, GS, 170. Abuses perpetrated under this system are described from a liberal viewpoint by Eduard Lasker, *Zur Verfassungsgeschichte Preussens* (Leipzig, F. A. Brockhaus, 1874), pp. 179 ff.

18. Eugene N. Anderson, *The Social and Political Conflict in Prussia, 1858–1864* (Lincoln, Neb., University of Nebraska Press, 1954), pp. 382 ff.

ter Law of 1808 gave the District Officer more control over local government agencies.[19] The previously mentioned 1842 and 1854 laws on the jurisdiction of the courts freed the bureaucracy from judicial restraints. The 1848 revolution imposed only superficial changes in Prussia which failed to hamper bureaucratic control over Prussian politics. Although Liberal opponents to the autocratic regime organized in political parties and used the Landtag and its elections as a forum, their activity remained ineffectual until 1871. The resounding defeat of the Landtag in 1866, when it tried to control the army budget, underscored its political weakness. In Prussia more than in most countries those who administered also ruled.

The ability of the Junkers to retain their power and the persistence of the autocracy in unchanged form can be understood only when the economic development of North Germany is taken into account.[20] The slow pace of Prussia's social and economic development before the second half of the 19th century foredoomed the 1848 revolution, for Prussia (as well as Germany as a whole) did not feel the upward surge of the industrial revolution until the last decades of the 19th century.[21] The population of Prussia remained predominantly rural. In 1817, 73.5 per cent of the population was classified as rural; in 1852, this proportion was 71.1 per cent. As late as 1871, 67.5 per cent of the population still lived in rural areas.

Moreover, Prussian industry recovered only slowly from the

19. Revised City Charter Law of March 17, 1831, GS, 10.
20. The best descriptions of German economic development are J. H. Clapham, *Economic Development of France and Germany, 1815–1914* (4th ed. Cambridge, Eng., Cambridge University Press, 1955); Franz Schnabel, *Deutsche Geschichte im neunzehnten Jahrhundert* (Freiburg, Herder, 1934), *3;* and Anderson.
21. Clapham, p. 278. However, the population of Prussia as a whole almost tripled between 1816 and 1867, growing from 7.9 million to 22.6 million. Consequently, many of the cities became proportionately larger and for the first time grew into urban centers in the modern sense. See Koeniglichen Statistischen Bureau, *Jahrbuch fuer die amtliche Statistik des preussischen Staates* (Berlin, 1883), *5, 71;* Georg von Viebahn, *Statistik des zollvereinten und noerdlichen Deutschlands* (Berlin, Georg Reimer, 1862), *2, 40.* One should note, however, that 1.9 million of the 1867 population was acquired by annexation of Hanover.

destruction it had suffered during the Napoleonic wars.[22] Most of the new factories were small shops using few machines. The number of industrial workers increased only from 1.3 million in 1846 to 1.8 million in 1861.[23] The pace of industrialization quickened perceptibly only in isolated sectors. For instance, the number of laborers employed in hard coal mines more than doubled in these twenty years. The mines also became somewhat larger enterprises.[24] In textiles, however, the drive toward larger factories did not occur until later. Wool weaving was powerized only after 1850; cotton weaving remained a hand industry until 1870.[25] In short, numerous small firms remained characteristic of Prussia's major industries. Thus Prussia scarcely felt the acceleration of industrialization until the second half of the 19th century.

An equally slow pace of social change in rural areas limited the pressure for reforms in the structure of field administration. The Landrat and noble estate owner depended on the subservient status of the peasant for much of their prestige and power. Although Prussia began emancipation of its peasants in 1807–08, progress remained slow. By 1860, only 1.5 million farmers had been released from their manorial duties and given 56.7 million *Morgen* of land.[26] Other peasants won their freedom only at the cost of their land and even then not until the last quarter of the century. Indeed, Prussian efforts to solve its peasant problem continued well into the 20th century.[27]

The gradual freeing of the rural labor force led to changes in the ownership of noble estates upon which the whole social struc-

22. Clapham, p. 87, writes: "By 1816 the industry of Berlin had slid back into the state from which only an 'artificial and expensive governmental policy' had raised it—a state in which the typical figure was the independent master craftsman, with few employees or none. There were 10,000 fewer people in the town in 1810 than there had been in 1801. With the peace, its industries had to start afresh. . . . What is true of Berlin is to a great extent true of all Germany."

23. Anderson, p. 12.

24. While the labor force doubled, the number of soft coal mines increased only from 415 to 503, and the number of iron mines from 1,087 to 1,615 (increases of 21 per cent and 48 per cent respectively). Viebahn, pp. 363–415.

25. Clapham, pp. 289–97.

26. Anderson, p. 12. A *Morgen* was slightly less than an acre.

27. Clapham, pp. 196–98.

ture east of the Elbe depended. Wealthy merchants and industrialists gradually bought noble estates; by 1849, an average of 55 per cent of all noble estates in the eastern provinces and somewhat more in the rest of Prussia rested in bourgeois hands.[28] However, these changes came too gradually and too late to make themselves felt in the political arena before 1870. The noble Landrat continued to feel secure in his position for most of these years, although an observer like Bismarck noted that Landrat positions were gradually falling into the hands of career civil servants who hoped to advance to higher positions.[29] Changed social conditions were gradually eroding the monopoly of unambitious nobles who were satisfied with being a Landrat their entire life.

The slowly changing economic and social structure of Prussia is the key to the stability of its administrative structure during the 19th century. After the vigorous wave of reforms at the beginning of the century, the government made no significant further changes. Nor did it assume new functions which might have necessitated administrative innovations. Only the 1848 revolution challenged the Prussian administrative autocracy in a fundamental way. But lacking a politically oriented, economically powerful stratum to support its demands, the revolution failed, leaving a weak legislative body in its wake. Even Prussia's expansion with the acquisition of Hanover, Hesse-Nassau, and Schleswig-Holstein in 1866 did not lead to immediate administrative reforms. The administrative structure shaped by Stein and Hardenberg continued to support Prussia's autocracy. It survived until social and economic changes gathered sufficient momentum to force reforms. The first changes occurred after German unification in 1871 during the era of the Second Reich.

28. Anderson, p. 14; Viebahn, p. 309.
29. Otto von Bismarck-Schoenhausen, *Erinnerungen und Gedanke* (Stuttgart and Berlin, J. G. Cotta'sche Buchhandlung Nachfolger, 1928), p. 47. See also Kurt Jeserich, ed., *Die deutsche Landkreise* (Stuttgart and Berlin, W. Kohlhammer Verlag, 1937), *1, 43.*

3. THE CONSERVATIVE ERA:

FIELD ADMINISTRATION DURING THE SECOND REICH

The unification of Germany initiated a period of spectacular economic growth which transformed her from an agrarian society into one of the world's foremost industrial powers. But the swift pace of her industrialization created undercurrents of unrest which seethed beneath the apparently calm domestic scene of Bismarck's Germany. The industrial revolution spawned new social classes that imparted entirely new dimensions to German politics. On the one side stood the urban proletariat; on the other stood that broad bourgeois stratum that includes clerical workers, shopkeepers, and industrial tycoons.

The struggle for political recognition by these new social classes focused first on the electoral and legislative processes. Yet Germany's political system gave relatively little weight to electoral results or to the deliberations of such legislative bodies as the Reichstag or the Landtag. The initiation of policy proposals and the making of final political decisions rested exclusively with the Kaiser, the Chancellor, and the bureaucracy. Electoral results gave voice to shifts of national opinion, but they could not cause the resignation of a chancellor. On the contrary, he and the Kaiser (as well as the bureaucracy) viewed election campaigns and legislative bodies with contempt. It is true that the Reichstag and Landtage held lengthy debates; the outcomes, however, only occasionally affected policy by withholding budgetary grants or by suggesting amendments. Thus when the proletariat and middle classes won considerable representation in legislative bodies, they still found themselves excluded from the decision-making process.

The bureaucracy which initiated most important political decisions became the second target of attack. It had remained the exclusive domain of the Prussian Junkerdom. Proletariat and middle-class organizations, therefore, worked for the establishment of specialized autonomous agencies which would execute programs of direct concern to themselves. These specialized agencies were to be staffed by civil servants not recruited from Junker families. In addition, liberal parties worked for the establishment of judicial controls over the administration. They also sought the formation of elected executive committees who would administer local programs. Such committees would resemble the municipal institutions in which bourgeois representatives had already won a dominant position through election to advisory positions and through infiltration of the municipal civil service. The government viewed all these reform proposals with alarm for each would undermine the loyalty and responsiveness of the field administration to its mandates. Its fears were well grounded, for the partially successful struggle to establish these reforms did indeed produce serious barriers to responsiveness.

A second set of obstacles to responsive field administration arose from the functional demands of Germany's modernizing society. Industrialization attracted thousands of peasants to factory towns where they felt all the frustrations incident to social disorganization. Their traditional associations with friends and neighbors were disrupted; in case of illness, they had no relatives to help care for their family. They lived as strangers among thousands of similarly estranged workers. They were wholly dependent on their employers for their livelihood and survival. Neither custom nor the government offered effective protection against exploitation, accidents, illnesses, or other dangers inherent in an emerging industrial society. Out of these conditions arose the social discontent to which Marxist doctrines and organizations gave form.

Germany's conservative government looked with alarm at the ferment that brewed in its new cities. On the one hand it tried to suppress the revolutionary socialist creed. On the other, it attempted to regain the confidence and allegiance of the proletariat by acting to alleviate some of the worst conditions that industrialism had spawned. These programs imposed entirely new functions on the field administration. Both the novelty of the programs and the political tensions that accompanied their adoption strained the responsiveness of the field administration.

Even the unification of Germany itself presented novel problems of field administration which had to be solved if that union were to prove viable. Bismarck unified Germany with "blood and iron." The display of Prussian might not only defeated Austrian ambitions and French objections, it also awed Germany's smaller states into silent acquiescence. While broad strata of Germany's commercial classes in every state welcomed the creation of the Second Reich, many of the most influential politicians and bureaucrats in the smaller states looked with dread on the unification, fearing complete submergence into a Greater Prussia. Their suspicions were based not only on parochial patriotism. Religious, cultural, and linguistic differences emphasized and reinforced their apprehensions. In the context of the federal structure in which the new Reich operated, the fears and jealousies of non-Prussian governments constantly threatened to obstruct responsive field administration of national mandates.

Finally, the establishment of a national government and the appearance of the new social strata threatened to destroy the social bonds that linked Germany's administrators to the ruling oligarchy in Berlin and other Land capitals and promoted almost frictionless execution of central mandates. The new social order and the administrative reforms that followed the unification of Germany introduced new elements into the political arena which were alien to the conservative Prussian system. Their political programs threatened to undermine the effectiveness of central hierarchical controls and the loyal identification of field agents with central governments.

While the social system bred powerful new groups, the Prussian government continued to be controlled by the same agrarian interests that had ruled since Frederick the Great. Moreover, Prussia's economic and political hegemony (reinforced by guarantees of Prussian dominance in the new Reich constitution) allowed the same interests to control Reich policies as well. These interests were reinforced by conservative industrialists who looked to the Junker noble for prestige and status.

Industrialists found access to political and social influence through assimilation with the Junkerdom. Such assimilation was sped by several factors. The industrialists possessed sufficient wealth to buy estates which granted their owners status and local political power. Their daughters were sought after as wives by Junkers who possessed traditional access to power but lacked the wealth to support themselves. Finally, Germany's reliance on industrial power as the foundation of her world position spurred the social acceptance of industrialists as men of substance. Thus a considerable group of Germany's industrial elite joined Junker agrarians in conservative parties.[1]

The traditional character of the Prussian and Reich governments was underscored by their ideological position. The ruling princes of Germany's Laender and Bismarck and his successors possessed no systematic political ideology to govern their actions, yet they shared several overriding goals. They sought to preserve the traditional privileges of the aristocracy and landowners, to defend the monarchical form of government, and to maintain political stability in order to maximize Germany's influence in the international arena. Where compromises had to be made, the ruling elite preferred to accede to the demands of the industrialist liberals whom they hoped to absorb into the ruling class. They made concessions to the proletariat masses only to preserve political stability and to prevent a revolution. Bismarck hoped that any concessions that the government gave to the proletariat would entice workers to abandon revolutionary aims and would restore their loyalty to the state.

The governments of the Second Reich tried to limit their concessions to areas where the traditional privileges of the ruling class would be least affected. This condition precluded constitutional reforms which would have given the working class a dominant role

1. However, we must note that many of the less wealthy industrialists and merchants remained in the liberal camp which vacillated between support of Bismarck and opposition to him.

in national or Land politics. It also precluded the acceptance of parliamentary responsibility, for that would have limited the Kaiser's and princes' prerogatives in favor of the will of the masses. Adjustment to changing social conditions, therefore, occurred mostly in the administrative sphere.

Alterations in field administration took the form of remolding the controls over field agents so that field officials would be partly responsive to the demands of the new classes while also responding to the policy mandates of central governments which the traditional ruling elite continued to dominate. Such changes in the administrative structure and in the controls over field agents were intended to ameliorate political tensions which might otherwise erupt in revolutionary violence.

Administrative reforms took place both at the Reich and Land levels. We shall first examine the Reich administration to survey the controls that Bismarck originally established to assure responsive field administration and the changes he made to avoid a revolution by the proletariat masses. Then we shall turn to Land administration using Prussia as our example, for Prussia was the largest, most powerful, and—in every sense—hegemonical Land of Imperial Germany.

THE REICH AND FIELD ADMINISTRATION

The Second Reich was the first truly national government that Germany possessed. Bismarck superimposed it on the governments of the twenty-five states which composed the Second Reich, most of whom had fully developed political and administrative institutions. However, Prussia alone occupied two-thirds of the Reich's territory and had three-fifths of her population. These unique conditions gave rise to a number of peculiar problems when the Reich established its own governmental and administrative machinery. First, Bismarck had to overcome the suspicions of the smaller states who feared that the national government would be used as a veil for Prussian domination. He did this by establishing the Reich on the federal principle. Thus, the Laender retained certain essential functions, the most important of which was administering national programs through Land agencies. This sort of functional federalism in which the Reich legislated and the

Laender executed domestic programs, however, led to a second problem: the Reich had to establish a set of procedures to guarantee responsive field administration when national programs were delegated to the Laender. Finally, the Reich had also to establish an administrative structure flexible enough to absorb novel functions.

Bismarck designed the constitutional structure of the Second Reich to ameliorate the suspicions of the smaller Laender and establish conditions that would promote administrative responsiveness. The Second Reich was a federal union of twenty-five Laender. Each Land retained its identity and existing political institutions but surrendered to the Reich jurisdiction over foreign affairs and effective control over the armed forces. The 1871 constitution also gave the Reich broad legislative powers: it could adopt laws in the field of commerce, establish tariffs, regulate banking, issue patents, control rail and water transportation, stipulate the requirements for citizenship, control immigration, establish a criminal and civil law code, and operate the postal and telegraph systems. A two-chamber legislature exercised these powers. The lower house, the Reichstag, was popularly elected by universal, secret suffrage. The upper house, the Bundesrat, represented the princes and rulers of the Reich's member states. In it each Land had at least one vote; Prussia had seventeen out of a total of fifty-eight. A legislative measure required a majority in both houses to become law.[2]

The Kaiser, Bundesrat, and Chancellor shared the vague executive powers that the constitution granted the Reich. The Kaiser supervised the execution of laws; the Bundesrat—in addition to its legislative functions—issued regulations (*Verordnungen*) supplementing the laws' contents and specifying administrative procedures. The Chancellor as Bundesrat chairman guided the Bundesrat's administrative function while as Prussian representative, he controlled Prussia's seventeen votes. Aside from distributing these supervisory powers among the Kaiser, Bundesrat, and Chancellor, the constitution failed to specify how Reich laws were to be executed.[3]

These constitutional provisions gave the smaller Laender limit-

2. Constitution of April 16, 1871, Articles 4, 5, 11, and 61.
3. Ibid., Articles 7, 15, and 17.

ed guarantees against Prussian domination. All laws and most administrative arrangements required the assent of the Bundesrat. Prussia received only 29 per cent of the Bundesrat's votes although her share of Germany's territory and population would have entitled her to more than 60 per cent of its votes. In actual practice, however, Prussia never had any difficulty in winning a working majority, for she normally commanded the votes of satellite states that were enclaves in Prussia or that habitually looked to Prussia for leadership. Yet the Bundesrat constituted a formal guarantee against roughshod Prussian domination and gave those Laender who most feared Prussia a forum in which to express their misgivings. The constitution's silence in designating who should administer Reich laws became another guarantee against complete submergence in a Prussianized Reich.

The constitutional silence was utilized to good advantage by Bismarck. Both for reasons of economy and political expedience, he delegated most administrative tasks to the Laender rather than establishing Reich field agencies. This proved economical, for all the Laender possessed fully developed administrative structures; the delegation of Reich functions simply placed an additional burden on existing agencies.

Political reasons, however, constituted the major attraction for this policy of administrative delegation. Allowing the Laender to execute Reich programs gave substance to the federal form and left the Laender with at least one set of governmental tasks. The Reich had already stripped them of the more glamorous governmental duties: control of foreign affairs, the army, and most legislative functions. The Laender, therefore, demanded the retention of their administrative functions. As the administration of laws had always been the most powerful governmental function in Germany, many Land politicians felt that they could retain influence over most governmental programs by controlling their administration. Land control of administration appeared to them to be the essence of a federal system. Any proposal to establish a Reich field administration would have met determined opposition in the Bundesrat.[4]

4. James H. Robinson, *The German Bundesrath*, Publications of the University of Pennsylvania, Political Economy and Public Law Series, 10 (Philadelphia, 1891), pp. 55–58.

Bismarck also favored the policy of administrative delegation, for he feared outside intervention in Prussian affairs. He realized that a Reich field administration would have to include some officials from other Laender; this would break the Junker monopoly over administration in Prussia. Moreover, together with Prussia's ruling class, Bismarck regarded the Reichstag with great misgivings. Prussia itself restricted the legislative influence of Liberals and Socialists by its three-class voting system; these groups, however, had considerable influence in the Reichstag. Prussia feared that if the Reich established administrative agencies of its own that operated in Prussia, the Reichstag would eventually win some control over them and use them to undermine the Junker domination of Prussia.[5]

As the Reich matured, anxiety that the Reichstag would become an influential policy-making organ became the decisive factor in convincing the Reich government to continue the practice of delegating traditional administrative functions to the Laender. Bismarck had succeeded in maneuvering the Reichstag out of control of the army by convincing it to accept a seven-year budget. As long as the Reich delegated all other administrative matters to the Laender, this seven-year army budget remained the only substantial one the Reichstag could rule on. Establishment of a Reich field administration would have changed that situation. It would have given the Reichstag other budgets with multiple opportunities to exert control; it would have raised the Reich's need for taxes and made the Reich government more dependent on Reichstag approval of new tax levies. The policy of keeping administration in the hands of the Laender reduced the danger of increased democratic control by a hostile Reichstag. Federalism and the policy of administrative delegation were thus a corollary of the conservative predispositions of the Reich government.[6]

For all these reasons, the Reich delegated the administration

5. See especially Johannes Ziekursch, *Politische Geschichte des neuen deutschen Kaiserreiches* (Frankfurt a/M, Frankfurter Societaetsdruckerie Gmb H, 1927), *1*, 319.

6. Bismarck made this argument himself in a letter to Prince William on January 6, 1888. Bismarck-Schoenhausen, *Erinnerungen und Gedanke, 3*, 15–16. See also Ziekursch, 2, 388.

ot most field functions to the Laender. The Laender, thus, enforced Reich health laws, administered uniform weights and measures, collected Reich taxes, and executed a host of other Reich measures. Reich laws usually delegated field administration to the Laender by stating: "The execution of this law is the function of the Land governments. The Bundesrat shall issue the necessary basic regulations (*Grundsetze*) to assure uniformity of execution. . . . Other regulations which are necessary for the execution [of this law] will be issued by the central agencies of the Laender."[7] The Laender, in turn, assigned Reich programs to their own field agencies. The Landrat in Prussia, the *Amtsmann* in Bavaria, and their equivalents in all the other Laender executed Reich mandates in addition to their assignments as field agents of their Land government.

Delegation of field administration to the Laender forced the Reich to seek effective ways to assure itself that Land administrators would be responsive to Reich policy mandates. Constitutional provisions created some channels to promote responsive field administration. The establishment of central administrative agencies by the Reich provided others. In addition to the formal procedures which these measures afforded, the Reich depended heavily on Prussia's hegemonical position and on the Kaiser's and Chancellor's powers of persuasion to avoid clashes between the Reich and Laender and to insure effective as well as responsive Land administration of Reich mandates.

The constitution granted a number of broad executive powers to the Kaiser which the Chancellor exercised. The Kaiser was responsible for supervising the execution of Reich laws and could demand information from the Laender about the performance of their duties. He could also appoint inspectors to assure uniform collection of Reich taxes and to check observance of Reich standards in equipping and training Land contingents of the army.[8]

In addition, the Bundesrat was responsible for "the general administrative provisions and arrangements" necessary for the execution of Reich laws and could issue basic regulations to guide Land agencies. As a last resort, if a Land refused to execute a law, the

---

7. Wine Law of April 7, 1909, RGBl, 393, paragraph 25.
8. Constitution of 1871, Articles 17, 36, and 63.

Bundesrat could authorize armed intervention *(Bundesexekution)* to compel it to meet its obligations.[9]

The Reich never threatened a Land with armed intervention; less drastic measures sufficed. The Kaiser and Chancellor established central administrative offices *(Reichsaemter)* in order to exercise their general responsibility for the execution of Reich laws. These Reich Offices lacked all facilities for field administration; instead, they were designed to aid the Chancellor in supervising the execution of Reich laws, hearing appeals, and drafting new legislation. Bismarck established these Reich Offices as subdivisions of his Chancellor's Office. In 1872 there were Reich Offices for the Interior, for Foreign Affairs, and for Marine Affairs in addition to a General Accounting Office *(Rechnungshof fuer das Deutsche Reich)* and a High Court for Commercial Law *(Oberhandelsgericht)*. Combined they employed only 79 officials and 112 clerks in 1872–73.[10] Although the Reich greatly expanded the scope of its activities in later years, these agencies never acquired a field organization. However, by 1914, the Reich found it necessary to establish five new central offices and increase the staff of its Berlin agencies almost tenfold. Just before World War I, 749 officials and approximately 1,587 clerks staffed the Reich Offices in Berlin.[11]

The Reich Offices performed two functions for the Chancellor. First, they drafted all legislative proposals that he submitted to the Bundesrat and Reichstag. Second, they maintained communications with Land ministries and tried to guide them to a correct interpretation and execution of Reich laws. Effective performance of this second function was crucial for obtaining responsive field

9. Ibid., Articles 7 and 19.

10. Reichstag Verhandlungen, 1873, vol. 4, 4th Session, Aktenstueck zu Nr. 125, pp. 701 ff. The only fully developed agencies of the Reich, complete with a field organization, were the postal and telegraph offices which reached every corner of the Reich except Bavaria and Wuerttemberg, which retained their separate postal administrations until 1919. The Reich postal and telegraph system employed 3,573 officials and 22,885 clerks in 1872–73. Ibid.

11. *Handbuch fuer das deutsche Reich* (1914), pp. 46 ff. The new Offices included ones for Justice, Treasury, Colonial Affairs, a Post Office, and a Railroad Office. In addition, the Office for Interior increased from 13 divisions in 1884 to 27 divisions in 1914.

administration. In most instances, however, the limited grant of powers under which the Reich Offices operated hindered them from performing their supervisory duties with optimal efficiency. The Reich Offices, with two exceptions, relied entirely on the voluntary cooperation of Land ministries when seeking information about the execution of Reich programs. In most cases, the Laender barred Reich inspectors from contacting Land field agents; the Reich could only send inspectors to the Land central ministries to check the operation of Reich programs. Even when complaints of inequitable or inefficient Land administration arose through the press or Reichstag debates, the Reich Offices had to depend on the cooperation of the affected Laender for an investigation and for corrective action. At other times, the Chancellor advised, guided, and warned Laender when their administrative actions deviated from the desired administration of a Reich law. Such communications, however, carried no legal force.[12]

When the constitution authorized it, the Reich supplemented indirect supervision by the Reich Offices with on-the-spot field inspections. The constitution allowed this practice in only two cases: to regulate army training and equipment and to check on Land collections of Reich taxes. The latter illustrates the procedures the Reich evolved.

The Laender collected all national taxes during the Second Reich. The Reich relied heavily on direct inspection to insure uniform collection of its taxes and tariffs. Through the Bundesrat it appointed representatives and inspectors to check Land collections at key points. As the Reich lacked qualified personnel of its own, it appointed officials from Land tax agencies (see Table 1). These representatives and inspectors conducted audits, checked tax records, and observed collection practices. They themselves could not correct abuses; they could only send reports to the Chancellor and Bundesrat. The Chancellor then could attempt to resolve the matter through discussions with the Land in ques-

---

12. The most thorough discussion of Reich control over delegated functions is found in Heinrich Triepel, *Die Reichsaufsicht* (Berlin, Verlag von Julius Springer, 1917), passim, but especially pp. 645–46. Unfortunately, Triepel, like most German students of administration, restricted his analysis to an examination of legal authority and precedents.

TABLE 1

*Mean Number of Reich Tax Representatives and
Inspectors Appointed from the Land and
Reich Civil Service Corps,
1874–1914*

Home Civil Service Corps	Reich representatives	Reich inspectors
Reich	1	1
Bavaria	3	8
Prussia	5	20
Saxony	2	4
Wuerttemberg	1	3
Hesse	1	2
Baden	1	3
Oldenburg	0	1
Mecklenburg	0	1
Totals	14	43

Source: *Handbuch fuer das deutsche Reich,* 1874, 1879, 1884, 1894, 1899, 1904, 1909, and 1914.

tion.[13] As a last resort, the Chancellor could refer the disagreement to the Bundesrat for action by administrative regulation.[14]

The Bundesrat occupied a central role in promoting responsive field administration. The Bundesrat issued supplemental and administrative regulations which guided the Laender in executing Reich programs. During the first decade of the Reich's existence, thirty-five Reich laws authorized the Bundesrat to issue supplemental regulations; in later years the practice became a routine one.[15] Moreover, the Bundesrat could issue administrative regulations without legislative authorization. Indeed, Bundesrat regu-

13. The most complete description of the functions of these inspectors is in Kaiserlichen Statisches Amt, *Statistik des deutschen Reichs,* vol. 6, part I (Berlin, 1874). See also Mabel Newcomer, *Central and Local Finance in Germany and England* (New York, Columbia University Press, 1937), pp. 21 ff.

14. *Vertrag zwischen dem Norddeutschen Bund, Bayern, Wuerttemberg, Baden, und Hessen ueber der Fortdauer des Zoll-und Handelswesen,* June 8, 1867, BGBl, 81, Article 20; *Schlussprotokoll,* July 8, 1867, BGBl, 110 f., paragraph 15; Triepel, pp. 185–86.

15. Albert Jaenel, *Die organisatorische Entwicklung der deutschen Reichsverfassung* (Leipzig, 1880), p. 85 n.; Robinson, p. 53.

lations became one of the basic tools by which the Reich obtained responsive field administration, for they carried great weight with German bureaucrats who were primarily trained as lawyers. However, such regulations could only be addressed to the central ministries of a Land. They in turn interpreted and forwarded Reich directives to their field agents. Once again the Reich was held at arm's length from Land field offices; it could not exert direct pressure on Land field agents who administered Reich laws at the local level.

The Chancellor also turned to the Bundesrat when a Land persisted in administrative practices that seemed injurious to Reich interests. In routine cases, the Chancellor could hope for success; in cases that involved a vital interest of several Laender, the outcome became more dubious.[16] After all, the Laender themselves were represented on the Bundesrat. It was unlikely that they would adopt a measure against their own interests.

The obstacles inherent in Bundesrat action and the lack of direct contact between Reich central offices and Land field agencies might well have immobilized the entire administrative structure but for the unique ties that bound the Reich and its largest Land, Prussia, together. Most of the Reich's senior civil servants came from the Prussian bureaucracy. Consequently, Reich civil servants often had personal knowledge of Prussia's field administration and had personal contacts with Prussian officials. Moreover, many of the chiefs of the Reich Offices held Prussian ministerial posts at the same time.[17] They therefore had direct access to Prussian field agents despite the constitutional division between Reich and Land administration. Finally, except for two brief periods, the Reich's Chancellor was the Minister President of Prussia as well. Under these circumstances, there was no danger that Reich and Prussian administrative policies would clash. As long as the Reich and Prussian administrative structures were united through dual office-holding by leading officials, the Reich possessed many of the

16. Triepel, pp. 694 ff.

17. *Handbuch fuer das deutsche Reich* (1884). In 1884, the chiefs of the Reich Office for Foreign Affairs and of the Reich Office for Internal Affairs were Prussian ministers at the same time. Four of the highest officials in the Reich Office for Internal Affairs served simultaneously in the Prussian Ministry of Interior.

advantages of having its own field administration without inviting any of its dangers. In the two-thirds of Germany ruled by Prussia, the Reich possessed the complete range of hierarchical controls to promote responsive field administration. Yet Reichstag influence was not enhanced nor did outsiders penetrate the Junker monopoly of the Prussian field administration.

The administrative union between the Reich and Prussia was broken only twice during the Second Reich's existence. In 1872, Bismarck resigned the Minister Presidency while remaining Chancellor; in 1893–94, Caprivi also served only as Chancellor and not as Minister President. Both times the Reich's control over Prussian administration quickly gave way to intense rivalry between the Reich's central offices and Prussia's central ministries. In both cases the breakdown of cooperation between the Reich Offices and the Prussian administration hastened the reunion of the offices of Chancellor and Minister President.[18]

Administrative delegation thus constituted the central element in German federalism. The Reich constitution allocated legislative powers to the national government but allowed the Laender to execute most laws. The Reich retained only supervisory powers over administration. The Bundesrat formulated regulations and sought to arbitrate disputes between the Reich and the Laender; the Reich Offices and their inspectors supervised the enforcement of Reich standards; the Chancellor advised and chided Land administrators to comply with Reich mandates. The distinctive feature of this policy was the lack of Reich field officials operating under the direct control of the Reich's central offices. Instead, the Reich relied exclusively on existing Land agencies. It ordinarily made no effort to specify the structure of the Land field administration; the Laender assigned Reich programs to whatever agencies they deemed appropriate.

These administrative arrangements served well for ordinary purposes. In novel situations, however, they had to be altered. Exceptions to the policy of administrative delegation occurred in

18. Ziekursch, 2, 268–69; Hans Goldschmidt, *Das Reich und Preussen im Kampf um die Fuehrung* (Berlin, Carl Heymanns Verlag, 1931), pp. 17–19, 158–62; J. Alden Nichols, *Germany after Bismarck* (Cambridge, Mass., Harvard University Press, 1958), pp. 184–87, and 327 ff.

two instances. The Reich established a direct field administration in Alsace-Lorraine; it organized specialized autonomous agencies to operate its social insurance programs.

The administration of Alsace-Lorraine posed a unique problem to the Reich. Although the territory was claimed for Germany because of its German character, it had been under French rule for more than one hundred seventy years. Bismarck and many other Germans did not trust the Germanic character of this district sufficiently to give it the status of a member state of the Reich. On the other hand, to offer the territory to the Laender as war booty would invite intense rivalry between Prussia, Bavaria, and Baden, each of whom could lay claim to parts of the province. Rather than allow such conflicting claims to divide the Reich in the first year of its existence, Bismarck decided to give Alsace-Lorraine the special status of a *Reichsland*.[19] It was to be a province of the Reich, belonging to no individual Land. Consequently, the Reich itself had to provide for all the administrative needs of the district. Tax collection, police, education, welfare, highway construction, and all other governmental tasks became direct Reich responsibilities in Alsace-Lorraine while they remained Land functions in the rest of Germany. To meet this need, the Reich established a field administration on the Prussian model. A Reich Governor (first called *Oberpraesident,* then *Reichsstatthalter*), responsible to the Chancellor, served as the Reich's regional representative. Three District Officers directed district administration; twenty-two counties and two cities served as local units of the field administration.[20]

Although unique, this field organization had little effect on the rest of Germany. As Alsace-Lorraine was a small area, its Reich field administration had no influence on other Laender. The establishment of a Reich field administration in Alsace-Lorraine raised none of the problems that blocked its organization in the

19. Erich Marcks, *Der Aufstieg des Reiches* (Stuttgart and Berlin, Deutsche Verlags Anstalt, 1936), 2, 518–20; Friedrich Darmstaedter, *Bismarck and the Creation of the Second Reich* (London, Methuen, 1948), pp. 388–89.

20. Georg Wolfram, *Verfassung und Verwaltung von Elsass-Lothringen, 1871–1918* (Berlin, Verlag fuer Sozialpolitik, Wirtschaft und Statistik, 1936), pp. 178 ff.; *Alsace-Lorraine,* Handbooks Prepared under the Direction of the Historical Section of the Foreign Office, No. 30 (London, 1920), pp. 29–67.

rest of Germany. It did not injure vested interests of the established Laender; it scarcely increased the influence or prestige of the Reichstag. The direct Reich field administration in Alsace-Lorraine remained an anomaly throughout the existence of the Second Reich. It failed to spur an extension of direct Reich field administration; instead, Alsace-Lorraine officials made repeated attempts to eliminate Reich controls and to establish the territory as an autonomous Land.[21]

The administration of Germany's social insurance program constituted the second exception. Although the Reich delegated the execution of the novel insurance measures to Land agencies, it specified agency structure in great detail. In each case, the Reich ordered the Laender to establish specialized autonomous agencies. The laws gave neither the Reich nor the Laender direct hierarchical control over their operation. Eventually, however, the Reich established a new central office which exercised a broad and increasingly detailed supervision over the autonomous insurance agencies. In 1911, the Reich finally established an insurance program for white collar workers which functioned under direct Reich supervision without the participation of Land agencies.

The technical demands of these social welfare programs were partly responsible for the Reich's insistence that specialized autonomous agencies be established. No country in the world had ever operated a health insurance, an accident insurance, or a disability and old age insurance program before Germany adopted these measures in the 1880s. It seemed unreasonable to burden the general administrative structure with such novel functions. Moreover, special wage deductions and assessments on employers rather than general taxes financed the insurance programs. Finally, the areal boundaries of the general administrative structure seemed inconvenient. The occupational groups covered by the health insurance required a variety of local agencies other than local government units to provide the necessary coverage. With the accident insurance, regional occupational organizations were established in order to overcome the anticipated actuarial risks; these organizations could not be conveniently fitted into the confines of Prussia's provinces or the boundaries of the smaller Laender.

21. *Alsace-Lorraine,* pp. 34–35 and 54–55.

Concern for the political impact of the social insurance program contributed much to the decision to establish autonomous agencies. Two elements played a particularly influential role in shaping the administrative structure of these programs. First, Bismarck designed the program to undermine working-class support of the Socialist party.[22] Second, the Catholic Center party and many Liberals in the Reichstag insisted that the insurance program be administered by autonomous agencies that promoted citizen participation and minimized bureaucratic control.[23] This coalition of Catholics and Liberals, who joined forces for somewhat different reasons, controlled a majority in the Reichstag. For once, Bismarck was forced to negotiate with the Liberals and Catholics, for the Conservatives, who usually provided Bismarck's parliamentary support, labeled these measures as "state socialism" and greeted them with reluctance bordering on outright opposition.[24]

The tensions accompanying Germany's rapid industrialization occasioned Bismarck's social insurance program. In November 1878, assassins who were alleged to be Socialists twice attacked the Kaiser. Bismarck and the Junker elite in Germany were shocked into action. The government first passed strong repressive legislation against the Socialist party. Its meetings and organization were outlawed; it became an outcast in the German political system. However, these exceptional anti-Socialist laws, which remained on Germany's statute books until 1890, brought only limited success. They hampered Socialist organization and underscored the alienation of the working class from the political process. Yet, after some initial setbacks, the party attracted increasing support in Reichstag elections.

Bismarck shrewdly recognized the positive appeal of the socialist doctrine. To combat it effectively, he realized that Germany would

22. For Bismarck's motives in supporting the insurance programs see Hans Rothfels, *Theodor Lohmann und die Kampfjahre der staatlichen Sozialpolitik 1871–1905* (Berlin, E. G. Mittler und Sohn, 1927), especially pp. 48–83. See also Hans Rothfels, "Zur Geschichte der Bismarckischen Innenpolitik," *Archiv fuer Politik und Geschichte*, 7 (1926), 284–310, and Otto Quandt, *Die Anfaenge der Bismarckischen Sozialgesetzgebung und die Haltung der Parteien*, Historische Studien Nr. 344 (Berlin, Verlag Dr. Emil Ebering, 1938), pp. 15–18.

23. Quandt, pp. 31 ff.

24. Ibid., pp. 50–55.

have to offer the workers an alternative. The German government should provide compulsory insurance against some of the hazards of an industrial civilization. The insurance would grant medical care in case of illness, compensation for accidental injury and permanent disability, and pensions in old age.

Bismarck hoped to place these programs under direct Reich control, for delegated administration sometimes proved awkward. Moreover, Bismarck believed that the Reich could reap the political benefits of its program only if it were administered by civil servants whose uniforms and official positions clearly identified them as agents of the Reich. According to Bismarck's plans, the Reich would also contribute substantial sums to support these measures so that workers would recognize that the largesse came from the Reich and no one else.[25]

Bismarck's plans for Reich administration of the insurance programs met the concerted opposition of the Catholic Center party and many Liberals. These groups shared a lively distrust of the German bureaucracy. They demanded that the insurance programs be operated by autonomous agencies instead of centrally directed Reich offices. Autonomous administrative agencies (*Selbstverwaltung,* they called it) appealed to Liberals because of their apparent similarity to the English governmental structure they so admired. The Catholics favored autonomous agencies for two quite different reasons. First, they opposed strengthening the bureaucracy, for they had just felt the brunt of bureaucratic oppression during Bismarck's fight against Catholicism in the so-called *Kulturkampf.* The Catholics feared that a strengthened bureaucracy might once more be turned against them. Second, Catholics preferred the establishment of autonomous bodies, for their doctrine favored "natural" occupational groupings rather than "artificial" bureaucratic structures. Their fears and doctrinal preferences led Catholics to support Liberal demands for autonomous agencies to administer the social insurance measures.[26] The Liberal and Catholic demands were coupled with opposition to Reich agencies and Reich contributions from Bavaria and Baden and coolness to the entire

---

25. Ibid., p. 25.
26. Heinrich Heffter, *Die deutsche Selbsverwaltung im 19. Jahrhundert* (Stuttgart, K. F. Koehler Verlag, 1950), pp. 683 ff.

scheme by the Conservatives.[27] The consequent lack of Reichstag support forced Bismarck to accept compromises proposed by the Catholic and Liberal opposition. As a result, the Reich authorized the Laender to establish autonomous administrative agencies for each of the insurance programs. The Reich contributed a small share only to the disability and old age insurance; the others were supported by contributions from workers and employers. The Laender received authority to supervise the agencies, but laymen rather than career civil servants controlled their daily operations.[28]

Lay administrators became especially entrenched in the Health Funds which administered the health insurance and in the Industrial Insurance Corporations (*Berufsgenossenschaften*) which operated the accident insurance. There were seven types of Health Funds, each of which had slightly different administrative arrangements. The most prevalent type, the Local Health Fund (*Ortskrankenkasse*), was controlled by workers.[29] Employers controlled the Industrial Insurance Corporations.[30]

Worker control of the Local Health Funds had especially important political implications. The government, employers, and medical associations frequently charged that Socialist party functionaries found refuge from official persecution and black-listing by winning appointments to staff positions in the Health Funds.[31] On the basis of this allegation, the 1911 Insurance Code gave

27. Quandt, p. 21.

28. The original statutory provisions may be found as follows: Health Insurance—Law of June 15, 1883, RGBl, 73; Accident Insurance—Law of July 6, 1884, RGBl, 69; Disability and Old Age Insurance—Law of June 22, 1889, RGBl, 97. A more detailed account of the administrative structure of the social insurance agencies may be found in Herbert Jacob, "Field Administration in Germany, 1871–1959," Unpublished Ph.D. Dissertation, Yale University, 1960, pp. 59–82.

29. Law of June 15, 1883, RGBl, 73, paragraphs 23, 34, 35, 38, 41, and 45. Thirty-five per cent of all insured workers in Germany and 50 per cent of insured workers in Prussia belonged to such Local Health Funds. *Statistisches Jahrbuch fuer das deutsche Reich* (1887), pp. 159–60.

30. Law of July 6, 1884, RGBl, 69, paragraphs 16 and 22.

31. See for instance the allegations in Wilhelm Moeller, *Die Herrschaft der Sozialdemokratie in der Krankenversicherung* (Berlin, Reichsverband gegen die Sozialdemokratie, 1910). Unfortunately, none of the historians of the Socialist party have sought to verify or invalidate the assertion.

employers a veto over appointees to Health Fund staffs.[32] This measure blocked the only opportunity Socialists possessed to gain administrative experience in semipublic agencies. At any rate it is clear that the existence of the Health Funds did not decrease Socialist revolutionary fervor or ameliorate proletarian distrust of Germany's political system as Bismarck had hoped. The social insurance system's political goal was never attained. The program failed to undermine working-class support for the Socialist party; indeed, the party polled an increasing number of votes until in 1912 it became the single largest party in the Reichstag although still far short of a majority.[33]

The establishment of autonomous insurance agencies aggravated the Reich's difficult task of holding field officials responsive to national policy mandates. Laymen who lacked the legal training of civil servants as well as their long apprenticeship in bureaucratic discipline operated the Health Funds and Industrial Insurance Corporations. Partly in response to control problems with these agencies, the 1890 statute that established the Disability and Old Age Insurance program vested its administration in the hands of career bureaucrats who worked under the supervision of existing administrative agencies in Prussia and the other Laender.

Central control over insurance programs was also made difficult by compromises that the Reichstag forced on Bismarck when the programs were enacted. The original statutes gave the insurance agencies a considerable degree of independence. Operating budgets and personnel appointments were entirely free from bureaucratic control of Land or Reich agencies until the 1911 Insurance Code gave the Reich and Laender some marginal controls over these aspects of the insurance operations.[34] Premium rates and benefit payments were likewise beyond the reach of central controls except when field agencies trespassed the limits prescribed by law or when a worker or employer brought a complaint to one of

32. Reich Insurance Code, July 19, 1911, RGBl, 509, paragraphs 332, 335, and 349. Heffter, p. 692, mistakenly asserts that employers got equal representation on the Health Fund Executive Boards. This was the government proposal, but it was not adopted by the Reichstag.

33. *Statistisches Jahrbuch fuer das deutsche Reich* (1915), p. 340.

34. Heffter, p. 692; Friedrich Kleeis, *Die Geschichte der sozialen Versicherung in Deutschland* (Berlin, Verlag der Arbeiter Versorgung, 1928), pp. 187 ff.

the special arbitration courts which the insurance system established. Reich and Land Insurance Offices served as final courts of appeal for such cases. Their decisions slowly created a body of case law that provided guideposts to the insurance agencies.[35]

The Reich was denied *direct* control of insurance programs until 1911 when the Reichstag established the White Collar Insurance. As white collar workers constituted a small and widely scattered group, the Reich overcame Land objections to the establishment of a centralized Reich Insurance Authority. The Authority operated under the Chancellor's direct control and was staffed by Reich civil servants. The White Collar Insurance, however, never matched the disbursements or political importance of the other insurance programs.[36]

Despite Bismarck's original intentions, the social insurance program produced almost as many obstacles to responsiveness as it overcame. The Reich established autonomous agencies that were staffed by lay personnel rather than civil servants in response to the political demands of an otherwise excluded group of citizens: the Liberals and Catholics. Yet the program failed to accomplish its primary goal: it did not attract widespread proletariat support for the Reich. Moreover, the administrative concessions Bismarck gave to the Liberals and Catholics made it difficult for the Reich to obtain responsive field administration. Lay personnel proved less tractable to Reich demands than professional civil servants. Untrained administrators often misunderstood central mandates; they neglected bureaucratic tasks that a career civil servant would not question. As a result, the Reich slowly increased its controls; it granted greater authority to Land governments to supervise the administration of social insurance programs; it attempted to promote the bureaucratization of the insurance agencies.

The lack of institutionalized guarantees for responsive field administration—blatantly evident in the social insurance programs—was typical of national field administration during the Second Reich. What was unusual were the Reich's eventual efforts to gain more direct influence on the operation of the social insurance agencies. In all other spheres, the Reich contented itself with

35. Heffter, pp. 689–91.
36. Law of Dec. 20, 1911, RGBl, 989; Kleeis, pp. 146 ff.

marginal controls. It delegated the administration of all its other programs to the Laender even though it lacked guarantees that the Laender would administer its policies energetically or uniformly. Even the Bundesrat provided only nominal assurance of responsive administration, for the Laender would have had to have voted sanctions against themselves to make Bundesrat supervision effective. If Bavaria or Prussia had ever refused to execute a Reich mandate, the Reich would have been powerless to act. However, institutional arrangements avoided such conflicts between the Reich and Prussia by combining in one man the offices of Reich Kaiser and Prussian King and in another the offices of Reich Chancellor and Prussian Minister President. As long as Prussia was loyal to the Reich, the danger of conflict from other quarters remained minimal.

A still more effective guarantee of responsive field administration lay outside the formal assurances of the constitution. It came from the knowledge that the Reich and most Laender pursued similar goals. The Reich's weak formal controls only sufficed because the similar political aims of the Reich and Laender obviated most conflicts. Indeed, Bismarck harbored greater fears that the Reich would fall under democratic control through an increase in the Reichstag's power than that a Land would refuse to execute a Reich law. He accepted the policy of administrative delegation as the lesser of two evils.

In the end, the Reich's policy of delegating field functions to the autonomous Laender rested to a large extent on the Reich's confidence that the Laender themselves would hold their field agencies under firm hierarchical control and prevent neglect of Reich policy mandates. We must, therefore, turn our attention to Land field administration to examine the degree to which this expectation was justified.

FIELD ADMINISTRATION IN THE LAENDER: THE PRUSSIAN EXAMPLE

As the Reich failed to establish field agencies of its own, the field administration of the Laender assumed an ever increasing operational burden. Land field agencies became the local agents for the Reich in the collection of taxes and supervision of the social insurances. They administered the Reich's Commercial Code (*Gewerbeordnung*) and executed emergency health measures when epidemics threatened. They suppressed the Socialists under the Reich's anti-Socialist laws of 1878–91 and carried out other police orders under the provisions of Reich law. During World War I, they recruited for the armed forces and administered the food rationing program. All these activities were in addition to their tasks as Land administrators, for under Land law they exercised general police powers, operated the country's schools, administered welfare funds, undertook all public works, and raised Land and local taxes. In short, the twenty-five Laender composing the Second Reich administered or supervised all government-sponsored programs.

We need not, however, study the administrative structures of each of these twenty-five Laender. The Laender differed greatly in size and influence. Prussia overshadowed all the rest; it had 64.5 per cent of the Reich's territory and 60 per cent of the Reich's population. It was almost six times larger than the next largest Land, Bavaria, which had only 14.1 per cent of the Reich's area and 11.7 per cent of its population. No less than twelve Laender were completely surrounded by Prussia.

Other factors than mere size contributed to Prussia's importance. Prussia provided the initiative in uniting Germany and in founding the Reich. The Prussian King was always to be the Reich's Kaiser; his representative chaired the Bundesrat and became Chancellor of the Reich. Prussia retained a veto in the Bundesrat on matters of defense, taxation, and on amendments to the constitution.[37] Even though Prussia had only seventeen of the fifty-eight Bundesrat votes, she could usually muster a majority with support from some of the small Laender that she surrounded.

The administrative structure of the other Laender reflected Prussia's territorial and political hegemony. Most of the other Laender broadly approximated Prussia's pattern of central and field administration. Of course, there were differences as well. South German Laender used different names for their officials; for instance, the Prussian Landrat's equivalent was called *Amts-mann* in Bavaria, *Kreisdirektor* in Hesse and Brunswick, and

---

37. Constitution of 1871, Articles 5, 7, 37, and 78.

TABLE 2

Population, Area, and Bundesrat Votes of Laender
Expressed as Percentage of Reich Total, 1871

Land	Population[a]	Area[b]	Bundesrat vote[c]
Prussia	60.0	64.5	29.3
Bavaria	11.7	14.1	10.3
Saxony	6.2	2.8	6.9
Wuerttemberg	4.4	3.6	6.9
Baden	3.6	2.8	5.2
Hesse	2.1	1.4	5.2
Mecklenburg-Schwerin*	1.4	2.5	3.3
Saxony-Weimar	0.7	0.7	1.7
Mecklenburg-Strelitz*	0.2	0.5	1.7
Oldenburg*	0.8	1.2	1.7
Brunswick	0.8	0.7	3.5
Saxony-Neiningen	0.5	0.5	1.7
Saxony-Altenburg	0.3	0.2	1.7
Saxony-Coburg-Gotha	0.4	0.3	1.7
Anhalt*	0.5	0.4	1.7
Schwarzburg-Rudolfstadt	0.2	0.2	1.7
Schwarzburg-Sonderhaus*	0.2	0.2	1.7
Waldeck*	0.1	0.2	1.7
Reuss-Older-Line	0.1	0.1	1.7
Schaumberg-Lippe*	0.1	0.1	1.7
Reuss-Younger-Line	0.2	0.2	1.7
Lippe*	0.3	0.2	1.7
Luebeck*	0.1	0.1	1.7
Bremen	0.3	0.1	1.7
Hamburg*	0.8	0.1	1.7
Alsace-Lorraine†	3.8	2.7	—

* Indicates Laender that were enclaves in Prussia.
† Alsace-Lorraine was no Land and had only advisory votes.
Sources:
  [a]*Statistisches Jahrbuch fuer das deutsche Reich,* 1880, p. 1.
  [b]Ibid.
  [c]Constitution of 1871, Article 6.

Amtshauptmann in Saxony and Oldenburg. Their duties, however, were essentially the same. No Land except Prussia had provinces, for none was large enough. The southern Laender tolerated
more political opposition than Prussia; these Laender also had
no Junker class to dominate the civil service. Therefore, the antith-

esis between state administration by professional civil servants and local government by lay personnel remained relatively subdued in the southern Laender.

With these exceptions, however, Prussian developments in field administration not only governed the activity of three-fifths of Imperial Germany but also set the pattern for most other areas. Our focus on Prussian field administration, therefore, will instruct us about the most significant organizational structures and administrative practices that the Laender developed during the Second Reich.

Prussia faced the same problem as the Reich in accommodating new social classes in a traditional political system. But Prussia chose to ignore working-class demands for equal representation. Prussia retained the three-class voting system until the November 1918 revolution.[38] This electoral system barred the election of Socialist deputies in the Landtag until 1908. The voting system, however, did not preclude the election of representatives from the liberal parties supported by industrialists and merchants. Their Landtag deputies formed a large block in the legislature and held at times a majority. Their policy included demands for less police interference with economic and political affairs and more lay participation (*Selbstverwaltung*) in local administration. As a direct consequence the Prussian government was forced into a series of administrative reforms beginning in 1872—a year after the unification of Germany—which gave local citizens a greater voice in local affairs while the Berlin government maintained sufficient

38. The three-class voting system operated as follows. The population was divided into three categories in each electoral district according to the property taxes they paid. The few wealthy, who paid one-third of the taxes, elected one-third of the electors; those who paid the next third of the taxes selected another third of the electors; those who paid few or no property taxes elected the last third. The electors from each district then met and selected the Landtag representative. Though this electoral system succeeded in blocking the election of Socialist representatives to the Landtag until 1908, in Reichstag elections the Socialists polled 963,000 votes in Prussia as early as 1893. A. Lawrence Lowell, *Governments and Parties in Continental Europe* (3d ed. Boston, Houghton, Mifflin, 1896), *1*, 303 ff.; Fritz Specht, *Die Reichstag-Wahlen von 1867 bis 1896* (Berlin, 1898), p. 101; *Statistisches Jahrbuch fuer das preussische Staat, 9* (1911), 581.

controls to assure a field administration responsive in the main to central policy mandates.

Before the reforms were initiated Prussian field administration still retained the same shape as given it by Stein and Hardenberg half a century earlier. In its thirteen provinces,[39] a Provincial Governor (*Oberpraesident*) represented the King and supervised provincial administrative agencies. Each province was divided into one to six districts; the district office (*Bezirksregierung*) coordinated the execution of most functions assigned to the field by Berlin ministries. In the ten or more counties each district possessed, the Landrat executed the Prussian government's policies or supervised their execution by towns and villages. City governments performed the same functions in the largest cities. The Governor, District Officer, and Landrat constituted the Prussian all-purpose field administration. These all-purpose field agents operated under the direct hierarchical control of the Ministry of Interior. Functional ministries such as the Finance Ministry, the Ministry for Religion, Education, and Public Health, and the Ministry for Commerce and Trade could also delegate field functions to the all-purpose field agencies. The functional ministries, however, channeled their policy mandates through the Ministry of Interior and its field hierarchy; they were not authorized to communicate directly with the Landraete.[40] In addition, some functional ministries also had their own field agents for collecting indirect taxes, managing public lands, inspecting factories, and performing certain other technical tasks. Most of the specialized field agents were attached to one or another of the all-purpose field agencies.

Liberal representatives in the Landtag made vigorous efforts to end the Junker monopoly in the all-powerful administrative structure in order to give bourgeois elements an opportunity to influence policy-making and execution. The reformers did not seek to reshape the entire administrative structure nor did they attempt

39. In addition to the thirteen provinces, Prussia possessed the district of Hohenzollern which ranked administratively in between the district office and province.

40. Instruktion, Oct. 23, 1817, GS, 248; Rudolph von Valentini, *Kaiser und Kabinetschef*, ed. Bernhard Schwertfeger (Oldenburg in Oldenburg, Gerhard Stalling, 1931), p. 88; Muncy, *The Junker in Prussian Administration*, p. 169.

to alter civil service recruiting procedures. Rather, they sought to introduce two nonbureaucratic controls on the activities of field officials. First, a devolution of functions to self-governing bodies at the provincial and county levels was to increase lay participation in administration and bring field officials under the supervision of their lay advisers. Second, the establishment of administrative courts was to provide a judicial curb on the legally trained but autocratic Prussian field service.

The devolution of field functions to self-governing agencies began with the County Organization Act of 1872. This law abolished the traditional police powers of the estate owners east of the Elbe River and substituted a state-appointed police magistrate (*Amtsvorsteher*). The reform also allowed broader popular participation in county affairs by giving town dwellers a heavier representation in the county councils. The law authorized the largest cities (over 10,000 inhabitants) to form counties of their own (*Stadtkreise*). In addition, the act established an executive body, the county committee (*Kreisausschuss*), elected by and from the county council to control the execution of the county's local government measures, to guide the work of the county council, and to assist the Landrat in the administration of the Land's field functions.[41]

Contrary to Liberal expectations, these measures posed no immediate threat to Junker authority—as represented by the Landrat—in rural areas. Indeed, the substitution of an appointed police magistrate for the hereditary estate owner strengthened the grip that the Junkers held on local affairs. Under the new provisions, the Provincial Governor appointed the police magistrate after nomination by the county council. In most cases, the same noble who had previously exercised traditional power was appointed to continue his functions as a state official.[42] However, his power no longer rested on custom alone; the central bureaucracy could

---

41. Kreisordnung, Dec. 13, 1872, GS, 661, paragraphs 4, 36 ff., and 133 ff. Technically, this law applied only in the seven eastern provinces. Parallel laws, however, extended its provisions with few changes to the other provinces. One should also note that despite the increased representation of towns on the county councils, rural areas still retained a majority in the councils. Cf. Frido Wagener, *Die Staedte im Landkreis* (Goettingen, Verlag Otto Schwartz, 1955), pp. 45–46.

42. Heffter, p. 555.

remove him or refuse to reappoint him on political grounds as well as for incompetence after his six-year term had expired. This aspect of the reforms, thus, strengthened central control over local police. As long as Junker families dominated the bureaucracy, they could use the administrative structure to remove mavericks, whereas before they had had to tolerate them.

The activities of the county council as established under the 1872 Kreisordnung also failed to undermine the Landrat's leading position in the county. The scope of the council's functions remained very limited; it concerned itself primarily with the county welfare program and road construction. The Landrat often dominated the council even though he could not formally control its decisions. He chaired its meetings and sat in the council as the King's representative. His prestige as a civil servant and as an expert (*Fachmann*) in administrative matters normally carried great weight in council deliberations.[43]

The activities of the county committee impinged more directly on the Landrat's duties as field administrator. The establishment of the committee institutionalized the set of advisers that most Landraete already possessed. However, committeemen could demand more frequent consultation than before as new laws constantly gave them additional statutory duties. The Landrat also needed the committee's consent to issue police regulations and to exercise his tutelary powers over the towns and villages.[44] Contrary to the expectations of the Liberals, however, most Landraete

43. The statements about the Landrat's relationship with the county council and county committee are based on comments by two Landraete of this period who wrote their memoirs: Valentini who became chief of the Kaiser's civil cabinet and Michaelis who became Chancellor during World War I. As both rose to high office, they are not representative of the Landraete of Prussia. However, it appears likely that all Landraete could more or less influence the council and committee. The author noted in interviewing contemporary Landraete that they now control and initiate proposals even though they are in a far weaker hierarchical position and possess less social standing than Landraete of Imperial Germany. See Valentini, p. 40; Georg Michaelis, *Fuer Staat und Volk* (Berlin, Furche Verlag, 1922), passim.

44. ALVG, July 30, 1883, GS, paragraph 127. Cf. Jurisdictional Catalogue in Max von Brauchitz, *Die preussischen Verwaltungsgesetze* (Berlin, Carl Heymanns Verlag, 1884), *1*, 555–614.

assumed command of their county committee for the same reasons they dominated the county councils. The small landowners and city merchants who sat on the committee could not challenge the Landrat's prestige or expert knowledge except in the few cases that concerned matters affecting themselves. Such issues arose when the Landrat proposed a police regulation affecting farming or trade practices; only then could the lay competence of the committee members evaluate the Landrat's proposals critically.

Consequently, even though the reforms enacted by the County Organization Act of 1872 were the result of great Liberal pressure, they failed to undermine Junker control of Prussia's administrative structure. The Liberals had attempted to win influence in the administrative system through local, elective councils which would be powerful enough to force career bureaucrats to listen to their wishes and ameliorate the directives sent out by the central ministries. To attain their goal, the Liberals needed to succeed in two tasks. First, they would have to capture a majority in these local councils in order to control their actions. Second, they would need to exercise council powers with such vigor that the Landrat would obey the council rather than the council following the Landrat. In both tasks the Liberals failed. Thus, the 1872 County Organization Act had little immediate impact on the distribution of power between Junkers and Liberals.

The County Organization Act, however, did loosen central control over the Junker Landrat. The Berlin ministries viewed him as *their* local agent, but he also served as executive officer of the county's local government. The Landrat's dual position as local official and Land field administrator was a vestige of the times when the Landrat was elected by the local nobility to look after local affairs and was only secondarily appointed by the King as a royal field official. The Landrat's dual position survived the Stein-Hardenberg reforms and assumed real significance through the 1872 reforms.

The Landrat in the Second Reich often found his local government activities more challenging than his Land duties. The Landrat's local functions allowed him wide areas for independent action which were denied him in the execution of Land policies, for local government was a sphere in which the Landrat could creatively guide the destiny of the people in his county. At the end of his term, he could see railroads, highways, hospitals, and welfare homes as visible testimony to his activity.[45]

The Landrat's preoccupation with local government functions caused the central ministries occasional concern, for the Landrat let subordinates administer Land programs while he concentrated on local projects. In 1912, for instance, the Prussian Minister of Interior wrote the Landraete that he expected them personally to direct energetic efforts to insure a satisfactory collection of direct taxes.[46] In the same year, the ministry also had to chide Landraete for delegating to subordinates their responsibilities regarding the rural police forces (*Gendarmerie*). The minister wrote:[47] "I must demand that the Landraete maintain the closest personal contact with the police in their county and personally attend police meetings." The records indicate that such admonitions were not unusual.

The consequences of expanded local government at the county level were, therefore, twofold. On the one hand, the Landrat had to share some of his decision-making powers with a county council and county committee. Even if the Landrat mostly dominated these bodies, the committee's statutory participation in decision-making made it necessary for the Landrat occasionally to negotiate rather than command. Second, the Landrat's local government functions sometimes caused him to neglect his duties as Land field administrator.

The Liberals sponsored a second reform which limited the activities of the Junker-dominated field administration more effectively. In 1875, the Landtag enacted the Administrative Court Act which gave Prussia a system of courts to adjudicate complaints against administrative measures. The law established three tiers of courts: a county administrative court, a district administrative court, and for all of Prussia, the Supreme Administrative Court

45. Valentini, p. 39.

46. Duesseldorf Staatsarchiv, Rep. LA Muelheim/Rhein 514, Letter from Minister of Interior MdI Ia 3051 I Ang., dated Jan. 9, 1912. In an interview with the author on March 24, 1959, at Arenberg, Rhineland-Palatinate, the former Finance Minister von Krosigk recalled that, when he was a Landrat, tax collection work was always delegated to a subordinate, for it was dull.

47. Duesseldorf Staatsarchiv, Rep. LA Muelheim/Rhein 514, Circular from Minister of Interior MdI IIc 65 dated Feb. 2, 1912.

(*Oberverwaltungsgericht*).[48] For eight years the Landtag tinkered with the composition of these courts; by 1883, the administrative courts finally emerged as closely integrated adjuncts to Prussia's field agencies.

In the counties, the county committees—which already possessed local government functions and shared some of the Landrat's administrative powers—sat as administrative court.[49] In the district office, a similar district committee (*Bezirksausschuss*) was established. Four laymen elected by the Provincial Landtag plus an appointed civil servant and judge constituted the court. The District Officer presided over it.[50] No lay judges but only career officials of the administrative and judicial civil service staffed the Supreme Administrative Court.[51]

These courts exercised a potentially powerful curb against abuse of administrative authority. Before their establishment, no appeal for judicial review of administrative acts had been possible. One could only appeal to the next higher echelon in the administrative hierarchy, normally the District Officer, for rescission of an order. As the District Officer usually relied on the judgment of the local official—who had issued the original order—this practice failed to provide safeguards against bureaucratic autocracy.[52] With the new administrative courts, appeals to semi-independent, quasijudicial bodies were possible.

The new courts were not free from bureaucratic influence. At each level, career officials of the administrative service chaired the court and undoubtedly influenced its decisions. Yet administrative immunity to court actions was clearly broken. The courts frequently reversed administrative decisions. A body of case law emerged from the decisions of the Supreme Administrative Court which established limits to administrative discretion.[53]

The fact that administrative courts imposed an external curb on the field administration can hardly be disputed. It is much

---

48. Administrative Court Act, July 3, 1875, GS, 375.
49. Kreisordnung, March 19, 1881, GS, 179, paragraph 130.
50. ALVG, July 30, 1883, paragraph 28.
51. Administrative Court Act, July 3, 1875, paragraphs 17–18 and 20–21.
52. Michaelis, p. 139; Lasker, *Zur Verfassungsgeschichte Preussens*, pp. 179 ff.
53. Cf. *Entscheidigungen des koeniglichen Oberverwaltungsgerichts* (Berlin, 1877–1918).

more difficult to estimate exactly how strong that curb was. The same factors that allowed the Landrat to dominate the county committee in local government matters probably gave him great influence when the committee sat as an administrative court. The same is true of the district committee where three career officials sat with four lay members on the administrative court. Moreover, many of the lay members of the district committees came from social strata that had no political reason to oppose the administrative bureaucracy. Indeed, as Table 3 indicates, lay members often

TABLE 3

Composition of District Committees, 1892
(Expressed as Percentage)

	Seven eastern provinces	All other provinces
Estate owners	54	41
Mayors and city councilmen	22.6	24.4
Merchants and industrialists	6.4	28.1
Other	9.0	11.5
Total	100.0	100.0

Source: Compiled from *Handbuch ueber den koeniglichen preussischen Hof und Staat,* 1892.

came from the same social classes as the civil servants.[54] Furthermore, both the county committees and district committees performed purely administrative functions in addition to their judicial duties. Thus, they were neither independent of the field administrators who made the decisions causing the litigation nor were they unfettered with administrative duties which might bias them against a plaintiff. German observers believe that such ties kept administrative courts free from impractical, ivory-tower decisions.[55] But the structural bonds between the administrative courts and field offices surely made the courts a less effective curb

54. No similar data are available on the composition of the county committees. There is every reason to believe, however, that the role of estate owners was still greater than in the district committees.

55. Statements in interviews with author by Professor Hermann Dersch, Berlin, Nov. 26, 1958, and Professor Hans Peters, Cologne, Jan. 15, 1959.

on administration than they might have been had they been established completely independent of the field administration.[56]

The Liberals intended these external controls to make field agents less responsive to the central ministries, for Prussia's central ministries remained relatively untainted by Liberal influence; only in local areas where the Liberals expected to muster a majority did they see an opportunity to ameliorate the autocratic rule of Prussia's field officials. In fact the new external controls did reduce field responsiveness to central demands, but not nearly to the degree for which the Liberals had hoped.[57] The field agents' prestige, their expert knowledge of administrative lore, and the election of numerous Junkers and landowners to county and district committees weakened the impact of the reforms.

Moreover, the Prussian central ministries retained a set of hierarchical controls over their field agents which promoted responsiveness to central demands. A review of the ministerially directed activities of Prussia's field agents will illustrate the ways in which the Prussian central government continued to control its field organization.

In all his activities as Land field administrator, the Landrat was subject to direct hierarchical control by the District Officer. The District Officer determined the Landrat's budget and the assignment of personnel to the Landrat's office. The Landrat himself depended on the District Officer's recommendation for promotion. Unlike most Prussian civil servants (*Beamte*), who had tenure in their position, the Landrat's post was considered a "political" assignment according to Prussian legal usage. He could, therefore, be removed at will and placed in retirement.[58] Landrat commissions, however, were not patronage appointments; when a new Minister of Interior came into office, he never dismissed the Landraete his predecessor had appointed. Rather, the govern-

---

56. The question of bias in the German administrative court system has never been studied; in fact, to the author's best knowledge, the problem has never been raised by German scholars. A detailed and systematic examination of the composition and decisions of the courts would contribute greatly to our ability to evaluate the German administrative court structure from 1875–1940.

57. Cf. Heffter, pp. 554–55; Wagener, pp. 45–46; Muncy, p. 24.

58. Disciplinary Law of July 21, 1852, GS, 465, paragraph 87. Other officials in the same category were the District Officer and Provincial Governor.

ment used its dismissal powers to discipline individual Landraete and to control those Landraete who sat as deputies in the Landtag.[59]

Through such controls, the Prussian ministries obtained responsive field administration of numerous programs. The Landrat remained the principal local field agent of the Prussian government. As county police superintendent, he supervised the performance of all police functions, particularly the work of the uniformed rural police (*Gendarmerie*). As agent of the Minister of Interior, he conducted all elections in his county. As agent of the Prussian Finance Minister, he collected all direct taxes. Upon instruction from any ministry or from the district office, he collected statistics and sent reports.[60]

Of these myriad functions, the Landrat's activities as police official were the most important to the central government. In Prussia, all prohibitions, whether they concerned criminal activities, trade practices, violations of the labor, mining, or construction codes, or acts threatening the security of the state, were in the form of police decrees. The law usually established general standards[61] and authorized the administrative officials to secure adherence by issuing detailed regulations (*Verordnungen*). Such regulations were issued by every level of the administration—by ministers, governors, district officers, and Landraete. The Landrat, of course, had to assure compliance with regulations issued by his superiors; but numerous problems remained which required the issuance of local regulations. Such police regulations were decreed by the village mayor or by the Landrat upon gaining approval from the county committee. If the county committee withheld its approval, the District Officer could issue the regulation with the approval of the district committee.[62]

In addition to his "legislative" role in decreeing prohibitions, the Landrat had operational control over the Gendarmerie and

59. Muncy, pp. 185–87.

60. Hue de Grais, *Handbuch der Verfassung und Verwaltung* (21st ed. Berlin, Verlag von Julius Springer, 1912), p. 232. A detailed description of the structure of field administration in a single province is given by Max Baer, *Die Behoerdenverfassung der Rheinprovinz seit 1815* (Bonn, 1919), pp. 354 ff.

61. Cf. Brauchitz, 5, passim, for examples of such skeletal legislation.

62. ALVG, paragraphs 127 and 142–43; Police Administration Law, March 11, 1850, GS, 265.

over police magistrates and town mayors. Towns within the county that had their own policemen were also subject to the Landrat's control.[63]

The Gendarmerie was the police force for rural Prussia. It recruited its policemen from noncommissioned officers who had completed nine years of active service in the Prussian army. After two months' schooling, these men were assigned to a police post in a county and placed under the supervision of a more experienced Gendarmerie officer. The Ministry of War paid and clothed the Gendarmerie; the Landrat directed its daily work. The Landrat was the only civil official in the county who could direct the Gendarmerie to enforce a police order.[64]

Through the Landrat's direction of the Gendarmerie and his issuance of local police regulations, the central government remained sure of its control over internal stability and of faithful execution of national and Land regulatory statutes. The Landrat's work as police official, thus, contributed greatly to the maintenance of a responsive administrative structure in Prussia.

Prussia's central ministries attained a responsive field administration not only by assigning tasks to the Landrat directly but also by sending specialized field agents to the counties and placing them under the Landrat's coordinating authority. Every county had a publicly paid doctor and veterinarian; all had school inspectors responsible to the district school office; in many counties there were mining and factory inspectors and sometimes state foresters. These specialists were equals of the Landrat in civil service rank; like the Landrat, they operated under the control of the district office.

Despite the presence of such specialists, the Landrat remained principally responsible for a balanced governmental program in his county. He acted as general coordinator. He was able to assume such a role even though he possessed no hierarchical authority over the specialists. Rather he capitalized on various characteristics of his office which gave him a commanding position in the county.

63. Kreisordnung, 1881, paragraph 77.
64. Ernst Kraker, *Gendarmerie und Schutzmannschaft* (Ph.D. Dissertation, University of Griefwald, 1912), pp. 14–16; Alfred Schweder, *Politische Polizei* (Berlin, Carl Heymanns Verlag, 1937), pp. 32–33.

For one thing, the Landrat's position as all-purpose county field administrator for the Land and as executive officer of the county's local government gave him wide access to information on social and economic conditions in his county. In addition, many Landraete held their office for long terms, even though the Landrat's post was increasingly becoming a wayside stop along a civil service career. As Table 4 illustrates, one-half or more of the Land-

TABLE 4

Tenure in Office of Landraete in
Selected Districts, 1894–1914
(Expressed as Percentage)

District	Less than 8 years	8–19 years	20 years and more	Total*
Aachen (Rhine Province)	50.0	20.0	30.0	100 (10)
Cologne (Rhine Province)	40.0	40.0	20.0	100 (10)
Muenster (Westphalia)	10.0	70.0	20.0	100 (10)
Frankfort/O (Brandenburg)	33.2	61.2	5.6	100 (18)
Gumbinnen (East Prussia)	81.2	12.5	6.3	100 (16)

* Figures in parentheses indicate total number in each district.
Source: Compiled from *Handbuch ueber den koeniglich preussischen Hof und Staat,* 1894, 1906, and 1914.

raete (except in East Prussia) remained at their post eight or more years; in three of the districts shown, one-fifth or more remained twenty years or longer. Such long tenure gave the Landrat a broad factual foundation upon which he could evaluate, assist, and coordinate specialists' activities.[65]

65. No direct evidence exists that Landraete became captives of their locality and refused to execute central mandates which violated local customs. In the eastern provinces, officials were often sent to their home locality to serve as Landrat; in the Rhineland, Berlin often sent Junkers from the east to avoid having to appoint local Catholics. See Baer, passim. Generally, the threat of dismissal and continual supervision by the district office averted the danger that local loyalties might bar field responsiveness.

While long tenure gave a Landrat some prestige, he owed most of his prestige advantage over specialists to his social position. The Landrat was often a Junker or noble; the technical specialist was almost always a commoner.[66] This meant that the best social circles were open to the Landrat while often remaining closed to the specialist. The Landrat usually counted army officers among his friends; the specialist rarely socialized with this elite group of Prussian society. The resulting social advantage added authority to the Landrat's coordinating efforts.

Finally, the Landrat controlled some of the facilities which specialists needed to execute their functions. The Landrat's authority to issue police regulations and his control over the police force became particularly strategic instruments to promote coordination. If the veterinarian wanted to quarantine cattle, he needed a police regulation which only the Landrat—with the county committee's consent—could issue. When a factory inspector wanted a regulation enforced, only the Landrat could order the Gendarmerie to assist. These powers made it necessary for specialists to consult the Landrat and to submit to a modicum of coordination.

The blend of formal direction (through control of facilities) and informal, deferential adjustment (through the Landrat's information, prestige, and social position) apparently resulted in successful coordination of Prussia's field agents at the county level. Neither the administrative literature nor Landtag budget debates reveal complaints about a lack of coordination at the county level. When combined with the ministries' hierarchical controls over the Landrat, these conditions gave the Prussian government assurance that local agents would execute central mandates as the ministries directed.

The district offices—which operated as an intermediate link between the ministries and Landraete—offered no particular problems of control to the central government. The Ministry of Interior possessed full authority to direct the activities of the district offices. Except for the administrative courts, no lay agencies existed to impose outside pressures leading to unresponsive field administration.

66. Muncy, p. 43 n., and pp. 173–74.

The district offices supervised the activities of most local agents operating in their district. Each district covered about half a Prussian province, or an average of twelve counties. As before, the district office was divided into three divisions which included most governmental tasks performed at the local level: 1) the division of internal affairs which dealt with organizational and police matters and was responsible for county administration and the execution of all general laws; 2) the division for religious and school affairs; and 3) the division for administration of state lands (*Domaenen*) and agricultural matters. These divisions encompassed most of the specialized field agents whom the Berlin ministries sent to the district. In addition, after 1911 the district office housed the District Insurance Office; this bureau supervised the Industrial Insurance Corporations and Health Funds in the district and served as arbitration court for social insurance matters.[67] Only two important activities remained outside the district offices' control. After 1823, the collection of indirect taxes fell into the hands of a provincial agency of the Finance Ministry which sent out its own district and county agents. The Ministry of Finance controlled these tax agents with almost no reference to the Provincial Governor or District Officer during the Second Reich. Postal and railroad administration were also never integrated with the district offices.[68]

For those activities which the district office controlled, coordination primarily resulted from hierarchical direction. All ministries sent their requests for field activities to a District Officer who referred them to the specialists in one of the three divisions of his office. Instructions to county field agents (the Landrat or county specialists) were issued from the district office alone. Routine communications were issued by division chiefs; more important matters required the District Officer's personal approval.[69]

Despite this reliance on direct hierarchical controls, the District

---

67. ALVG, paragraphs 17–27; *Circularverfuegung betreffend die Geschaefts-fuehrung der Regierungen* . . . (Feb. 9, 1884), reprinted in Brauchitz, *1*, 384–89; Reich Insurance Code, July 19, 1911, RGBl, 69, paragraphs 61–80.

68. De Grais, pp. 240 ff.

69. Heffter, pp. 591–92; Muncy, pp. 167–70; the only detailed study of a district office is H. Schubert, *Die preussische Regierung in Koblenz, ihre Entwicklung und ihre Wirken* (Bonn, Kurt Schroeder Verlag, 1925).

Officer's ability to control the manifold activities of his office declined, for the office grew to an unwieldy size. In 1831, nineteen higher civil servants sufficed on the average to staff a district office; in 1897, thirty-five were needed.[70] The District Officer was given no additional staff assistance nor was he relieved of the responsibility of personally leading the division for internal affairs. The result was that specialists in the district offices increasingly initiated important activities without consulting their chief. Consequently, the District Officer's failure to coordinate field activities aroused increasing criticism after 1900 and demands for reform—demands which remained unmet for 30 years.[71]

The highest Prussian field official, the Provincial Governor, only gradually became part of the administrative hierarchy. Originally his position was a symbolic one with the function to represent the Prussian King in the provinces and to act as liaison to the provincial diets. The reforms of 1872–85, however, gave him important administrative duties. He appointed the local police magistrates; he was the final court of appeal on matters involving town or county self-government. He also ruled on administrative disputes that involved the district offices. The Old Age and Disability Insurance Authorities were attached to a provincial autonomous agency which the Governor supervised; and the regional indirect tax offices were attached to the governor's office.[72] All reports to the ministries from the district offices and all instructions from the ministries to field offices came through the governor's bureau. However, the sheer volume of paperwork and the unclear authority of the governor over the district officers continually plagued the governor's attempts to coordinate field activities on a provincial level.[73] Almost all reform proposals circulating after 1900

70. Computed from *Handbuch ueber den preussischen Hof und Staat*, 1831 and 1897.

71. See, for instance, *Stenographische Berichte, Hause der Abgeordneten* (1900), *1*, 1323–24; Frhr. von Zedlitz und Neukirch, "Neueinrichtung der preussischen Verwaltung," *Preussische Jahrbuecher*, *107* (1902), 38.

72. Hartung, *Der Oberpraesident*, pp. 48–49; Heffter, p. 599; Kube, *Die geschichtliche Entwicklung der Stellung des preussischen Oberpraesidenten*, pp. 46 ff.; Guenter Lenz, *Die Wandelung der Stellung des preussischen Oberpraesidenten* (Ph.D. Dissertation, University of Goettingen, 1936), pp. 36–38; Muncy, pp. 62–67.

73. Hartung, pp. 48–49; Heffter, pp. 599–600.

sought to eliminate either the District Officer or Provincial Governor as the existence of both served to increase confusion rather than coordination.[74]

Prussia's field administration during the Second Reich, therefore, may be summed up as consisting of a structure of ministerially controlled all-purpose and specialized field units. Lay councils and administrative courts diminished responsiveness to central mandates to some extent but never seriously undermined the authority of the central ministries.

The same field agencies executed most of the functions that the Reich delegated to Prussia. The field agents, however, had no contact with Reich officials except for the finance inspectors. The Reich addressed all its requests to the Prussian central ministries in Berlin. The Prussian ministries then assigned Reich functions to the Prussian field agents in the same manner as they assigned purely Prussian functions. The Landrat and city governments assumed the execution of most Reich functions. They scarcely distinguished between Reich and Prussian functions, for central controls over the Reich programs were exactly the same as over Prussian functions. Existing Prussian field agencies absorbed all Reich activities except supervision over the social insurance programs. For that task Prussia established Insurance Authorities for Disability and Old Age Insurance in the Provincial Executive's office in 1889; it established Insurance Offices in the Landrat's and mayor's bureaus and District Insurance Offices in the district offices in 1911. With these minor exceptions, the Prussian field administration assimilated Reich functions without structural changes or signs of stress.

In addition to the hierarchy of bureaucratically controlled local and regional officials, Prussia possessed self-governing administrative bodies at the local and provincial levels. In the larger cities, a locally appointed mayor (*Buergermeister*) performed the Landrat's functions; in the county, county councils provided aid to the poor and built local roads; at the provincial level, roads and canals

---

74. The reform proposals are summarized by Hugo Preuss from a liberal position in "Verwaltungsreform und Politik," *Zeitschrift fuer Politik, 1* (1908), 95–126; von Zedlitz und Neukirch is a representative of reform proposals from the conservative vantage point.

were built according to the instructions of the Provincial Landtag by the Provincial Executive (*Landeshauptmann*). Each of these bodies was an all-purpose, autonomous field agency. All were staffed by lay personnel or by civil servants who came from a quite different social background than did Land bureaucrats. City officials were notably liberal in contrast to the conservative tradition of the Prussian bureaucracy; moreover, most municipal civil servants were commoners rather than Junkers or noblemen.[75]

Prussia maintained control over these autonomous all-purpose field agencies by a variety of devices. In the county, the Landrat served as the county's executive for local government functions as well as for Land field functions. The bureaucratic controls which impinged on the Landrat as Land official affected his county activities too. The Landrat remained subject to civil service discipline; his career depended on the ministry's evaluation of his activities. Few Landraete would spoil their civil service careers by persisting in local policies not approved by the ministry.

Control over city administration remained less direct. The District Officer supervised city governments. Budgets for delegated functions required district office approval. Police administration in the largest cities was entrusted to a Land civil servant (*Polizeipraesident*) rather than to the locally appointed mayor. The District Officer's most important control instrument, however, was his authority to approve candidates a city wished to appoint to the post of mayor. A candidate whom the District Officer considered incompetent or politically unreliable (i.e. too liberal) was rejected. This control over the mayor's selection, however, remained a considerably weaker instrument than the ministry's control over Landraete, for the mayor, once appointed, was immune to ministerial controls over his career.[76]

Supervision of the Provincial Executive's office rested with the Provincial Governor. His control always remained marginal. The governor could only guard against *ultra vires* acts by the Provincial Executive. However, the central ministries paid little attention to their lack of effective controls over this agency as the scope of its activities remained nominal.

75. Heffter, pp. 610–12 and 614.
76. For central controls over municipal administration, see ibid.

Prussia thus sought to guarantee itself responsiveness to central mandates by placing most of its field agents in a hierarchical structure which gave central officials multiple opportunities to direct local activities. The Provincial Governor and District Officer were tools to promote better supervision of Landraete and municipal officials. The administrative structure provided clear channels for directives to flow from Berlin to each locality; it enabled the central ministries to apply pressure by threatening the budgets of local agencies and the careers of local field agents.

In addition to all these techniques, Prussia's civil service recruitment policies contributed greatly to the attainment of a responsive field administration. During the Second Reich, the government continued to seek civil servants from the nobility and from those upwardly mobile elements of the bourgeoisie who enthusiastically supported the monarchy.[77] Such preferential recruitment in itself promoted loyalty to the central regime, for whenever outside groups sought to win a voice in controlling the bureaucracy, the civil service proved to be a valuable ally in the government's struggle to retain monopolistic control over administration.

Not only the recruiting but also the prior training of civil servants contributed to responsive administration. While proper social credentials helped enormously in winning an appointment to an administrative agency, each recruit also had to pass a series of examinations and undergo a period of apprenticeship. In order to pass these examinations, attendance at a university became mandatory. The usual academic curriculum for the prospective official almost always included law and administrative law.[78] These legal studies had great influence on the future civil servant. The law and administrative law he studied sometimes emphasized the rights of citizens and thus helped curb the autocratic power of the bureaucracy. Without exception these studies attempted to inculcate unquestioning loyalty to the State, the Crown, and to bureaucratic superiors. While administrative law emphasized the

77. Theodor Eschenburg, *Der Beamte in Partei und Parlament* (Frankfurt a/M, Alfred Metzner, 1952), pp. 33–38; Muncy, p. 109.

78. Marx, "Civil Service in Germany" in White, ed., *Civil Service Abroad,* pp. 204 ff.; Muncy, p. 101.

special privileges of civil servants, it also stressed the duty of a
civil servant to obey his superiors.[79]

All civil servants went through this common legal training.
After winning a degree (usually in law), the neophyte sought an
apprenticeship with an administrative agency—usually with a
Landrat or District Officer.[80] In this apprenticeship, he was introduced to the bureaucratic routine and also learned the norms
of bureaucratic behavior, the most important of which was obedience to superior officials. It was also during this apprenticeship
that most prospective civil servants fulfilled their military obligation by serving as a reserve officer in the Prussian army.[81] Their
army experience was still another occasion to learn obedience and
to acquire the pride of status that was typical of the Prussian ruling elite. By the time the prospective civil servant passed his final
examinations, he usually had completely assimilated the legalistic
perspective of the Prussian bureaucrat and had learned the unquestioning loyalty that the Prussian government required. The
whole training and recruiting process might be compared to a
concentrated exposure to preventive medicine, for through it most
candidates internalized the values sponsored by the monarchy and
therefore offered little opposition to central mandates when working as field agents. As an official observed during those years:[82]

> How is it possible to have a liberal government? Since fifty
> years no Landrat, no *Regierungsrat,* nor District Officer,
> almost no Provincial Governor either, no Police Magistrate,
> almost no village mayor east of the Elbe was appointed who
> was not conservative to the bones. We find ourselves in an
> iron net of conservative administration and self-administra-
> tion.

79. See especially Georg Meyer and Gerhard Anschuetz, *Lehrbuch der
Deutschen Staatsrechts* (7th ed. Munich and Leipzig, Verlag von Duncker und
Humblot, 1919) as this was probably the most influential text on administra-
tive law written during the Second Reich.

80. Muncy, p. 101.

81. Ibid., pp. 107–08.

82. This statement is attributed to Clemens von Delbrueck by Gustav
Schmoller, "Die preussische Wahlrechtsreform von 1910 auf dem Hintergrunde
des Kampfes zwischen Koenigtum und Feudalitaet," *Schmollers Jahrbuch fuer
Gesetzgebung, 34* (1910), 1268; also see Muncy, p. 109 n.

SUMMARY

In summing up the development of Prussian field administration during the Second Reich, it is important to note that the Prussian government maintained control over its field administrators despite the reforms it initiated under pressure from the Liberals. The Liberals had hoped that the extension of self-government and the establishment of administrative courts would loosen the central government's grip on its field officials and allow Liberal influence to penetrate the administrative system. These hopes remained unfulfilled because the new institutions—notably the county committees which served both as self-government organs and as administrative courts—were dominated by the same Junker officials who staffed the central ministries and the field service. Moreover, the Prussian central government maintained a set of effective hierarchical controls over its field officials which promoted responsiveness to central policy mandates. The Berlin ministries retained their authority over appointment, transfer, and promotion of field officials; central budgetary controls remained intact; the District Officer continued to supervise the Landraete and cities in their performance of Land functions. Thus the Prussian government conceded little indeed to Liberal demands for an effective role in administration. Unlike the Reich, it conceded nothing at all to the working classes.

The Prussian experience justified the Reich's confidence that Land administration would remain under the strict hierarchical control of the Land central ministries and that these ministries would remain under the control of the conservative ruling class. The Reich needed no direct field administration of its own as long as the Land governments remained as conservative as the Reich.[83] Prussia's retention of the three-class voting system, her refusal to make her cabinets responsible to the Landtag, and the continued

---

83. The political and administrative development of the other Laender was essentially similar. Nowhere did political events bar responsive field administration. See Heffter, passim, and Ziekursch, *Politische Geschichte, 1* and *2,* passim. The development of Bavarian administration is described by Max von Seydel, *Bayern* (Freiburg i.B., 1888); Wuerttemberg administration is examined by Alfred Dehlinger, *Wuerttembergs Staatswesen* (Stuttgart, W. Kohlhammer Verlag, 1951–53), *1* and *2,* passim.

dominance of the Junkers and the Junker spirit in the civil service were essential elements of the Reich's guarantee of responsive field administration. When the 1918 revolution destroyed these conditions, both the Reich and Prussia were forced to initiate substantial changes to retain a responsive field administration.

4. THE STRAINS OF ADMINISTRATION IN A NEWBORN DEMOCRACY: THE WEIMAR REPUBLIC

As the smoke lifted from the battlefields in November 1918, it drifted east and settled on a war-weary, strife-torn Germany. The end of the war stunned Germany. The army had collapsed; the Kaiser had abdicated; Germany was proclaimed a Republic. The November revolution stirred unbounded but heterogeneous hopes as well as bitter mistrust. Where order had reigned with a matter-of-fact inevitability, chaos now ruled. The Socialists who proclaimed the Republic began their rule in utter disbelief that the Kaiserdom and monarchy had fallen. It was a revolution that was neither expected, planned, nor entirely desired.

Overnight the Reich fell under the control of the Socialists, a party which had been systematically excluded from governmental power under the Second Reich. The new regime immediately severed its ties with Prussia and pledged to establish a parliamentary government. Thus at one swift blow, the Reich's conservative bias, its denial of parliamentary responsibility, and the bond between the Reich and Prussia were swept away.

In the wake of its defeat and the change of regimes, Germany faced a host of urgent problems. The Allies pressed for immediate withdrawal of Germany's troops and demobilization of its army. They also demanded the surrender of "war criminals" and the payment of uncalculated millions as reparations. At home, the new government had to control radicals who wanted to continue the revolution until it swept all bourgeois elements away. At the same time, the regime had to win the loyalty of a bureaucracy that had once sworn to protect the Kaiser but now found itself serving the same Socialists whom the Kaiser had branded enemies of the state a few years earlier. The new government, moreover, had to win sufficient popular support to execute the drastic demands of the Versailles Peace Treaty. When it moved too quickly, the regime faced a reactionary uprising; when it moved too slowly, it faced occupation of German territory by Allied troops.

Some of Germany's problems arose from her peculiar status as a defeated power, subject to the whims of sixteen victorious enemies. But many of its problems resulted from the sudden rise of a new elite by revolutionary means. As such, the situation had much in common with other revolutions. The Socialists who seized power had been suppressed by the Second Reich; as representatives of the proletariat, they had been denied an active role in policy-making. This denial, of course, contributed to the tensions that caused the revolution. But, in addition, it branded the Socialists as untrustworthy radicals in the eyes of many bourgeois elements who also opposed the autocratic regime of William II. Therefore, when the Socialists seized power, they did so with a large segment of the German public predisposed against them. This distrust was the heritage of the Second Reich's failure to assimilate the working class into its political system. The Socialists' problem of winning loyal support was thus not only the result of the revolution but also of the rapid economic development of the previous forty years which had not been matched by a broadening of Germany's political base.

Obstacles to responsive field administration arose from this situation and in turn aggravated it. The Second Reich left the new regime no field agencies of its own. After the revolution the Reich did not even control Prussia any more, for it had cut its bonds with the Prussian government upon seizing power. Instead, Berlin housed two autonomous central governments—one legislated for all Germany while the other controlled the administration of three-fifths of Germany. This split imposed new risks to the traditional Reich policy of delegating administration to Land agencies. Moreover, some Land governments overtly opposed the republican regime; they actively pursued a policy of disloyal administration of Reich mandates. Under these new conditions, Germany's federal structure imposed loyalty barriers and communication impediments of unprecendented proportions.

Even Land governments that were loyal to the Republic had difficulty rendering faithful administration, for they themselves could not always exact responsive field administration from their own agents. Their civil service was composed of Junkers and aristocrats who lacked sympathy—not to speak of enthusiasm—for the new order. Moreover, the revolution had placed the Laender in a new legal position to which they had to accustom themselves. Finally, the chaos created by the revolution, demobilization, inflation, and the demands of the Allies so spawned organizational bottlenecks and communication impediments that responsive field administration became a remote goal.

THE REPUBLICAN REICH AND FIELD ADMINISTRATION

The Reich faced the most critical obstacles to responsive field administration. It lacked its own field units and yet lost many of the controls that assured responsive administration by the Laender during the Second Reich. The republican structure of the Reich and the political crises that it faced forced the government to search for new guarantees of responsive field administration.

Postwar Germany abandoned Kaiser, King, and Junker domination.[1] The new government quickly called a National Assembly to draft a constitution for the Republic. Elected in January 1919, the assembly completed its task in August.

The new constitution confirmed the events of November 1918; it prescribed a republican, parliamentary government for the

1. General histories of the Weimar Republic which give a balanced coverage of domestic affairs include: Theodor Eschenburg, "Die improvisierte Demokratie der Weimarer Republik," *Schweitzer Beitraege zur allgemeinen Geschichte, 9* (1951), 161–211; Albert Schwartz, *Die Weimarer Republik* (Konstanz, Akademische Verlagsgesellschaft Anthanaeum, 1958). For the origins of the Republic, see Arthur Rosenberg, *Die Enstehung der deutschen Republik 1871–1918* (Berlin, E. Rowohlt, 1928); an indispensable reference for the last years of the Weimar period is Karl D. Bracher, *Die Aufloesung der Weimarer Republik* (Stuttgart and Dresden, Ring Verlag, 1955).

Reich. Under its provisions, the Reich's Chancellor and the cabinet became individually and collectively responsible to the Reichstag. No cabinet was to rule without Reichstag confidence.

The constitution retained the Reichstag but replaced the Bundesrat with a *Reichsrat*. Like its predecessor, the Reichsrat represented the Laender; unlike the Bundesrat, the Reichsrat had no veto over legislation. The Reichsrat's principal function was to give expert advice on legislation in order to simplify delegation of administrative functions to Land agencies.

The constitution also provided for a popularly elected Reich President. The President was to be a symbolic substitute for the Kaiser in the German Republic. His duties, therefore, were primarily ceremonial. Yet, some paragraphs of the constitution vested the President with functions that could become critically important during national emergencies. Article 47 of the constitution made the President supreme commander of the armed forces. Article 48 gave him the power to compel Laender to execute Reich laws; during emergencies, it also gave the President the right to issue decree-laws without Reichstag approval.

The constitution also made important changes in the national government's formal authority to establish its own field administration. In contrast to the 1871 constitution's silence on the matter, the new charter specifically authorized the creation of a national field administration for tax collection and, by implication, for other purposes as well.[2] However, Article 14 indicated a continued partial reliance on the Reich's old policy of delegating most functions to the Laender; it stated: "National laws are to be executed by Land authorities, in so far as national laws do not provide otherwise."

These structural provisions destroyed some of the guarantees for responsive field administration that the Second Reich had relied upon. The diminution of the Laender's role through reform of the Reichsrat lessened the likelihood that national laws would be acceptable to the Land governments; by the same token, it increased the likelihood that Land governments would seek to amend national laws through administrative interpretations if the Laender were allowed to execute national policies. Moreover, the

2. Constitution of Aug. 11, 1919, Articles 14 and 83.

substitution of a President for the Kaiser finalized the divorce between the Reich and Prussian governments, for, unlike the Kaiser
who was King of Prussia, the Reich President held no position in
the Prussian government. This divorce between the Reich and
Prussia removed another of the mechanisms by which the Second
Reich had sought to assure itself of responsive field administration.

While changed political conditions created new barriers toward
the attainment of a responsive field administration, they also removed some of the objections that had prevented Bismarck from
establishing Reich field agencies. The 1871 constitution had not
forbidden the Reich to establish a field administration of its own.
Bismarck and his successors, however, considered such action un-
wise, for they wanted to minimize Reichstag power. Bismarck had
also viewed the Laender, especially Prussia, as more reliable de-
fenders of the old order than the Reich. None of these reasons
remained valid in 1919.

Political conditions in 1919 redefined Reich policy. The republican government no longer found it profitable to restrict Reichstag influence. On the contrary, the Socialists, Catholics, and
Democrats who formed the government derived their most effective support from it. On the other hand, the Land bureaucracies
—the bulwark of Bismarck's regime—at best gave only lukewarm
aid to the Republic. Even though all the ruling princes had been
driven out, the Laender provided the Reich only mixed support.
While the Socialists held firm control over Prussia, left-wing radicals seized power in Saxony, Thuringia, and Bavaria. When the
Soviet Republic (*Raeterepublik*) collapsed in Munich, a reactionary government which stood on a platform of noncooperation with
the Reich replaced it. The loyalty of Land governments could
never be taken for granted by the Weimar Republic as it had been
by the Second Reich, for German politics had turned a somer-
sault. Therefore, the republican government found it advanta-
geous to develop new administrative policies. Because it desired
Reichstag support and because it feared disloyal administration
by the Laender, the Reich government felt free to establish its
own field organization.[3]

3. These considerations were reflected in the National Assembly debate on
the establishment of a Reich Finance Administration. See *Verhandlungen der
Nationalversammlung, 329,* 2367 ff.

Moreover, Land opposition to the establishment of a Reich field administration was weaker in 1919 than ever before. The National Assembly possessed no second chamber representing the Laender. After the constitution went into effect, the Reichsrat represented the Laender, but they found themselves without the absolute veto that they possessed in the old Bundesrat. These changes in the formal powers of the Laender reflected a change in their actual position. The Allies negotiated exclusively with the Reich for a peace treaty and sent directives for its execution to the Reich government. Such foreign pressures forced the Reich to seize enough power to enable it to fulfill armistice and peace treaty obligations. At the same time, the Land with the strongest particularistic tradition, Bavaria, found itself paralyzed in the throes of civil war. The Bavarian government even appealed to the Reich for troops in April 1919, to help defeat the Soviet Republic which leftist radicals had proclaimed in Munich. Not until 1920, when an ultra conservative government re-established itself in Bavaria, could Bavaria once more try to defend states' rights in the national forum.

The structural changes embodied in the Weimar constitution and the emergence of a new political balance made the establishment of a national field administration a realistic option for the Reich. A Reich field organization offered the national government opportunities to bypass obstreperous Land governments in addition to affording the Reich a full range of hierarchical controls to obtain responsive field administration.

The Reich exercised its option only twice. In 1919 it established a Reich Finance Administration with specialized, ministerially controlled field agencies operating throughout Germany. In 1927 the Reich created the Reich Unemployment Insurance Authority, a specialized, autonomous field unit. The Laender continued to administer all other national programs, for the proponents of federalism were able to ward off Reich ambitions by appealing to the federalistic proclivities of the Catholic supporters of the Weimar coalition and by utilizing the recurrent national crises to stalemate Reich designs for more extensive field operations. The Republic thus combined the use of centrally controlled agencies with the continued utilization of the autonomous Laender in order to carry out national programs. Each of these administrative procedures encountered obstacles to responsive administration which the regime had to overcome.

THE NEW REICH AGENCIES

The aftermath of World War I and the provisions of the peace treaty forced Germany to reorganize her tax system. Germany had financed 84 per cent of her war expenditures from loans,[4] for in 1914, the Reich had postulated its financial plans on a short war. When a quick victory became impossible, the government failed to adjust its financial policy to the exigencies of a long war of attrition.[5] Not only did the Reich neglect to raise existing tax rates during the war, it also made no move to levy new direct taxes on a continuing basis. Instead, the Reich depended entirely on consumer taxes and tariff revenues even though the war choked off almost all income from the latter. As a result, Germany's national debt pyramided to unprecedented heights. Whereas Germany entered the war with a national debt of about 5.4 billion marks, she ended it with a debt of over 150 billion marks.[6] In addition, the Reich faced the dismal prospect of paying undetermined billions as reparations to the Allies. While a typical prewar Reich budget sought to raise 5 billion marks, the first budget presented to the National Assembly in August 1919 requested 27 billion. Before the war the Reich needed only 35 per cent of all tax receipts; in 1919 it required 75 per cent.[7] These changed conditions clearly required a reassessment of the Reich's standing policy of delegating the collection of Reich taxes to Land administrative agencies.

The 1919 constitution authorized the Reich to organize its own tax-collecting agencies;[8] the Reich Finance Ministry made the

---

4. Walter Lotz, *Die deutsche Staatsfinanzwirtschaft im Kriege* (Stuttgart, Deutsche Verlagsanstalt, 1927), p. 1.

5. Albrecht Mendelssohn-Bartholdy, *The War and German Society* (New Haven, Yale University Press, 1937), pp. 69–74.

6. Lotz, p. 102.

7. Finance Minister Erzberger, *Verhandlungen der Nationalversammlung,* 329, 2376.

8. Constitution of 1919, Articles 8, 83, and 84.

establishment of a Reich Finance Administration its principal
goal. It is symbolic of the crisis in which the Reich found itself
that Finance Minister Erzberger was a member of the strongly
federalistic Catholic Center party; in fact, he himself had opposed
national collection of taxes in 1909.[9] Yet once he proposed the
creation of Reich agencies for tax collection in August 1919, the
coalition parties quickly rallied behind Erzberger's proposals.
Erzberger brought the Catholic Center party with him while both
the Democrats and the Socialists were already strong adherents of
nationalizing administration as far as possible. The opposition of
the other parties in the National Assembly remained token. The
bill to establish a Reich Finance Administration passed all three
readings within a week.[10] The tax-collecting agency was functioning when new revenue laws were enacted in December 1919.[11]

The new legislation meant that responsibility for the collection
of Reich taxes henceforth rested with Reich agencies. Direction
of this activity centered in the Reich Finance Ministry in Berlin;
regional offices (*Landesfinanzaemter*) operated on the Land level;
at the local level finance offices (*Finanzaemter*) collected internal
revenues while customs offices (*Zollaemter*) collected tariffs. All
these agencies operated entirely on the Reich's budget and were
staffed by Reich civil servants.[12] The Reich, however, made some
concessions to the Laender. It respected Land boundaries in drawing the districts for the regional finance offices. In some cases a
single office served a group of the smaller Laender while the larger
Laender each possessed several regional finance offices.[13] The

9. Klaus Epstein, *Matthias Erzberger and the Dilemma of German Democracy* (Princeton, Princeton University Press, 1959), p. 81.

10. *Verhandlungen der Nationalversammlung, 329*, 2376 ff. See also Margarete
Seibert, *Die grossen politischen Parteien und die Erzbergische Finanzreform*
(Ph.D. Dissertation, University of Griefwald, 1934), pp. 15–19.

11. *Verhandlungen der Nationalversammlung*, pp. 2622 ff., and RFBl, 1919,
pp. 11–12.

12. Franz A. Medicus, "Reichsverwaltung," *Jahrbuch des oeffentlichen Rechts
der Gegenwart*, 20 (1932), 52 ff. Twenty-six regional finance offices, 1,025 finance offices, and 1,691 customs offices were originally established.

13. For instance, the regional office of Hanover served the Laender Brunswick, Schaumburg-Lippe, and Waldeck-Pyrmont in addition to the Prussian
province of Hanover. The larger Laender, especially Prussia and Bavaria, each
had several regional finance offices.

Laender were also given the right to be consulted on the location of the finance offices. Indeed, Erzberger had offered a more important concession when he proposed that the Laender be given a veto over appointments to the position of chief of the regional finance office. The National Assembly, however, amended this provision to allow Land consultation instead of a veto.[14]

These concessions caused Erzberger little concern because they were necessitated by administrative convenience as well as political prudence. It was impossible to establish a far-flung tax administration overnight, for the Reich possessed no pool of qualified officials. Therefore, the law authorized the Reich to nationalize the existing tax-collecting agencies of the Laender wherever practicable.[15] However, only the southern Laender possessed specialized agencies to collect all taxes. Prussia had divided tax collection between the specialized Indirect Tax Directorates and the Landraete who collected direct taxes in addition to their other duties. Erzberger, therefore, could only take over the tax agencies of the southern Laender. He nationalized the entire finance administration of Bavaria, Wuerttemberg, Baden, Hesse, and Saxony.[16] Land agencies, with their entire office staffs, were transferred to the Reich Finance Administration and formed regional finance offices and local finance offices for the Reich. In seven of the twenty-six offices, the chief of the regional finance office was the

14. *Verhandlungen der Nationalversammlung, 329,* 2613–15; Law of Sept. 10, 1919, RFBl, p. 2, paragraphs 4 and 14.

15. *Verhandlungen der Nationalversammlung, 329,* 2615; Verordnungen of Sept. 15, 1919, Sept. 27, 1919, and Sept. 29, 1919, RFBl, pp. 9–10. See also Franz Schiffmann, *Verwaltung, Verausserung, Belastung des Staatsvermoegens in Bayern* (Ph.D. Dissertation, University of Wuerzburg, 1931), pp. 56–57.

16. The Laender whose tax-collecting agencies the Reich nationalized were left with no means of collecting local and Land taxes. Consequently the Reich Tax Code obligated the Reich to collect Land taxes as well as Reich revenues until the Laender reorganized themselves. Most of the Laender eventually reestablished their own tax agencies. Only Bavaria allowed the Reich's offices to collect its revenues until the end of the Republic. Reich tax offices in Bavaria were therefore always the most overworked, and Bavarian officials felt that their Land taxes were neglected. See Reich Tax Code (*Reichsabgabeordnung*), Dec. 13, 1919, RGBl, 2, 1993 ff., paragraph 19; Metz, "Die Ueberlastung der bayerischen Finanzaemter," *Der deutschen Sueden* (July 10, 1927), pp. 149–53; also Schiffmann, p. 68.

Finance Minister of the Land in which the office was located.[17]

Despite these drastic moves, the Reich's finance administration took several years to become firmly established. The transition from a Land position to the Reich civil service was especially difficult for top-level officials. Before 1919, such officials held policy-making posts in a Land ministry; after 1919, they found themselves in a regional office adapting decisions made in Berlin. Such officials had to be placated. Moreover, the inflation of 1922–23 aggravated the normal troubles of a new agency by making tax collection virtually impossible. Indeed, the Reich financed as much as 90 per cent of its expenditures by printing money.[18] In the spring of 1923, nonnationalized tax agencies of the Laender (chiefly in Prussia) still collected more than 40 per cent of the income tax and 20 per cent of the turnover tax for the Reich. It took until 1925 before the Reich's own agencies were able to collect all national taxes.[19]

The circumstances under which the Reich established its network of field agencies confronted the Finance Ministry with numerous barriers to responsive administration. The ministry had to promote loyalty to national policies in a civil service that had been recruited and trained by the Laender and that had learned to identify with particularistic rather than national goals. Moreover, as the first—and, for some years, only—Reich field organization, the Finance Administration faced peculiarly difficult problems in coordinating its operations with parallel Land agencies. All these difficulties were aggravated by the inflation of 1922–23, the depression after 1928, and the recurrent political crises which undermined confidence in the central government.

The Reich Finance Ministry met some of these problems by holding its field units under a tight rein. The ministry specified the organizational structure of the regional and local finance offices through circulars sent from Berlin. It assigned and transferred all but the least important personnel. In-service training

17. RFBl, 1919, 13. Indeed, until 1921 several of these officials retained their position as Land Finance Minister. See Gerhard Lasser, "Reichseigene Verwaltung unter der Weimarer Verfassung," *Jahrbuch des oeffentlichen Rechts*, *14* (1926), 143.

18. Lasser, p. 136.

19. Ibid., p. 153.

remained carefully regulated by central directives.[20] The assignment of key personnel accentuated central control. Replacements for retired chiefs of regional finance offices after 1927 came predominantly from the ministry rather than from the field service. Eight of the ten appointees in the years 1927 to 1932 came from positions in the ministry; the other two were promoted from positions as division chiefs of a regional finance office.[21] The closest the Finance Ministry came to decentralizing personnel functions was when it delegated its authority to recruit field personnel to two of the twenty-six regional finance offices in 1927.[22] On the whole, these controls operated effectively. For instance, when field offices in Prussia adopted the customary Prussian practice of hiring apprentices who worked without pay upon expectation of gaining appointment at the end of their training period, the ministry quickly learned of it. A ministerial directive prohibited the practice by pointedly remarking that it was against the social policies of a democratic regime.[23]

The Reich Finance Ministry also sought to control operational decisions. The ministry used two methods to direct its field officials. It issued detailed instructions on collection procedures and required central approval of administrative interpretations of tax clauses in the law.[24] The ministry also designated which decisions could be made by field offices and which had to be referred to the ministry.[25] A system of special administrative courts gave an additional guarantee for uniform collection of taxes by the field offices of the Reich Finance Administration. The 1919 law established a tax court at each regional finance office; a central tax court

20. *Geschaeftsordnungen,* July 7, 1920, RFBl, p. 311; Aug. 19, 1924, RFBl, p. 73. For the local finance offices a *Geschaeftsordnung* was specified in RFBl, 1925, p. 127. For personnel policies, see RFBl, 1923, p. 3.

21. Tabulated from announcements in RFBl, 1927–32. Confirmed by statement of former Staatssekretaer of the Reich Finance Ministry, Hans Schaefer, in personal interview, Cologne, March 20, 1959. No information on replacements before 1927 could be obtained; however, most of the original appointees served until 1927 or after.

22. Special Directive of July 31, 1926, RFBl, pp. 93 ff., paragraphs 17–18.

23. RFBl, 1922, p. 240.

24. Johannes Popitz, *Einfuhrung in das Abaenderungsgesetz vom 8. April 1922 zum Umsatzsteuergesetz vom 24. Dezember 1919* (Berlin, Verlag von Otto Liebmann, 1922), pp. 33–34.

25. RFBl, 1925, pp. 82 ff.

(*Reichsfinanzhof*) which sat in Munich ruled on appeals.[26] These courts rendered authoritative interpretations of the tax laws.

Central control of the field offices of the Reich Tax Administration sometimes became inordinately great. Trifles, as well as more important matters, were regulated to the smallest detail. When economy was necessary, the ministry gave instructions on how to use envelopes three or four times. When economic conditions grew better, the ministry gave field offices permission to acquire soap and other washroom articles "when really needed."[27]

The Reich Finance Administration was the first Reich-established, Reich-controlled field organization. Its field agents had less independence than most Prussian field administrators in similarly organized agencies. Yet, the Finance Ministry's controls apparently promoted responsive administration, for Reichstag debates reveal almost no complaints about regional or even political favoritism in tax collection. But while the organizational structure of the Reich Finance Administration solved control problems, it left coordination difficulties unsolved. The field officials of the Reich Finance Administration were specialists; they remained the only field agents under direct Reich control until 1927. Their organizational isolation from other local officials made coordination a troublesome task. No all-purpose field structure existed which could adjust the activities of the Reich's tax collectors to the operations of Land administrators. Yet they frequently needed assistance from Land officials in order to enforce tax closures by police actions and to acquire information about the local economy. As there was no common hierarchical superior who could resolve local conflicts and promote cooperation, Reich officials had to rely on *ad hoc* bargains with local Land officials whenever assistance from them was needed. Such cooperation by agreement depended greatly on the personal tact of the officials involved; it sometimes sufficed to overcome coordination problems.

The Reich Finance Administration successfully hurdled most barriers to responsiveness by subjecting its field agents to the hierarchical controls inherent in a bureaucratic organization. The Reich had to find other means to control the Reich Authority for Unemployment Insurance and Employment Service, Germany's

26. Law of Sept. 10, 1919, RFBl, p. 2, paragraph 7.
27. RFBl, 1923, p. 405; ibid., 1926, p. 35.

second national field organization. The Authority was organized as a specialized, autonomous agency and, therefore, was not subject to the usual hierarchical controls.

The program assigned to the Unemployment Insurance Authority originated immediately after World War I when the government sponsored a public employment service to place demobilized soldiers in new jobs; those who could not be placed were granted unemployment compensation.[28] The Reich delegated both functions to the Laender who in turn assigned the programs to their autonomous field agents, the city and county governments. The cities and counties operated under extremely loose supervision and freely improvised administrative organizations to manage the employment services and to dispense benefit payments to the jobless.[29] To bring some order to the program, Reich legislation in 1922 specified the organizational structure of the employment service offices.[30] In 1923, administrative regulations by the Reich Ministry of Labor assigned to the employment service offices the additional task of dispensing unemployment benefits from funds paid by workers holding regular jobs, their employers, and the county and city governments.[31] All these provisions, however, were makeshift measures; the Reich had hoped that unemployment would be a temporary problem rising from postwar demobilization and the inflation of 1922–23. The Reich was disappointed in that hope. Unemployment remained high in 1924 and rose to new peaks in 1925–26.[32]

28. Verordnung, Nov. 13, 1918, RFBl, p. 1305; Martha Driessen, *Die Entwicklung der Reichsarbeitsbehoerden 1919–1929* (Cologne, Gilde Verlag, 1932), p. 48. Already in 1914, the Reich had established a central advisory agency for job placement, the *Reichszentral fuer Arbeitsnachweis.*

29. Ludwig Preller, *Sozialpolitik in der Weimarer Republik* (Stuttgart, F. Mittelbach, 1949), p. 276.

30. Employment Service Act of July 22, 1922, RGBl, *1*, 657.

31. Verordnung, Oct. 15, 1923, RGBl, *1*, 984. See also Verordnung, Feb. 13, 1924, RGBl, *1*, 121, and Driessen, p. 50.

32. According to Preller, pp. 166 ff., the average number of unemployed for the years 1920–32 was as follows (in thousands):

1920	346	1925	606	1929	1,476
1921	269	1926	1,456	1930	2,245
1922	59	1927	986	1931	3,989
1923	594	1928	1,106	1932	4,572
1924	542				

The system of employment service offices established in 1922 operated far too inefficiently to serve permanently. The districts which the employment service offices used—the counties and cities —proved to be totally inappropriate for such a program, for these general administrative areas did not correspond with the economic bounds of the labor market. For instance, a county seat that had its own city government possessed two employment offices, one for the city and one for the county, even though many workers commuted from the county to work in city factories. Because the city had its own office, the county could not directly refer jobseekers to the factories; rather it had to negotiate with the city office through their common superior, the Land central office.[33] In the Ruhr such problems were particularly acute. Large factories drew their labor supply from several counties each of which had its own employment office with no central card files. The employment offices' areal limits, thus, complicated the administration of the unemployment compensation program.[34]

Financing methods also retarded the program. Local revenues collected from workers and employers provided most of the funds, but rates varied according to the local incidence of unemployment. Businesses in depressed areas (with high unemployment) had to pay more than their competitors in more prosperous regions. This simply added to the difficulties of bringing new jobs to depressed areas.[35] To aggravate these problems still further, the city and county employment service offices operated under extremely loose controls. The Reich had no direct means to guide their operations, and the Laender did not concern themselves greatly because no Land funds were involved.[36]

33. Friedrich Syrup and Otto Neuloh, *Hundert Jahre Staatliche Sozialpolitik 1839–1939* (Stuttgart, W. Kohlhammer Verlag, 1957), pp. 305 ff.; Preller, pp. 371 ff.

34. *Reichstag Verhandlungen, 391,* 8927–30; Driessen, pp. 79–83; Syrup and Neuloh, pp. 308–10.

35. Workers and employers paid 4/9 each while cities and counties paid the last 1/9. If all necessary revenues could not be raised locally, the Laender and Reich pledged themselves to contribute the remainder. Verordnungen of Oct. 15, 1923, RGBl, *1,* 984; of Feb. 13, 1924, RGBl, *1,* 212; and of Feb. 16, 1924, RGBl, *1,* 127.

36. *Reichstag Verhandlungen, 413,* Aktenstueck Nr. 2885, p. 45; Preller, p. 371.

The Reich sought to correct these shortcomings in 1927 by establishing the Reich Authority for Employment Service and Unemployment Insurance. The Authority was to operate the employment service and administer an unemployment insurance program that replaced the existing charity-like jobless benefits. The Reich Authority was an autonomous agency on the model of the White Collar Insurance Authority. The Reich, however, had no control over the Authority's budget or over its policy decisions. Moreover, it was not financed by taxes but by workers' and employers' contributions; the Reich only pledged itself to cover emergency deficits with tax funds. Once the Reichstag set insurance premiums, the Reich had no further control over the Authority's finances. The Reich's control over the Authority's administrative policies remained equally marginal. The president of the Authority was appointed by the Reich, but the president's influence on policy decisions was limited by a tripartite board consisting of employers, workers, and government representatives; this board had to approve all policy decisions. The government members on this board did not even represent the Reich; instead the Laender, counties, and cities selected them. The Reich, therefore, lacked the means to influence policy decisions of the Authority.[37]

The Authority's field organization operated in entirely new districts. The districts respected neither Land, city, nor county boundaries; instead the Authority created regional offices in areas chosen for their economic congruity. Thirteen regions served the eighteen Laender; only the Bavarian region coincided with a Land's boundaries. The Authority showed the same disregard for existing administrative boundaries in creating local districts. The Authority's only criterion was whether the district encompassed an area in which a real labor market was operative. Consequently the Reich Authority established only 363 local districts to serve 869 local government units.[38]

The autonomous position of the Unemployment Insurance Authority raised acute problems of control for the Reich government. The Authority's income matched expenditures only during the first year of its existence. Thereafter, the depression prevented it

37. Unemployment Insurance Act of July 16, 1927, RGBl, *1*, 187.
38. *Handbuch fuer das deutsche Reich* (1929), p. 285; Syrup and Neuloh, p. 307; Preller, pp. 374–75.

from building up a reserve fund from which it could grant unemployment compensation without subsidies from the Reich's
general treasury. The Authority's deficits became so large that the
Reich could no longer balance its own budget. In those pre-
Keynesian years, the Reich Finance Ministry still insisted on governmental economy and a balanced budget to combat the depression and save the solvency of the government. This policy forced
the Reich to demand that the Authority decrease its deficits either
by cutting payments or by raising premium rates. Yet, because of
the Authority's autonomous status, the Reich government could
not impose these measures on it through administrative channels.
Instead the government had to seek remedial legislation. The necessity of transferring the struggle into the legislative arena in
order to reduce the Authority's deficit cost the Republic dearly,
for the issue divided the tenuous coalition supporting the Reich
cabinet. As a result, the Republic's last democratic government—
led by a Socialist Chancellor—lost its parliamentary mandate. The
next cabinet under Chancellor Bruening ruled only by the grace
of presidential emergency decrees.[39]

One cannot argue with certainty that if the Authority had been
subject to normal hierarchical controls, the government would
have avoided the fatal crisis. The depression remained and might
have swept the government away despite such changes. Yet, hierarchical controls would have avoided this particular affray; they
would at least have delayed the final cleavage between labor and
management, between the political Right and Left which
deepened in the following years. On other issues, the government
might have been able to weather the storm.

The internal structure of the Authority raised different problems of responsive administration. The Authority's field offices
were a hybrid of autonomy and hierarchy. While local tripartite
boards consisting of representatives of workers, employers, and
county governments advised on operations, they did not possess
the veto power held by the tripartite board at the Reich level. On
most matters the Reich Authority possessed effective controls over
its field units. The Authority appointed the chiefs of the local and

---

39. The sequence of events is brilliantly narrated by Helga Timm, *Die
deutsche Sozialpolitik und der Bruch der Grosse Koalition im Maerz 1930*
(Duesseldorf, Droste Verlag, 1952). See also Preller, pp. 424 ff.

regional offices; both were explicitly bound to follow the directives of the Reich Authority. In policy matters, the Reich Authority guided regional and local operations directly by issuing regulations, by controlling local budgets, and by making appointments to key positions in the field organization.[40] As a result of these arrangements, the Authority's field units usually responded satisfactorily to policy mandates sent to them by the Authority. While responsiveness to demands of the Reich government remained tenuous, responsiveness within the hierarchical structure of the Authority was attained.

Once again, however, Germany's federal structure raised difficult coordination problems. As the boundaries of most of the regional offices of the Authority did not coincide with Land boundaries, cooperation with Land governments was complicated. At the county level the problem was even more acute, for most operational activities took place there. Many unemployment insurance districts included several counties; others included only parts of some counties. Such disregard for county boundaries complicated cooperative arrangements with Landraete. When a local unemployment insurance office, for example, needed assistance from the police, the office had to deal with several Landraete. Obversely, when a Landrat wanted help from an unemployment insurance office, he had to negotiate with several local offices, each of which operated only in part of the county. In case of conflicts between the unemployment insurance offices and counties, no common superior existed to mediate, for the one was a Reich agency and the other a Land unit.[41]

Such arrangements would not have raised serious administrative problems if the execution of the unemployment insurance program had not conflicted with county efforts to remain solvent during the depression. When the Authority restricted the scope of its coverage in 1930, unemployed workers who lost their benefits turned to county welfare programs for emergency help. The counties, however, lacked the financial resources necessary to grant such widespread assistance. The Landrat, therefore, sought to convince his local unemployment insurance office to dispense grants

40. Unemployment Insurance Act, paragraph 34.
41. Kurt Jeserich, ed., *Die deutschen Landkreise* (Stuttgart, W. Kohlhammer Verlag, 1937), pp. 912 ff.

more generously than the Authority's policy permitted. When a local office refused to disregard its central mandate, the Landrat left embittered and in no mood to assist the local office when his cooperation was needed. Thus, responsiveness to Reich mandates by the local offices led to a breakdown of local coordination. Responsiveness in one sphere of the program led to inefficiency in another![42]

The experience of the Reich Finance Administration and the Reich Unemployment Insurance Authority shows that the establishment of Reich field agencies brought only mixed results. It is true that the Reich Finance Administration operated effectively throughout the republican years. Berlin secured responsive field administration through its use of hierarchical controls; the field units usually maintained cordial relations with local Land agencies so that voluntary coordination could be achieved. However, the Reich Authority for Unemployment Insurance met an unhappier fate. Its autonomous position balked the government's plans to impose economies in its program and led to a parliamentary crisis that brought the government's downfall. Moreover, the Authority's field units, while remaining responsive to central mandates, aroused such fierce conflicts with county agencies that cooperation was often hindered.

DELEGATED ADMINISTRATION

The Reich established only these two field organizations during the Weimar Republic; it continued to delegate all other programs to Land agencies. The 1919 constitution left the Reich with the same powers over delegated administration as it had possessed since 1871. The cabinet and Reichsrat took the Bundesrat's place in issuing administrative regulations to guide the Laender in executing Reich laws. The Reich could send inspectors to the Land field agencies only with Land permission. In case of a grave violation of a Reich law, the Reich President could compel a Land to comply with Reich orders through the use of troops.[43]

The Reich possessed another instrument to promote compliance

42. Ibid.; Preller, pp. 449–50.
43. Constitution of 1919, Articles 15, 48, and 77.

with its directives which the constitution did not include. By reserving most taxes for Reich use and compensating the Laender with grants-in-aid, the Reich won financial control over Land governments. Land reliance on Reich grants reached its peak during the inflation of 1922–23, for the Laender depended entirely on Reich grants of newly printed marks to meet their payrolls. When normalcy returned, the Laender continued to rely on Reich grants for more than half their revenues.[44] The Reich could, therefore, try to obtain more responsive field administration by threatening to reduce its contributions to Land budgets.[45]

Obtaining responsive field administration, however, remained more difficult for the Weimar Republic than for the Second Reich. The Republic lost a most valuable instrument when it severed its ties with Prussia during the 1918 revolution. Neither the Reich Chancellor nor any Reich minister held a position in the Prussian government. Such bonds had assured the Second Reich of faithful administration of national mandates in Prussia. Lacking them, the Republic was never certain of responsive administration of its policies. Yet the separation of Reich and Land governments continued until the last days of the Republic when the authoritarian government of Franz von Papen attacked Prussia's democratic regime, beginning an assault on Germany's republican institutions that the Nazis later completed.[46]

The lack of effective institutional guarantees forced the Reich to depend principally on the political loyalty of the Laender for assurance of faithful execution of Reich laws. Unfortunately, the Reich often had reason to doubt the loyalty of some Land governments, especially during the first years of the Republic. National government coalitions often included moderate Socialists; until 1925, the Reich President was a Socialist. In contrast, right-wing

44. Hans-Erich Hornschu, *Die Entwicklung des Finanzausgleichs im deutschen Reich und in Preussen* (Kiel, Forschungsberichte des Instituts fuer Wirtschaft an der Universitaet Kiel, 1950), pp. 12–13; Newcomer, p. 355.

45. In 1930, when the Nazis gained control over the police in Thuringia, the Reich cut off its police grants-in-aid. *Reichstag Verhandlungen, 444*, 118.

46. In July 1932, the Reich government under Papen removed the Prussian government and installed its own Reich Commissioners in an act of dubious legality. Papen took this action precisely because of the lack of institutional links between Prussia and the Reich. As this incident was a prelude to Nazi measures which came six months later, we will discuss it in the next chapter.

Conservatives controlled the Bavarian government; these conservatives campaigned on a plank of resistance to Reich interference in Land affairs. At the same time left-wing Socialists and Communists gained control of another Land, Saxony. Yet when such Land governments refused to comply with Reich directives, the Reich could only react by compromising its position or by compelling Land compliance through the use of troops.

Overt refusal to follow Reich mandates plagued the Weimar Republic on several occasions. The most acute crises arose as a result of Reich attempts to control the activities of the Land police when subversive forces threatened the security of the Republic. These instances of Land resistance to Reich mandates dramatically illustrate how the Reich attempted to control delegated functions and what limits the Weimar constitution and political circumstances imposed on Reich efforts to obtain responsive field administration.

After the revolution of November 9, 1918, was victorious in Berlin, the new government's most imperative task was to restore order and assure itself power throughout Germany.[47] The new government had to restrain radical elements who hoped to extend the revolution along the Russian pattern. The radicals already had seized power in many localities. Following the sailors' mutiny in Kiel on November 3, 1918, Soldiers' and Workers' Councils on the model of the Russian soviets captured control of numerous German cities; in Bavaria and for a shorter period in Brunswick and Bremen, the councils proclaimed Soviet Republics. Acting spontaneously, these Soldiers' and Workers' Councils were able to take local control because they possessed the only armed force in the community. The regular administrative organization remained all but paralyzed by the Kaiser's abdication, for civil servants—sworn only to obey the Kaiser—were confused about which authority to obey. In any case, the police were neither equipped nor trained to cope with the armed mobs and troops under the control

47. A firsthand account of the events of the first weeks of the Republic is given by Gustav Noske who served as Reich Defense Minister from January 1919 until March 1920. See his *Von Kiel bis Kapp* (Berlin, Verlag fuer Politik und Wirtschaft, 1920), pp. 78 ff., and his *Erlebtes aus Aufstieg und Niedergang einer Demokratie* (Offenbach/Main, Bollwerk Verlag, Karl Drott, 1947), pp. 97–98 and 127 ff.

of the councils. The only other force capable of meeting the situation, the army, dispersed as quickly as units returned to Germany. Moreover, Soldiers' Councils seized control over most of the military formations that still existed and made them entirely unreliable for the new government's use. On the one hand, the Soldiers' Councils interpreted the revolution as eliminating discipline; they, therefore, chased their officers away. In addition, radical leftists often controlled these councils and used them to resist the new Reich government.[48]

Land governments were ordinarily responsible for maintaining order, but most of them were still preoccupied with the task of organizing themselves on a democratic basis in November and December 1918. The Reich, therefore, undertook the first measures to restore peace.

Even Berlin remained without real protection against radical mobs. The first act of the Reich's new Defense Minister, Gustav Noske, was to retreat to the Berlin suburbs and collect a small but reliable military force. This accomplished, Noske moved his motley assortment of troops into the city on January 15, 1919, and luckily met no resistance. In short order, the same troops, to which new, temporary formations were constantly added, "conquered" Bremen, Hamburg, Brunswick, and the industrial centers of the Rhineland and Westphalia.[49]

But Germany could not be ruled by troops. The presence of soldiers always threatened to cause new riots, for the working class viewed the army as representative of the old Prussia they had just overthrown. At the same time, the Allies were insistent in their demand that Germany dismember her military machine. A police force, therefore, had to be substituted for the provisional army troops and volunteer corps (*Freikorps*) who had fought for the government since January 1919. The Reich suggested to the Laender that they establish heavily armed police to cope with riots. The first such police force was a security police (*Sicherheitspolizei*) in Berlin, formed from one of the *ad hoc* units that had liberated the city in January 1919.[50] Hamburg organized a similar

48. Ibid.; Harold J. Gordon, Jr., *The Reichswehr and the German Republic, 1919–1926* (Princeton, Princeton University Press, 1957), pp. 8–9.

49. Noske, *Von Kiel bis Kapp*, pp. 70–75; Gordon, pp. 34–38.

50. Noske, ibid., p. 113.

police force in June 1919, after riots demonstrated that the old police units—even when augmented by soldiers—were too weak to battle armed mobs. In Hamburg, too, the personnel for the new police came from the volunteer corps stationed in the vicinity.[51] Prussia followed suit by establishing a city police during the first months of 1919.[52] In Bavaria the same developments were made more dramatic by the bloody battle to retake Munich from Communist revolutionaries in May 1919. When order was restored, the city commandant established the Bavarian police force.[53]

The security police consisted of large formations of heavily armed troops. In December 1919, the Bavarian state police consisted of 10,000 men with equipment that included 10 cannons, 15 mortars, 51 heavy machine guns, and numerous lighter weapons.[54] The Hamburg police had 5,000 men with equally heavy equipment;[55] Prussia's security police forces were similarly equipped.[56]

Such heavily armed police units, however, aroused the suspicions of the Allied Control Commission which had been established to supervise Germany's disarmament. According to Article 162 of the Versailles Peace Treaty, the police were to consist only of gendarmes and municipal police; their number was not to exceed the 1913 total except where a population increase could be shown. When Allied observers saw these entirely new, heavily armed security police formations, it is small wonder that they considered

51. Lothar Danner, *Ordnungspolizei Hamburg* (Hamburg, Verlag Deutsche Polizei, 1958), pp. 23–24. Danner was chief of the Hamburg security police during most of the Republic.

52. Carl Severing, *Mein Lebensweg* (Cologne, Greven Verlag, 1950), *1*, 312–17. Severing served as Prussian Minister of Interior for many of the Weimar years.

53. *Bayerische Hauptarchiv, Abt.* II, *Landespolizei Amtbund* I (1919). See also G. Sagerer and E. Schuler, *Die bayerische Landespolizei von 1919 bis 1935* (Munich, 1954), pp. 5–6.

54. Inspection report dated Nov. 22, 1919, *Bayerische Hauptarchiv, Abt.* II, *Landespolizei Amtbund* I (1919).

55. Danner, pp. 26–27.

56. Severing, *1*, 312–17; Hans Helfritz, "Die Entwicklung des oeffentlichen Rechts in Preussen seit inkrafttreten der neuen Verfassung," *Jahrbuch des oeffentlichen Rechts*, *14* (1926), 298–301; Horst-Adalbert Koch, "Zur Organisationgeschichte der deutschen Polizei," *Feldgrau*, *5* (1957), 142 ff.

them as "the skeleton around which [Germany] hoped to build up [its] main forces in case of mobilization."[57] The Allies, therefore, insisted on dissolution of the security police. After vigorous German protests, the Conference of Spa and the subsequent Conference of Ambassadors in June 1920 finally authorized a security police limited to 150,000 men if organized on a civilian-controlled basis and if divested of its heavy arms.[58]

Consequently the Laender reduced the size of their security police forces and stripped them of prohibited weapons. The Reichstag enacted additional restrictions. Policemen had to enlist in the security police for a period of twelve years after which they either transferred to the Gendarmerie or municipal police or retired from police service altogether. Moreover, all positions in the Gendarmerie and municipal police forces were reserved for security-police veterans.[59] In addition to its normal controls, the Reich possessed one special instrument to insure Land compliance with these standards—the Reich paid 80 per cent of the costs of the security police.[60] When a Land refused to abide by the statutory provisions for the security police, the Reich could cut this grant off. It did so only once, when a Nazi was appointed Minister of Interior in Thuringia in 1930.[61]

Aside from the above provisions, the Reich usually allowed the Laender full discretion in organizing and deploying their security police. The Laender usually stationed the security police in large cities where major riots were most likely to occur. A portion of the police were organized in companies and assigned to barracks to be available for emergency riot duty; the remainder manned police stations throughout a city and performed all the ordinary criminal, traffic, and preventive functions of a city police. In Prussia these police forces were controlled by the Provincial Gov-

57. London *Times* (April 19, 1919), p. 12.

58. U.S. Department of State, *The Treaty of Versailles and After* (Washington, Government Printing Office, 1947), p. 322.

59. Law of July 17, 1922, RGBl, *1*, 597. For Prussia see also Law of Aug. 16, 1922, GS, 241; Law of July 31, 1927, GS, 151. For Bavaria see Decree of Nov. 22, 1920, *Bayerische Hauptarchiv, Abt.* II, *Landespolizei Amtbund* I (1920), and Law of Aug. 26, 1922, GVBl, p. 427.

60. Danner, p. 24.

61. *Reichstag Verhandlungen, 444*, 118. Severing, 2, 229–32, 241–43, especially p. 231.

ernors and District Officers who directed security police actions according to ministerial directives from the Prussian Ministry of Interior. In each city a police commissioner (*Polizeipraesident*) directly responsible to the Ministry of Interior exercised command functions.[62] The field organization of the security police in the other Laender was similarly patterned.[63]

As long as Reich control over security police organization remained marginal, the Laender did not resist Reich supervision. On the other hand, when the Reich attempted to exercise active control over the police during emergencies in 1922 and 1923, it met such furious resistance from Bavaria that Reich actions were stymied.

The Reich's first attempt to control Land police occurred in 1922 after nationalist fanatics assassinated the German Foreign Minister, Walther Rathenau. Reich President Ebert issued an emergency decree under Article 48 authorizing the Reich Minister of Interior to send binding directives to any Land field official, including the police.[64] With this decree the Reich intended to initiate nationwide operations to break up extreme right-wing organizations that advocated violent overthrow of the Republic. A month later, the Reichstag replaced the presidential decree with the Law To Protect the Republic; this act defined political crimes against the Republic, ordered the Land police to apprehend all violators, and established a special Reich court to hear their cases. The law left execution to the Land police but withdrew political crimes from ordinary Land courts.[65] The Reichstag also adopted a bill to establish a Reich Investigation Agency (*Reichskriminalpolizeiamt*) which could send its agents to the Laender for on-the-spot investigations of important cases.[66]

These moves brought protests from many Laender and vigorous

62. Hans-Hugo Pioch, *Das Polizeirecht einschliesslich der Polizeiorganisation* (2d ed. Tuebingen, Verlag J. C. B. Mohr, 1952), pp. 52–53.

63. Ibid., p. 24.

64. Verordnungen of June 26, 1922, RGBl, *1*, 521, and of June 29, 1922, RGBl, *1*, 532. For a general discussion of the president's powers under Article 48, see Frederick M. Watkins, *The Failure of Constitutional Emergency Powers under the German Republic* (Cambridge, Mass., Harvard University Press, 1939), pp. 15–24.

65. Law of July 21, 1922, RGBl, *1*, 585.

66. Law of July 21, 1922, RGBl, *1*, 593; Pioch, pp. 54–57.

resistance from Bavaria. Bavaria countered the Reich Law To Protect the Republic with her own emergency decree which she claimed nullified the Reich's action.[67] Bavaria refused to execute the Reich law within her boundaries. The Reich had only two alternatives. It could compel Bavarian compliance through the use of armed force, or it could compromise its position by negotiating with Bavaria. The Reich chose the latter course because it feared Bavarian secession (a step the French were encouraging) and wanted to avoid the resulting bloodshed. In the ensuing negotiations, Bavaria promised to rescind her emergency decree on the condition that the Reich suspend execution in Bavaria of the most important provisions of the Law To Protect the Republic. The Reich also abandoned its plans to establish the Reich Investigation Agency.[68] The terms of this settlement were decidedly in Bavaria's favor.

A graver crisis in 1923 provoked the Reich's second attempt to control Land police in emergencies. In September 1923, the Reich decided to end Germany's passive resistance against the French occupation of the Ruhr. To prevent any outbreak of domestic violence, President Ebert proclaimed a state of emergency under the provisions of Article 48. The President first delegated his executive powers to the Reich Defense Minister and then directly to the Army Chief of Staff. The army's powers included the authority to issue direct orders to the Land police.[69] Many of the Laender protested against this application of the President's emergency powers.[70] The real test of strength, however, once more came in Bavaria. The army ordered Bavarian officials to prohibit publication of the Nazi newspaper, *Voelkische Beobachter*. Bavaria ignored the order and won to its side the commanding general in

67. Karl Schwend, *Bayern zwischen Monarchie und Diktatur* (Munich, Richard Pflaum Verlag, 1954), pp. 183 ff.; Werner G. Zimmerman, *Bayern und das Reich 1918–1923* (Munich, Richard Pflaum Verlag, 1953), pp. 113 ff.

68. The agreement is reprinted in Schwend, pp. 194–95. See also Zimmerman, pp. 107–09, 113–15, and 135–37, and Johannes Mattern, *Bavaria and the Reich: the Conflict over the Law for the Protection of the Republic* (Baltimore, Johns Hopkins Press, 1928), pp. 119–25.

69. Verordnungen of Sept. 26, 1923, RGBl, *1*, 905, and of Nov. 8, 1923, RGBl, *1*, 1084.

70. For Prussia see Otto Braun, *Von Weimar zu Hitler* (New York, Europa Verlag, 1940), pp. 105–06; for Hamburg see Danner, pp. 128–31.

Bavaria, who refused to obey his military superiors and declared his allegiance to Bavaria. Fortunately, Hitler chose this moment to stage his "Beer Hall Putsch"; he thereby drove the Bavarian government into a common front with the Reich against his Putschists.[71] After the Putsch was defeated and the Reich had successfully deposed an extreme leftist government in Saxony, Berlin was in a strong enough position to deal with the Bavarians. This time the Reich did not retreat. It retired the Bavarian army commander and annulled all special rights regarding army organization which Bavaria still enjoyed.[72] Moreover, the Bavarian government resigned in favor of a less militant group.[73]

These incidents clearly illustrate the limits to Reich control over Land agents. The constitution allowed the Reich to exercise direct control over the police only during emergencies. During such emergencies, however, the Reich was too weak to overcome resistance from Laender whose governments were ideologically opposed to the Reich. In 1922–23 Bavaria relied on the old federal argument that all police functions belong to the Laender and could point to several constitutional provisions and to the customary German practice to support her case. Moreover, political considerations bolstered Bavaria's position in these crises. The Reich lacked a reliable force of its own to crush Bavarian resistance. Allied insistence on disarmament not only shrunk the size of the German army to minute proportions but also directed the resentment of many soldiers against the Republic for agreeing to these limitations. In addition, the Republic had to fear Bavarian secession under French auspices at a time when France already occupied most of the Ruhr. The lack of loyal military forces and the failure of the Bavarian government to execute Reich mandates voluntarily thus stymied the Republic's attempts to stamp out subversive movements. The failure to overcome these loyalty obstacles marked a major defeat in the Reich's effort to establish a stable and effective government in postwar Germany.

Until the last months of the Republic, the Reich never again

71. Schwend, pp. 214–42; Gordon, pp. 235–51.

72. Otto Gessler, *Reichswehrpolitik in der Weimarer Zeit*, ed. K. Sendtner (Stuttgart, Deutsche Verlagsanstalt, 1958), pp. 277–78. Gessler was Reich Defense Minister during this incident.

73. Schwend, p. 255.

tried to seize direct control of Land police or any other Land agency.[74] One reason is that after 1923 a political calm descended over Germany which obviated the need for direct Reich action until the 1930s. During the last years of the Republic, the Reich was too weak to attempt such actions. Nor did the Reich need to intervene in police administration during the later years of the Republic, for the Laender were better able to maintain order than the Reich. The governments of the major Laender were far more stable than the Reich's. From March 1920 until January 1933, the Reich had seventeen cabinets. Most of the Reich cabinets rested on such fragile coalitions that they could not contemplate impulsive actions likely to inflame domestic politics. In contrast, Prussia had only three cabinets, one of which ruled eleven and a half years; Bavaria had only nine, one of which governed for six years. The most important Laender, thus, could themselves act to prevent major riots which might otherwise have necessitated Reich action.

Other programs that the Reich delegated to the Laender did not provoke such violent crises, even though the Reich supervised the Laender more closely than before. For example, a special decree in 1923 ordered all Reich offices to reduce their personnel; this decree applied to the social insurance agencies in the Laender as well. Moreover, during the inflation of 1922–23 and the depression after 1928, the Reich authorized the Laender to supervise the activities of the autonomous social insurance agencies in far greater detail than ever before. These decrees were executed without extensive opposition by the Laender, for they involved no precipitous change in the balance of power between the Reich and the Laender.[75]

The Reich's experiences with its own field organization and with the delegation of field functions to the Laender show how the political weakness of the Republic was reflected in its inability to evoke responsive administration. The Reich no longer could trust the Laender to execute all its policies effectively and loyally. Some of the Laender opposed the Reich regime on partisan

74. The notable exception was the Reich's seizure of the entire Prussian government in 1932 which we shall discuss at length in the next chapter.

75. Lasser, "Reichseigene Verwaltung," p. 63; RABl (1924), p. 18.

grounds; others considered it a usurper, lacking legitimate au thority to compel Land administration of Reich policies. Yet Germany's precarious financial, economic, and political position compelled the Reich to make greater demands for uniform execution of its laws than ever before. The Reich's financial condition led it to insist on the elimination of local variations in tax collection; Germany's economic crises made local deviations in the administration of unemployment assistance intolerable. Recurrent riots which bordered on civil war and widespread subversive movements made nationwide police actions imperative.

In two spheres of action—tax collection and the administration of the unemployment insurance—the Reich overcame most barriers to responsiveness by establishing its own field agencies. In each case the Reich vested a central agency with direct hierarchical controls over a field organization. These controls promoted uniform translation of national policies into effective administrative actions at the local level. The most serious loyalty barriers and communication impediments were surmounted by these nationally controlled, hierarchically organized field organizations. Yet some communication problems remained. The Reich's requirement that its policies be translated without deviation resulted in local hardships and the breakdown of coordination with Land agencies that operated at the same level. From the Reich's point of view, these problems remained minor; however, the Laender and particularly counties and cities regarded them as grave crises, for they endangered local programs that were to supplement Reich policies. These coordination problems remained unsolved during the Weimar Republic.

The Reich delegated police administration and many other national programs to the Laender despite the loyalty and communication barriers that threatened to impede responsive field administration. Allied insistence on Land administration of police and the convenience of using existing administrative organizations for programs that were not extremely urgent caused the Reich to overlook the potential dangers of this policy. The incidents described in relation to police administration show the Reich's fears to have been well founded. The Reich's controls over Land administration did not suffice to induce responsive field administration without Land cooperation. The constitutional provisions

that allowed the Reich to compel Land adherence to Reich standards proved ineffectual, for proposed Reich actions against recalcitrant Laender threatened to erupt into civil war.

When the Reich lacked its own field agencies, it had to rely on
the willingness of the Laender to execute Reich policies. We shall
see in Chapter 6 on the German Federal Republic that a national
administrative court system and federal intervention in Land
elections can sometimes supplement hierarchical controls over
Land administration. The Weimar Republic, however, failed to
adopt these tools, for it remained too weak to impose them on the
Laender. No Reich cabinet possessed a firm parliamentary base.
The most reform-oriented party, the Socialists, became weaker
with every cabinet change. After November 1922, the Socialists
were either excluded from the government or checked by right-
wing components of coalition cabinets.[76] The impetus of reform,
thus, was quickly stifled in Weimar Germany. Administration reforms and fundamental changes in Reich-Land relations remained
unfulfilled promises.

Throughout the Weimar Republic, the Reich remained heavily
dependent on Land cooperation to secure faithful execution of
Reich policies when the Reich did not possess its own field agencies. We have already shown how the Bavarian government refused to execute some Reich policies. However, responsive field
administration was also uncertain in Laender that loyally supported the Republic, for the Laender themselves encountered
loyalty and communication barriers to responsive field administration. We shall, therefore, examine Prussian administration to
see how Germany's largest Land—one that remained steadfastly
loyal to the Republic—attempted to surmount those obstacles.[77]

76. The second Wirth Cabinet, which fell in November 1922, was the last
government composed of the "Weimar Coalition" alone on the Reich level. It
consisted only of the Socialists, Democrats, and the Center party.

77. One should note that Prussia lost some of her territory as a result of
Germany's defeat in World War I; consequently, she accounted for only three-
fifths of Germany's population and area during the Weimar Republic. More-
over, some of Germany's smaller Laender were combined in 1918 so that the
Republic had only 18 Laender in contrast to the 25 of the Second Reich. See
Arnold Brecht, *Federalism and Regionalism in Germany* (London, Oxford
University Press, 1945).

FIELD ADMINISTRATION IN REPUBLICAN PRUSSIA

Prussia's administration keenly felt the impact of the November 1918 revolution. At one blow the monarchy and the special privileges of the nobility were swept away. Control of the army was taken over by the Reich whose leaders were workers' sons instead of Junker aristocrats. The only conservative institution that survived the first onslaught of the revolution was the civil bureaucracy.

The Prussian civil service posed an insoluble enigma to the new regime. In the face of the deep unrest that rocked the country and the pressing demands of the Allies, the government had to restore order as quickly as possible. The Socialist ministers were quite aware that the old civil servants viewed them with suspicion and even hatred.[78] In the field, Provincial Governors, the District Officers, and Landraete were often hostile to the new regime. But no other trained personnel were available. As long as the revolution was to be a limited one, the government could make gradual personnel changes only as soon as loyal and qualified officials could be found.[79]

In order to rid itself of the most recalcitrant bureaucrats, the new regime offered a ¾-full pension regardless of actual service seniority to officials who felt themselves unable to serve the new government. Approximately 10.5 per cent of all administrative civil servants made use of this opportunity. In the field service, 19.4 per cent of the Landraete in the eastern provinces resigned.[80] After the Kapp Putsch in March 1920, the new Minister of Interior, Carl Severing, forced another 19 per cent of the Landraete

78. Braun, pp. 43–45, vividly describes the attitude of the civil servants in the Ministry of Agriculture when he took office in November 1918.

79. This is essentially the argument of Paul Hirsch, *Der Weg der Sozialdemokratie zur Macht in Preussen* (Berlin, Otto Stollberg Verlag, 1929), pp. 162–66. Hirsch was Minister President of Prussia from November 1918 to March 1920.

80. Hans-Karl Behrend, "Die Besetzung der Landratsstellen in Ostpreussen, Brandenburg, Pommern, und der Grenzmark von 1919 bis 1933," Unpublished Ph.D. Dissertation, Free University of Berlin, 1956, pp. 9–10 and p. 131.

into retirement.[81] The new regime, however, continued to depend on some field officials appointed by the monarchy; in 1922 at least 33 per cent of the District Officers and 36 per cent of the Landraete in all of Prussia had been appointed before 1918.[82]

The government followed a cautious replacement policy because it lacked candidates for office who were both loyal and also met the statutory requirements for regular civil service appointments or who were otherwise qualified. Appointees for Landrat positions, for instance, had to possess a university education and have passed state examinations after an apprenticeship period. Candidates without these qualifications could only be appointed if they owned estates and had held a local government position over a number of years. This clause obviously qualified Junkers, not Socialists. To enlarge its pool of potential appointees and allow it to appoint "outsiders" (i.e. men who had not received the formal training of a civil servant), the Prussian government amended the County Government Act to eliminate all qualifications. The new provisions simply read: "The Cabinet (*Staatsministerium*) appoints the Landrat."[83]

Despite these liberal provisions, the Prussian government named few outsiders to Landrat posts. In 1925 only 18 per cent of all Landraete were outsiders.[84] Most who were appointed had gained their administrative experience in trade union posts and as party

---

81. Ibid., p. 132.

82. Computed by author from *Handbuch ueber den koeniglich preussischen Hof und Staat* (1918) and *Handbuch ueber den preussischen Staat* (1922). These percentages actually underestimate the number of officials who remained in office as they exclude those who retained a Landrat position but were transferred to a different county.

83. Verordnung, Feb. 18, 1919, GS, 23, paragraph 12; Behrend, p. 25. The government also amended the general civil service law to allow appointment of outsiders to other positions such as District Officer and ministerial councillor. The new provisions, however, required assent of both the Minister of Interior and Minister of Finance before an "outsider" could be appointed. As these two ministerial posts were not held by the same party after 1922, few appointments were made under these provisions, for such appointments would have required lengthy, delicate interparty negotiations. Cf. Ebehard Pikart, "Preussische Beamtenpolitik 1918–1933," *Vierteljahrshefte fuer Zeitgeschichte, 6* (1958), 127.

84. Behrend, p. 121.

secretaries—the only administrative positions open to Socialists in Imperial Germany.[85]

In spite of the few outsiders that the government appointed, avowed supporters of the Republic became more numerous among the civil servants. In 1919 only 20 of Prussia's 423 Landraete claimed affiliation with the Socialist party; in 1925, 58 did so; in 1929, between 55 and 63 claimed membership.[86] Of 398 Landraete on whom data are available for 1925 (out of a total of 423), 71 belonged to the Catholic Center party, 58 to the Socialist party, 22 to the Democratic party, and 7 to the rightist (but still republican) German People's party. Thus in 1925, at least 37.5 per cent of the Landraete openly acknowledged allegiance to one of the republican parties.[87] Many others rendered loyal service to the Republic despite political objections to a Socialist-dominated regime. Thus in March 1920, the Republic survived the Kapp Putsch only as a result of a general strike by workers and the refusal of officials in the central ministries to support the Putsch. However, in later years as rightist resistance to the Republic became more respectable, many officials in the ministries gave support to antirepublican parties. The Republic was never able to imitate the Second Reich's policy of limiting its personnel recruitment to those social groups that would render unquestioning loyalty to the regime. As a result, a hostile residue of civil servants always remained to plague the regime; the Republic never fully won the allegiance of its civil service.[88]

The changes that Weimar democracy brought to Prussian field administration were particularly noticeable at the Landrat's level. The Landraete found their status position changed; at the same time, lay bodies such as the county council won greater influence in administration.

The Landrat's prestige declined after the 1918 revolution. Deference was no longer paid quite so blindly to government of-

85. Pikart, pp. 124–25. Behrend, pp. 151–52, notes an interesting reason for the small number of outsiders appointed. Landrat positions paid less than the post of union or party secretary. Thus, the men most qualified in Socialist ranks were not interested in the government positions.

86. Behrend, p. 122.

87. Ibid.; Pikart, p. 214, gives a slightly higher estimate.

88. Cf. Severing, *1*, 286.

ficials. The government also appointed fewer noblemen as Land-raete than ever before. In 1916, 54 per cent of the Landraete were noblemen; in 1925, only 27 per cent belonged to the nobility.[89] Even when a Landrat was a Junker or nobleman, his title meant less to the populace than before, for the nobility occupied no special, privileged position in the Republic.[90] Elections to the Landtag demonstrated the lowered status of the Landraete. In the last prewar election twenty-seven Landraete won seats in the Landtag; in the first postwar election, only two were elected.[91]

At the same time lay bodies such as the county council became much more active in administrative affairs. The county councils won an important role in the appointment of Landraete. The new procedure required the Minister of Interior to send prospective appointees to the county to serve a probationary term after which the county council voted whether to accept the candidate or not.[92] The minister tried to find a candidate suitable to the county as well as to himself in order to avoid a conflict with the local council. If the county council objected to his candidate, the minister could still appoint him as Landrat. But the minister exercised this power reluctantly as a Landrat appointed under such circumstances usually had difficulties working with the council. In the eastern provinces the county councils rejected the proposed Landrat nineteen times (13.5 per cent of the possible instances). In these nineteen cases, six were left as Landrat while thirteen were transferred. Attempts by the county council to dismiss a

89. Pikart, p. 120 n. The difference would be even greater if we knew the percentage of noblemen *appointed* in 1916 and 1925, for Pikart's 1925 data include many noble Landraete appointed during the Second Reich but still holding office in 1925.

90. It is true that a good deal of prestige still accrued to the nobility, especially in rural areas. However, the argument here is that such prestige was lower than during the Second Reich.

91. Hirsch, pp. 149 ff. However, this measure of the change in the Landrat's status must be qualified. The elections in 1919 took place under universal suffrage which put conservative candidates at a disadvantage in comparison to the three-class voting system under which so many Landraete were elected to the Landtag during the Second Reich.

92. Technically, the question on which the council voted was whether it should nominate a different candidate for the post; in effect, this was a confidence vote on the minister's appointee.

Landrat—clearly an *ultra vires* act—were always rejected by the ministry.[93]

County councils and county committees also appear to have played a more active role in administrative matters than their predecessors of the Second Reich. Noske reports that while he was Provincial Governor of Hanover, Socialist Landraete continually complained of interference in administrative affairs by party representatives on the county council.[94] Moreover, the county councils apparently became an arena for partisan disputes for the first time after 1918. Under the previous election system, only Conservatives could normally win elections with the result that partisan cleavages rarely occurred at the county level. During the Weimar period, universal, equal suffrage and greater representation for towns gave liberals of various parties and the Socialists a real opportunity to win county council seats. No election statistics or membership data are available for county councils during the Weimar period. Data on the composition of town councils in 1926 for towns under 5,000 population, however, show distinct party alignments in many towns. In a sample of 92 such towns, only 19 (21 per cent) town councils were not split among party groups. In 61 towns, the council was split into a leftist bloc on the one hand and a *Buergerblock* of all bourgeois parties on the other.[95] There is no reason to believe that county council representation differed greatly from that of these small-town councils. Such a partisan council required the Landrat to negotiate extensively with right- or left-wing elements to secure a majority for his proposals. As a

93. Behrend, pp. 80–81. Before the county councils were newly elected in 1919, revolutionary Soldiers' and Workers' Councils tried to control the Landrat's actions. In the eastern provinces, these councils tried to remove Landraete in fifteen counties (14 per cent of all counties) and succeeded in nine. Ibid., p. 60.

94. Noske, *Erlebtes,* pp. 293–94.

95. The data and sample are taken from *Kommunales Jahrbuch,* Neue Folge, Vol. 1 (Jena, Verlag von Gustav Fischer, 1927). The volume contains information on all cities and towns that were members of the *Deutsche Staedtetag* (German Municipal League). This organization primarily catered to large cities but had 92 small-town members. Biases in this sample are admittedly unknown. However, this is the only information available short of extensive archival research which could not be undertaken in this study. The data are to be considered as indicative, not definitive.

consequence, the Landrat could no longer count on blind deference from the county committee and county council; he personally had to win their confidence. Robbed of his status advantage
and faced with organized factions in the council, the Landrat had
to rely on persuasion rather than simple command.[96]

While the Landrat's informal position thus was far less secure
than during the Second Reich, his formal authority did not suffer
great losses. He won new responsibilities in some functions but
more often had to share decision-making with the lay county
councils or county committees. These developments are particularly evident in the Landrat's supervision of the county's police
forces, in the issuance of police regulations, in the supervision of
cities located in his county, and in the operations of the county
local government.

The Gendarmerie's[97] connections with the Defense Ministry
were completely severed in 1919.[98] This move was partly necessitated by the Peace Treaty's limitations on the strength of the
German army. If the Gendarmerie had remained under the Defense Ministry, the Allies would have considered it part of the
army. Another consideration was that the 1919 constitution transferred the Defense Ministry from the Prussian government to the
Reich; separation of the Gendarmerie from the Defense Ministry
thus allowed Prussia to retain control over its rural police force.
As a consequence of these changes, the Landrat won the control
which military officials had previously exercised over the Gendarmerie. He now handled all discipline cases himself and had to insure proper housing and equipment for his police. In addition,
the Landrat controlled the deployment of the Gendarmerie in his
county and assigned them specific functions. Whenever an administrative agency needed police assistance, the Landrat was the
only county official who could authorize the Gendarmerie to act.[99]

96. Minister President Heine in *Verhandlungen des Landesversammlung, 3,*
3859.

97. The *Gendarmerie* was renamed *Landjaegerei* in 1919. However, as this
police corps regained the name "Gendarmerie" after 1933, we shall continue
to use the older name to avoid confusion.

98. Verordnung, March 19, 1923, GS, 55; Helfritz, pp. 301–02; Pioch, p. 50;
Jeserich, pp. 1030–32.

99. Duesseldorf Staatsarchiv, Rep. LA Gummersbach 114.

The Landrat also won additional authority in the issuance of police regulations under the provisions of the Police Administration Law of June 1931. This law withdrew from smaller towns and police magistrates the right to issue police regulations. Only towns with more than 5,000 inhabitants could henceforth publish their own regulations. All other police regulations were issued by the Landrat with the approval of the county committee.[100] The county committee's role in this function was not new, but took on added significance during the Weimar Republic. County police regulations not only governed public health matters and farming practices, they also determined whether political meetings should be allowed. In such matters, the Landrat acted on instructions from the District Officer. When the District Officer wanted a county regulation, the Landrat had to convince his county committee to approve it. The Landrat's added police powers were thus blunted by the necessity of gaining approval from a lay committee for their use.

The Landrat's tutelage powers over local governments also underwent changes which led in contradictory directions. On the one hand, the Landrat—and the state bureaucracy in general—lost authority to reject local officials because of their political affiliations. For the first time, a Socialist could become a *Buergermeister*. But this was a two-edged sword. The Socialist-Democratic coalition government of Prussia found it impossible to prevent the election of right-wing antirepublican mayors in the last years of the Republic. In other spheres such as financial matters, however, the central bureaucracy gained influence because localities were increasingly financed by state grants rather than by local taxes. The Reich reserved all major revenue sources for itself and returned some of the revenues to the Laender; the Laender, in turn, distributed some of their income to the localities. The Landrat, as local state official, supervised the local governments' use of these state funds.[101] The Landrat also exercised most of the District Officer's tutelage powers over cities in his county and became the

100. Police Administration Law of June 1, 1931, GS, 77, paragraphs 27–28; see also the justification for the legislative proposal reprinted in Erich Klausener, Christian Kerstiens, and Robert Kempner, *Das Polizeiverwaltungsgesetz* (Berlin, Verlag fuer Recht und Verwaltung, 1931), pp. 67 ff.

101. Hornschu, pp. 89–102, and 183.

actual supervisory authority over cities. Before 1932, the District Officer simply delegated his tutelage power to the Landrat; in 1932 the delegation was formalized by central decree.[102]

The Landrat's ability to coordinate the activities of other specialists operating in his county declined during the Weimar Republic. During the Second Reich, part of the Landrat's ability to coordinate other field agents lay in his superior status position. As fewer Landraete were nobles and as the nobility's prestige declined during the Weimar period, the Landrat lost much of his status advantage over specialized field agents; deferential adjustment to the Landrat's wishes was less likely to occur. The Landraete also did not stay at their posts as long as they had during the Second Reich. In the eastern provinces, only 10 per cent of the counties had the same Landrat for all fourteen years of the Republic in contrast to the 20 per cent that had been served by one Landrat for twenty years or more during the Second Reich.[103] Moreover, the Landrat more frequently had no better information than specialized field agents, for more of the new Landraete were novices in public administration. However, the Landrat did retain jurisdiction over facilities which other field agents in the county needed for their work. The Landrat's control over the issuance of police regulations and his command over the county police gave him tools which he could use to promote coordination.

The establishment of Reich field agencies directly affected the Landrat's position. The lack of formal ties with the Reich's new field units made the Landrat's coordinating task far more difficult than ever before. With specialized field agents of the Land, a dispute between them and the Landrat could as a last resort be referred to the district office. Disputes with Reich field officials could not be referred, for no common superior existed. However, Landraete and Reich officials seem to have developed a policy of coexistence. Normally the Landrat established *ad hoc* ties with Reich officials, furnishing them police assistance when necessary. No great difficulties appear to have arisen with the Reich's finance

---

102. Verordnung, Sept. 3, 1932, GS, 283; Frido Wagener, *Die Staedte im Landkreis* (Goettingen, Verlag Otto Schwartz, 1955), pp. 118–22. Cities which possessed the status of counties (i.e. *Stadtkreise*), however, remained under the supervision of the district office.

103. Behrend, pp. 128–29; cf. Table 4, p. 57, above.

offices even though the Gendarmerie was extremely hesitant to gain unpopularity by helping the Reich's revenue agents.[104] On the other hand, our earlier examination of the operations of the Reich Unemployment Insurance Authority revealed that cooperation between the Authority's local offices and the Landrat often broke down.

The lack of formal coordination between the Landraete and Reich field agents never provoked open conflicts which interferred with field operations. But it invited daily friction between field officials and produced confusion for the German public. In 1932 the Landrat's position had declined to such a degree that the Papen government, when it seized control of Prussia, formalized the Landrat's previously implicit authority in the county. The government's decree read:[105]

> The Landrat is charged with observing that the operations of the other state agencies in the county do not clash with the interests of the general state administration. For this purpose, the chiefs of the [other] county offices must maintain continuous contact with the Landrat. They must channel directives and reports through the Landrat or inform him of them according to more detailed instructions of the District Officer.

The decree even authorized the Landrat to suspend another agency's actions when he considered them detrimental to general policy. The matter would then be referred to the District Officer.[106] Six months later, however, one of the first decrees of the Nazi regime hastened to add that other field officials were not subordinate to the Landrat.[107] Thus the Landrat remained in an ambiguous leadership position in the county.

104. Duesseldorf Staatsarchiv, Rep. LA Gummersbach 114, Circular from the Prussian Ministry of Interior, dated June 7, 1921. In this circular all local police were asked to give "temporary" assistance to the finance offices though an attached report from the district office of Lueneberg proposed that the finance offices establish their own police. The Gendarmerie was already overworked and did not want to gain the unpopularity of revenue agents. However, the finance offices never acquired their own police force.

105. Verordnung, Sept. 3, 1932, GS, 283, paragraph 12.

106. Ibid.

107. Duesseldorf Staatsarchiv, Rep. LA Muelheim/Rhein 436.

The Landrat remained a subordinate of the Minister of Interior. He continued to receive his instructions through the district office. The district offices themselves underwent few formal changes during the Weimar period. But as with the Landraete, popularly elected local government bodies gained a voice in the appointment of District Officers. According to Article 86 of the Prussian constitution, the executive committee of the Provincial Landtag had to approve appointments to the position of District Officer and Provincial Governor. This occasionally multiplied the ministry's difficulties in employing loyal, efficient, yet locally acceptable civil servants in these key positions, for the Provincial Diets did not necessarily reflect the government's views. The Provincial Diet was elected by direct popular vote after 1919 and could easily be captured by radical or regional groups. Carl Severing, who served as Prussian Minister of Interior, recalls such difficulties when in the aftermath of the Erzberger murder in 1921 he sought to replace several District Officers in the Rhineland and Westphalia. Even though the proposed replacements belonged to the same political party as their predecessors, the Diet obstinately refused to confirm the appointments. It took several additional months to fill these important posts.[108] Under such conditions, the ministry had to balance party claims for leading administrative positions in a manner never before necessary. Some field positions had to be allocated to party adherents according to party strength in the Landtag.[109] This practice, while not necessarily corrupting, made personnel management a delicate task for the Minister of Interior.

Few changes in the Provincial Governor's office and in the use of autonomous all-purpose agencies such as local governments occurred during the Weimar period. The most significant reform took place in 1927 when the Landtag granted counties home-rule powers (*Kompetenz-Kompetenz*).[110] Under this authority counties could extend their activities to new functions without central approval. However, the depression a year later drained county treasuries so completely that they made no use of their new powers.

---

108. Severing, *1*, 286–87; Noske, *Erlebtes*, pp. 208–89.
109. Eschenburg, *Der Beamte in Partei und Parlament*, pp. 47–48.
110. Law of Dec. 27, 1927, GS, 211.

CONCLUSION

The principal barriers to responsiveness that the Prussian government encountered during the Weimar period were the disloyalty of field officials, the centrifugal force of popularly elected councils participating in field administration, and communication obstacles which impeded coordination of Land and Reich programs at the local level. Political circumstances forced the Prussian government to adopt moderate measures to overcome these barriers. It refrained from conducting a thorough purge of the field service because it possessed no trained replacements; in the face of economic, financial, and security crises that continuously occurred during the first years of the Republic, the government could not dispense with the technical skills of the incumbent civil servants even though they might be disloyal. Over the years the government gradually appointed qualified and loyal personnel; the regime thus won a relatively loyal field service. One index of the field administration's loyalty is the fact that the Nazis deemed it necessary to remove all Provincial Governors, 91 per cent of the District Officers, and 73.1 per cent of the Landraete appointed by the Weimar Republic.[111]

A second means of overcoming these barriers consisted in employing the hierarchical controls that the Ministry of Interior possessed. Landraete remained Land civil servants as before; they depended entirely on the ministry for appointment, transfer, and promotion. The Landrat's budget had to be approved by the District Officer; numerous policy decisions remained reserved to the district office and Ministry of Interior. These controls blocked many attempts to circumvent the execution of central mandates. Ministerial controls, however, proved insufficient to overcome the new communication obstacles which resulted from the appearance of Reich field agencies at the district and local level. Coordination with these agencies was extremely awkward and often remained unaccomplished, for no common superior linked the Reich and Prussian field agencies.

Like the Reich, Prussia failed to develop effective external re-

111. Behrend, p. 141. However, the Nazis removed field agents for reasons other than disloyalty; see pp. 138–41 below.

straints that could supplement conventional hierarchical controls when they proved insufficient to promote field responsiveness. The one external restraint on which the Prussian regime placed great hope—popularly elected county councils—had an uneven impact on the field administration. When county elections returned a council majority that favored the central government's policies, the council served as an effective check on potentially disloyal field officials. But even partisanly loyal county councils differed with the Berlin government on the execution of some policies. Moreover, in some cases the councils were captured by parties hostile to the Berlin regime. In these cases, county councils failed to promote field responsiveness to central mandates; on the contrary, they supported deviations from the central mandates by the Landrat.

Prussia's field administration was not as responsive to central policy mandates as during the Second Reich. The barriers encountered by the Weimar regime were both more numerous and more serious than those faced by the Second Reich. Yet in view of the tumultuous events that marked the Republic's thirteen-year reign, one must concede that the Prussian government surmounted its most serious barriers to responsiveness with remarkable success. Prussian field administration became sufficiently reliable for most tasks. When the Republic fell, it was not because the Prussian field administration had failed it. The Republic was simply overwhelmed by a tidal wave of economic and political crises.

5. THE SHIFT TOWARD TOTALITARIANISM:
FIELD ADMINISTRATION DURING THE THIRD REICH

The Weimar Republic began to crumble when the Great Depression descended on Germany. The economic crisis destroyed the fragile bonds that had held coalitions together during the republican years; after 1929 polarization of public opinion paralyzed Germany's democratic processes. The Republic drifted to disaster. In April 1930, President Hindenburg appointed Heinrich Bruening as Chancellor even though he did not command majority support in the Reichstag. Bruening consequently had to rule by presidential decree. In June 1932, Bruening lost Hindenburg's confidence and was forced to resign in favor of Franz von Papen, who not only lacked parliamentary support but aroused active parliamentary opposition throughout the entire spectrum of the hopelessly divided Reichstag. The Republic finally came to an end when Hindenburg appointed Adolf Hitler, leader of the revolutionary National Socialist German Labor party (NSDAP), to be Chancellor on January 30, 1933. On that day, a new era began for Germany. Field administration, like all segments of German life, had to adjust itself to the new regime.

The Nazi program portended extensive changes in the structure of German government. Hitler strove for total power in order to erect an authoritarian state in which all public organs would be submissive to the will of the *Fuehrer*. The National Socialists pledged themselves to revive German might and glory and to halt unemployment and economic stagnation. The Nazi program foreshadowed further changes by its vehement attacks on the existing governmental structure. The Nazis envisioned themselves as missionaries destined to save the German people from a malignant rot that had enveloped them. Hitler promised to violate the provisions of the "disgraceful" Versailles Peace Treaty by rebuilding Germany's army and expanding Germany's *Lebensraum*. The Nazis promised to purge the governmental structure of alleged corruption and incompetence; they vowed to eliminate the influence of Jews, Marxists, and trade-unionists. They proposed to replace the confused instability of the Weimar system with dynamic, unitary leadership of the Fuehrer, Adolf Hitler.[1]

The administrative structure that the Nazis inherited presented numerous barriers to the realization of their goals. The German administrative system was a highly fragmented one. The Reich Finance Ministry was the only national ministry that possessed a field organization operating in all corners of Germany. The Unemployment Insurance Authority also had a field organization, but it was an autonomous body free from direct control by a Reich ministry. The Laender—who were politically autonomous and free from immediate Reich direction—controlled all other administrative functions. In addition, external checks limited administrative action in opposition to the Nazi Fuehrer principle. Legislatures at the Reich (*Reichstag*), Land (*Landtag*), and county (*Kreistag*) levels sought to curb administrative activities. District committees and county committees participated in administrative decision-making and limited administrative discretion. Administrative courts at the county, district, and Land levels held administrative actions within legal bounds.

Another potential barrier to the faithful execution of Nazi policies lay in the degree of loyalty which civil servants rendered

1. Good summaries of Nazi aims are given by Walter Hofer, ed., *Der Nationalsozialismus* (Frankfurt/M, Fischer Bucherei, 1957); Jean F. Neurohr, *Der Mythos vom Dritten Reich* (Stuttgart, J. G. Cotta'sche Buchhandlung Nachfolger, 1957), pp. 95–115; Henri Lichtenberger, *The Third Reich*, trans. and ed. Koppel S. Pinson (New York, Greystone Press, 1937).

the Nazi state. The Nazis doubted the ardor displayed by government officials for National Socialism. The hated Weimar regime
had sought to mold the civil service in its own image; in Prussia,
Socialist Ministers of Interior had controlled administrative appointments for twelve years. Many civil servants belonged to democratic parties and presumably believed in their Liberal-Democratic
programs. But Nazi uncertainty of bureaucratic loyalty had still
deeper roots. The Nazis looked on bureaucrats as technicians
whose role consisted of executing orders but not formulating policies. Leadership was a party function; the civil service should
execute the leaders' orders. This allocation of roles clashed with
many a bureaucrat's self-image as the formulator of policy and
the expert in politics. In addition, differences in social status between Nazi leaders and civil servants threatened to undermine
the bureaucrat's respect for his Nazi superiors. Nazi leaders predominantly came from lower middle-class, marginal, and unsuccessful backgrounds; the higher civil servants, in contrast, usually
came from higher middle-class families, had enjoyed stable environments, and had achieved success early in life.[2] The seizure
of top positions by the previously scorned Nazi leaders aroused
the jealous animosity of many civil servants.

Responsiveness barriers were not the only cause for the Nazi
desire to increase control over the bureaucracy. The unprecedented programs inaugurated by the Nazi regime also necessitated
closer supervision of the civil service. The Nazi goal was a totalitarian state. Many activities performed by private organizations under the Weimar regime became government functions under the
Nazis. Labor unions were state controlled. The press, radio, and
all other mass media fell under the control of Goebbel's propa-
ganda ministry. The government made vigorous attempts to place
welfare and religious activities under state supervision. In addition, the regime intervened in business affairs more frequently
than ever before. In all these spheres, the regime imposed detailed
mandates which field agencies had to execute. German field agents,
therefore, labored under a greater work load than ever before and

2. Daniel Lerner, et al., *The Nazi Elite* (Stanford, Calif., Stanford University Press, 1951), pp. 34–52. We shall discuss these differences in more detail
below.

had to fulfill unprecedented demands by the central government. The increased demands necessitated stricter controls.

The barriers to bureaucratic responsiveness and the heightened demands of the Nazi regime in a large measure shaped the development of administration during the Third Reich. The Nazi regime responded to its difficulties by initiating two kinds of administrative reforms. First, it sought to reorganize the structure of German field administration to impose its hierarchical restraints on field officials more effectively. The regime strengthened its internal controls over the Reich bureaucracy; it stripped the Laender of their constitutional and political autonomy; it extended direct Reich controls over Land field agencies; it eliminated legislative and judicial restraints on field officials; and it conducted a thorough purge of Land field officials. Most of these measures extended the use of control instruments which the Weimar Republic had developed to a much lesser degree. Their application, however, did not satisfy the Nazi urge to direct the operations of German field officials more comprehensively. The National Socialists, therefore, developed new external controls. The Nazis infiltrated the bureaucracy by placing trusted party members in top-level administrative positions. Moreover, the party allowed its own field units to supervise the government's field agencies. In some cases, the party usurped public functions and allowed them to be performed by party units rather than by public agencies. These hierarchical and external controls were developed simultaneously; the Nazi regime fashioned them pragmatically rather than according to a grand program.

Our classification seeks to put in order a wild disarray of events. We will first examine the Nazi use of hierarchical controls in four contexts: 1) as changes in the Reich administration; 2) as a restructuring of Reich-Land relations; 3) as the reorganization of field administration in Prussia; and 4) as implementation of large-scale personnel changes. Second, we will discuss the growth of external controls by examining the operation of the Prussian Landrat's office and the organization of German police during the Third Reich. In a concluding section we shall briefly discuss the coordination problems that arose as a result of the frenzied, unplanned application of hierarchical and external controls on German field administrators.

HIERARCHICAL CONTROLS

Increased Centralization of Reich Administration The Reich possessed few administrative agencies with field organizations; these gave the Nazis only limited opportunities to increase central control. Yet even such a highly centralized organization as the Reich Finance Administration felt the impact of Nazi centralization efforts. The ministry increased supervision over all field operations, especially in regard to personnel policies. In addition to requiring the implementation of Nazi personnel laws, the ministry minutely prescribed training programs for its field officials.[3] The ministry also carefully regulated field relationships with local Nazi party organizations—largely in self-defense.[4] It was not unusual for local party leaders to demand contributions to party charities from finance officers, to command the presence of officials for party parades, to request the assignment of office personnel to party training schools, or to require assistance for other party projects. All these activities grossly interfered with the normal work of the finance administration. The chiefs of the local finance offices, however, often found themselves unable to withstand the pressure of local party or SS leaders.[5] Therefore, the ministry came to their help with detailed regulations restricting party activities of civil servants. Deviation from the ministry's directives could be authorized only by the ministry itself. The result of these regulations was that local party leaders were told to refer their requests to the party's national headquarters which would negotiate with the ministry. The ministry, whose State Secretary was an ardent and high-placed Nazi (Fritz Reinhardt), felt better able to resist petty interference with its work than did local field officials.[6]

3. RFBl (1933), pp. 76–77; (1934), pp. 85 and 286; (1935), pp. 35 and 143; (1936), p. 51; (1937), pp. 156 and 183; (1938), p. 10.

4. Ibid. (1933), pp. 69, 96, 101–02, and 155; (1934), pp. 26 and 150; (1935), p. 61; (1936), pp. 9 and 23; (1938), p. 621; (1940), p. 31.

5. The SS (*Schutzstaffel*, commonly Black Shirts) was an elite corps of bodyguards under the leadership of Heinrich Himmler. Local SS and SA (*Sturmabteilung*, commonly Storm Troopers) were under the control of their own hierarchy; local party leaders did not have jurisdiction over them.

6. Statements by Reichsfinanzminister a.D. von Krosigk, Arenberg, March 23, 1959, and Regierungsrat a.D. Otto Kaestele, Munich, July 22, 1959, personal interviews.

The Nazis had a greater impact on social insurance administration, the other sphere in which the Reich already had widespread administrative organs. The Nazis quickly subordinated the Unemployment Insurance Authority and its far-flung field organization to the Ministry of Labor.[7] Once the Authority's autonomy was breached, the Reich Labor Ministry tightened personnel and budgetary controls over all field offices. Eventually, the Authority simply became a branch of the Labor Ministry. During World War II, party agencies won great influence over the Labor Ministry's field offices. The regional boundaries of the Unemployment Insurance Division were changed so that the unemployment office regions conformed to party regions. In addition, the Reich placed the unemployment insurance regional offices under the general policy direction of the party's regional leaders, the *Gauleiter*.[8] Thereafter, the Ministry of Labor had to share supervision over the unemployment insurance field offices with party agencies.

The other social insurance agencies remained organized on a local or Land basis but also lost their autonomy. The Nazi regime altered the social insurance laws to subordinate the social insurance agencies to Land ministries, district offices, and Landraete. The Nazis also achieved the dismissal of the administrative chiefs of almost all social insurance agencies because they had had too close ties with the Social Democratic party. Nazi party members were appointed in their place.[9] In addition, the Reich Ministry of Labor won direct supervisory authority over all insurance agencies. The elected councils which had controlled administration of the Health Funds and Industrial Insurance Corporations were also abolished.[10] However, the increased supervision of the social insurance agencies by the Reich Labor Ministry sometimes served to restrain local party interference with social insurance adminis-

7. Social Insurance Law of July 5, 1934, RGBl, *1*, 577.

8. Decree of July 27, 1943, RGBl, *1*, 450. The party's regional organization is discussed below.

9. Statements by Ministerialrat a.D. Dormann, Berlin, Dec. 2, 1958, and Ministerialrat a.D. Knoll, Berlin, Nov. 19, 1958, personal interviews. Both served in the Reich Labor Ministry during the Third Reich.

10. Decree of Oct. 24, 1933, RGBl, *1*, 1105. A plethora of decrees followed; the best guide is Hans Engel and J. Eckert, *Die Reichsversicherungsgesetze in jeweils neuesten Stande* (Looseleaf Collection; Munich and Berlin, C. H. Beck'sche Verlagsbuchhandlung [c. 1942]), 2 vols.

tration rather than to give the Nazis unobstructed power. The Reich Ministry of Labor, while under the direction of an ardent Nazi, remained staffed by professional civil servants who apparently resisted Nazi pressures to implement party policies.[11] The officials in the ministry occasionally used their increased supervisory powers to prevent misallocation of funds by local party officials and the unjustified withholding of benefits to workers who had incurred the displeasure of the local party organization.[12] Increased centralization, the Nazis found, could impair responsive administration of their revolutionary demands as well as foster it. For this reason the Nazi regime quickly turned to an intensive program of placing trusted Nazis in key Land and field positions; moreover, they reorganized the structure of field administration in the Laender. The full impact of these measures can be best understood in the broader context of Nazi changes in Reich-Land relations and in the reorganization of the all-purpose field agencies of the Laender.

The Destruction of Germany's Federal System The independence of Land governments constituted an obvious barrier to the Nazi desire to gain total power over Germany and to implement Nazi policies through direct control by the Fuehrer. Abrogation of the Laender's autonomy, therefore, became an immediate objective for the Nazi regime. Hitler, however, was not the first to undermine the constitutional position of the Laender. The last months of the Weimar Republic produced ample precedents for Hitler's reforms. We must briefly return to the political developments in the Reich and in the Laender during the last years of the Republic to understand the success of the Nazi regime's strategy in carrying out its drastic changes in Reich-Land relationships.

After March 28, 1930, the Reich government ruled without Reichstag support. The last cabinet backed by a Reichstag coali-

11. J. Eckert, *Schuldig oder Entlastet* (Munich, Rechts- und Wirtschaftsverlag, 1947) effectively argues this viewpoint; personal interviews with key Labor Ministry officials (Dormann and Knoll as cited above; Professor Hermann Dersch, Berlin, Nov. 26, 1958) as well as the texts of central regulations tend to confirm the argument.

12. Eckert, pp. 196 ff.; statements by Knoll and Dormann, personal interviews.

tion split over the issue of unemployment insurance rates and benefits. The depression polarized public opinion and electoral support to such a degree that no new coalition became possible. In this emergency, President Hindenburg appointed Heinrich Bruening as Chancellor and allowed him to rule by emergency decrees. Under the provisions of Article 48 of the Weimar Constitution, Hindenburg countersigned laws and decrees which the Reichstag ordinarily would have enacted. Between April 1930 and May 1932 the depression continued its dismal course and political strife became fiercer. The only expression of political consensus between 1930 and 1932 came with Hindenburg's re-election to the Presidency by a narrow margin over Hitler in March 1932. The 85-year-old President, however, increasingly relied on a coterie of unofficial advisers who were hostile to Bruening. As Bruening had no Reichstag majority to support him, the Chancellor was forced to resign on May 28, 1932, when Hindenburg withdrew his confidence from him. Hindenburg then appointed the favorite of his camarilla, Franz von Papen, as Bruening's successor to the Chancellorship.[13]

The depression had forced the Bruening Reich government to intervene in Land affairs with increasing frequency. Bruening's government enacted a number of laws regulating Land budgets and personnel expenditures to an unprecendented degree.[14] The government also enacted special measures to prevent street riots between rival political factions, placing Land police under the obligation to ban open-air political meetings and to suppress publications that incited their readers to violence.[15] These infringements on Land autonomy reflected the inability of the Laender to overcome the economic and political crises of the depression years. The Bruening government, however, did not systematically attempt to destroy the Laender's autonomy.

Depression and political instability undermined democratic government in the Laender as well as at the national level. The coalition government that had ruled Prussia since 1920 fell on

13. Karl D. Bracher, *Die Aufloesung der Weimarer Republik* (Stuttgart and Dresden, Ring Verlag, 1955), gives the best account of this period. See especially pp. 571 ff.

14. Decree of Aug. 24, 1931, RGBl, *1*, 453.

15. Emergency Decree of March 28, 1931, RGBl, *1*, 79.

May 24, 1932, after Land elections returned a Landtag in which the only possible majority was an obstructionist coalition between the Communist party and Hitler's National Socialists. As this Landtag majority refused to support the existing government but could not agree on a new one, Minister President Braun's cabinet provisionally remained in office. Parliamentary elections in other Laender also led to deadlocked legislatures; provisional governments ruled in Bavaria and Saxony after the summer of 1930, in Hamburg after October 1931, and in Hesse after December 1931.[16]

The Papen government, which succeeded Bruening on June 1, 1932, took a more radical approach to the question of Land-Reich relations. Papen's cabinet was thoroughly reactionary; it represented right-wing elements just short of the National Socialists. Papen's program included a reorganization of Germany's constitutional structure. The principal goal of such a reorganization was to eliminate the Reichstag as a participant in the political process and to unite the Prussian and Reich governments under his own leadership.

Papen soon found pragmatic grounds for plotting against the Prussian government. As the Prussian Landtag remained unable to elect a successor to the coalition cabinet under the Socialist Minister President, Braun's government continued to rule in Prussia. It obstructed Papen's revolutionary plans at every opportunity. When Papen revoked the ban on rightist para-military organizations—Hitler's SS and SA—Papen assured himself a conflict with the Prussian government. In response to Papen's revocation, Prussia—together with Bavaria, Baden, and Hesse—reenacted the prohibition on the basis of their own police powers. Papen, consequently, turned to the President's emergency powers under Article 48 and revoked the Land prohibitions as well.[17]

Prussia and the other Laender opposed revocation of the ban against the SA and SS on two counts. Braun and his colleagues knew that open activity by the SA and SS would strengthen Hitler's National Socialists who had perfected the technique of winning votes by a combination of bland promises and ruthless terror. The Laender also opposed revocation of the ban, because

16. Bracher, p. 575.
17. Ibid., pp. 571 ff.

without it their police forces could not prevent armed clashes between the SA and SS and Communist militants. Despite the threat of civil war, Papen continued his policy. On the one hand, he hoped to buy Hitler's support with a lenient attitude toward the SA and SS; on the other hand, Papen hoped to provoke a crisis which might allow him to depose the Prussian government.[18]

On July 19, 1932, especially bloody riots in Altona, a Prussian suburb of Hamburg, gave Papen the pretext he had sought. Declaring that Prussia had been unable to keep peace and order, Papen convinced Hindenburg to issue a presidential decree by which the Reich took over the Prussian government. It declared the Prussian government deposed and appointed Papen as Reich Commissar for Prussia; additional commissars were appointed for each of the Prussian ministries. Papen's move caught Prussia totally unprepared; it offered no resistance and indeed could not. The army, through the good offices of General von Schleicher, the Defense Minister, supported Papen. The police, even if they had been well enough armed to resist the army, were no longer entirely loyal to Braun's government.[19] Other Laender sympathized with Prussia but feared the same fate and stood idly by. A Bavarian official later wrote:[20] "Everyone hesitated (*scheuten davor zurueck*) in these circumstances to heighten tensions and left the matter for time and the Supreme Court (*Staatsgerichtshof*) . . . [to decide]." Prussia indeed appealed to the Supreme Court. The court, however, waited for three months to decide the case.[21] Its decision then condemned Papen's deposition of the Prussian government but conceded that the Reich could appoint commissars to control Prussian administrative agencies. The proposal of legislation and other sovereign acts, such as representation of the Reichsrat and dissolution of the Landtag, were to remain with the old Braun cabinet. These restrictions on the Reich Commissars were insignificant. No legislation was possible as long as the Prussian Landtag remained paralyzed by a Communist-Nazi obstructionist majority; the right to dissolve the Landtag and call

18. Ibid., pp. 577–80.
19. Severing, *Mein Lebensweg*, 2, 354; Bracher, pp. 591 and 597–99.
20. Schwend, *Bayern zwischen Monarchie und Diktatur*, p. 507.
21. The legal argument is reproduced in Arnold Brecht, ed., *Preussen contra Reich vor dem Staatsgerichtshof* (Berlin, Verlag J. H. W. Dietz, 1933).

for new elections remained meaningless as long as the prospects of returning a workable majority stayed dim; and representation in the Reichsrat had no practical consequences, for the Reichsrat lay dormant as long as the Reichstag was also paralyzed by the lack of a majority. The Supreme Court's decision, therefore, was a decisive victory for Papen; after slapping his wrist, the court left him in control of the executive organs of the Prussian government—the ministries, the field organization, and the police.

Papen's move sounded the death knell for Prussia even though her autonomy was not legally revoked. Prussia could no longer act independently of the Reich. Her administration lay completely in the hands of the Reich government. Papen's Reich regime now proceeded to rule Prussia according to his own policies. Prussian field agencies became Reich offices in fact though not yet in law.

Papen's deposition of the Prussian government paved the way for Hitler's total seizure of power six months later on January 30, 1933. When Hitler became Chancellor, he not only won legal control over the Reich government, its army, and its predominantly Berlin-centered administrative corps; by virtue of Papen's coup d'état against Prussia, Hitler also won control over Prussia with its 100,000-man police force and its network of field agencies that constituted the core of Germany's administrative system. Without making an illegal move himself, Hitler won control over both the Reich and Prussia.

As soon as Hitler became Chancellor, he hastened to extend the precedents that Papen so obligingly had established. Hitler first sought to secure Nazi control over Prussia and to extend his power over the other Laender. Hitler appointed Papen as Reich Commissar and Hermann Goering as Commissar for the Prussian Ministry of the Interior.[22] Defying the Supreme Court order which had reserved certain powers with Minister President Braun's coalition cabinet, Hitler ordered the Prussian Landtag dissolved and new elections scheduled to coincide with the Reichstag elections on March 5. These elections gave the Nazis a majority in

22. Papen held this post only until April 7, when he was replaced by Goering. *Schulthess' Europaeischer Geschichtskalender 1933* (Munich, C. H. Beck'sche Verlagsbuchhandlung, 1934), p. 91.

the Prussian Landtag after the Communists were excluded because of their alleged complicity in the Reichstag fire.

Having thus secured his control over Prussia, Hitler moved to abrogate the autonomy of the other Laender. He applied the emergency decree issued after the Reichstag fire[23] and appointed Reich Commissars for Hesse on March 6, for Hamburg on March 8, for Bavaria, Bremen, and Luebeck on March 11.[24] The Reich dissolved the legislatures of all these Laender and reconstituted them according to the March 5 Reichstag election results which, by excluding Communist votes, left the Nazis in firm control.[25] The remaining Laender were already ruled by National Socialist governments.[26]

After installing commissars, the Reich proceeded to divest the Laender of all autonomous powers. The Government Reorganization Act of March 31, 1933,[27] gave each Land cabinet the right to issue decree laws and constitutional amendments. As these cabinets were appointed by the Reich Commissars, the Reich won indirect control over all forms of Land legislation as well as administration. In April 1933, the Reich replaced the commissars with Reich Governors (*Reichsstatthaltern*); these governors represented the Reich and appointed Land governments and Land civil servants.

By the end of 1933, the Laender had effectively lost all autonomous powers. The final step in the abrogation of Land autonomy came with the Governmental Reorganization Act of January 31, 1934.[28] This law officially divested the Laender of their constitutional and political autonomy and abolished the Reichsrat as their organ in the national legislative process.

From the very beginning the Nazi regime relied on two channels of communication for exercising its control over the field ad-

23. Decree of Feb. 28, 1933, RGBl, *1*, 83.

24. Walter Baum, "Die 'Reichsreform' im Dritten Reich," *Vierteljahrshefte fuer Zeitgeschichte, 3* (1955), 37–38; for Wuerttemberg, see Alfred Dehlinger, *Wuerttembergs Staatswesen* (Stuttgart, W. Kohlhammer Verlag, 1951–53), *1*, 191 ff.

25. The legal authority for these actions was the law of March 31, 1933, RGBl, *1*, 153.

26. The Laender already under Nazi control were Thuringia, Mecklenburg-Schwerin, Bruswick, Oldenburg, Anhalt, Lippe, and Mecklenburg-Strelitz.

27. RGBl, *1*, 153.

28. RGBl, *1*, 75.

ministration of the Laender. The Reich had the normal administrative hierarchy at its disposal; the Nazi leaders in Berlin could direct Land field activities through the Reich Ministry of Interior and the Reich Governors. In addition, the Nazis could use their own party channels to direct Land field operations, for all the Reich Governors, except those in Bavaria, were also party regional leaders *(Gauleiter)*.[29] In Bavaria, which had six party regions, Hitler appointed an old party member who was not a Gauleiter, General von Epp, to be Reich Governor. Epp, however, appointed two regional leaders of the party to the Bavarian cabinet; Adolf Wagner, the Gauleiter of Munich and Upper Bavaria became Minister of Interior, and Hans Schemm, Gauleiter of Bavaria's *Ostmark,* became minister without portfolio.[30] As a result of those appointments, the regime could use the party hierarchy to communicate its plans to the field if bureaucratic channels proved resistant to Nazi desires.

In the ensuing years, the Nazi regime strengthened the party's role in Land central administration. Originally the Gauleiter-Reich Governors could only supervise the Land governments; they did not participate in the normal administrative routine. After 1935, however, an increasing number of Gauleiter also became Minister President and thus won an active role in Land administration. In 1935, the Saxon Reich Governor and Gauleiter, Martin Mutschmann, took over direct control of the Saxon government by becoming Minister President of Saxony in addition to holding his other posts.[31] In 1936, Jakob Sprenger, the Reich Governor and Gauleiter of Hesse, became Hesse's Minister President, and Alfred Meyer, Gauleiter of North Westphalia, became Minister President of Lippe.[32] In 1939, the Hamburg government was taken over by the Reich Governor-Gauleiter Karl Kaufmann.[33] When the Bavarian Minister President Siebert died in 1942, an-

---

29. Artur Norbeck, *Die Formen der Zusammenarbeit von Partei und Staat auf dem Gebiet der Verwaltung* (Ph.D. Dissertation, University of Munich, 1937), pp. 29–30; *Nationalsozialistisches Jahrbuch* (Munich, Verlag Franz Eher Nachfolger, 1934).

30. *Schulthess' Europaeischer Geschichtskalender 1933,* p. 99.

31. *Nationalsozialistisches Jahrbuch* (1936), p. 120.

32. Ibid. (1937), p. 135.

33. Ibid. (1940), p. 428.

other of the party's Gauleiter, Paul Giesler, assumed the Bavarian Minister Presidency although General von Epp retained his position as Reich Governor throughout the Third Reich's existence.[34] In each of these cases, the Gauleiter combined his party position with governmental responsibilities. The practice placed fanatic Nazis who were subject to party as well as government discipline in key executive positions.

Reich and party controls over Prussian administration developed somewhat differently, for Prussia—in contrast to the other Laender—did not retain central ministries of her own. All Prussian ministries, except the Finance Ministry, were merged with their Reich counterparts.[35] Frick and later Himmler, for instance, became both Reich and Prussian Minister of the Interior. Similarly, the ministries for education, economics, food and agriculture, labor, transportation, religious affairs, and the forest office were merged with the parallel Reich ministry.[36] These mergers signified a unification of top-level central leadership; moreover, most of the ministers were high-ranking Nazis rather than bureaucrats. The consolidation of the Reich and Prussian ministries gave the Reich control over Prussia's central ministries and direct access to Prussia's field agencies. Party control was exercised directly through the Reich ministries.

The measures we have described so far only assured the Nazi Reich government top-level control. The Reich also increased its direct control over Land field agencies by broadening the supervisory authority of Reich Governors over the Land agencies, by increasing Reich control over Land civil servants, and by making

34. Ibid. (1943), p. 327. One should note, however, that not all Gauleiter held government posts, for there were far more party regions than administrative areas. The lack of congruity between party regions and administrative areas raised thorny coordination problems. This topic is discussed separately in the final section of this chapter.

35. The grounds for excluding the Finance Ministry from these mergers remain obscure. However, the Prussian Finance Ministry's jurisdiction was increasingly restricted to formulating budgets for Prussian field agencies which were then forwarded to the Reich Finance Ministry. Prussia lost its powers to assess and collect taxes at the same time as the other Laender.

36. The last of the mergers occurred in July 1935. The exact dates are given in the *Handbuch ueber den preussischen Staat* (1938), pp. 14, 36, 107, 125, 147, and 148.

the Laender completely dependent on annual Reich grants-in-aid.

The Reich Governor's Act of January 1935 placed the Reich Governors in the regular administrative hierarchy subordinate to the Reich's functional ministries.[37] Although the law revoked the Governor's power to name Land cabinets and Land civil servants, it made the Governor responsible for the execution of Reich policies by Land agencies. In 1939, Land field agencies officially became Reich offices subject to the direct control of the Reich's central ministries.[38] By this progression of edicts the Reich extended its hierarchical control over local administrative agencies. They received their policy mandates from Reich ministries and were responsible to the Reich for their execution.

Moreover, Nazi personnel laws ignored the traditional distinction between Reich and Land civil servants. The Law To Restore a Professional Civil Service of June 1933 initiated a comprehensive purge of Land as well as Reich civil servants.[39] A decree of February 2, 1935, obliterated the historical boundaries between the two; thereafter, Reich officials could be used for Land functions and Land officials, for Reich functions.[40] The Reich Civil Service Code of January 1937 minutely regulated the recruitment, conditions of employment, personal and political qualifications, and dismissal procedures of all government officials in Germany.[41] The code effectively eliminated major local variations in personnel management. Even the civil service nomenclature became uniform throughout the Reich.[42]

Finally, the Reich tightened its control over Land finances. The Reich Finance Administration began to collect Land taxes as well as Reich levies. Slowly the Reich revoked the Laender's right to levy taxes and gave them grants-in-aid instead.[43] The Reich distributed its grants according to a fixed formula which provided

37. RGBl, *1*, 65; Baum, p. 44.

38. Law of July 5, 1939, RGBl, *1*, 1675.

39. RGBl, *1*, 389. The impact of this purge is discussed in the following section of this chapter.

40. RGBl, *1*, 81, paragraph 5.

41. RGBl, *1*, 39.

42. Decree of Nov. 28, 1938, RGBl, *1*, 1675.

43. Karl Groth, *Die Reichsfinanzverwaltung* (Berlin, Industrieverlag Spaeth und Linde, 1937), pp. 89–92.

the Laender the same yield as they had previously collected for their taxes. When the Laender ceased to perform some of their traditional functions—notably police—and assumed many new ones during World War II, the grants lost their relationship to the financial needs of the Laender. Finally in 1944, the Reich changed the grant-in-aid formula to give Laender funds according to their actual administrative work loads.[44] This change made the Laender entirely dependent on annual changes in the Reich budget.

Thus, the Reich's constitutional and administrative reorganization transformed the Laender from autonomous states to administrative regions. The Reich abrogated Land political autonomy and integrated the Laender's administrative structure with the Reich bureaucracy. The Reich itself appointed top-level Land officials. Other Land civil servants were appointed according to provisions of Reich laws; they could be transferred at will to Reich offices. Reich ministries directed the activities of Land field agencies by detailed regulations which the ministries could send directly to the field offices. Like all administrative units, the Laender depended entirely on fluctuating Reich grants for their financial support. In place of the traditional fragmentation of administrative functions along federal lines, the Nazi regime erected a thoroughly integrated administrative machine with all formal lines of authority leading to Berlin.

Reorganization of Prussian Field Administration   The developments we have described made the Laender directly responsible to the Reich. Within each Land similar changes were necessary to assure loyal administration of Nazi policies by field agencies at the district and county level. The Nazis sought to assure themselves of an effective field organization in Prussia by inaugurating three kinds of reform: 1) the Nazi regime eliminated legislative and judicial restraints on field agents; 2) it applied more stringent hierarchical controls on field officials; and 3) it purged the civil service in an effort to assure itself a loyal corps of field officials. Each of these measures represented a partial solution to the Nazi quest for a field organization that would effectively respond to

44. Hornschu, *Die Entwicklung des Finanzausgleichs im deutschen Reich und in Preussen*, pp. 32–37.

central directives. Although similar changes occurred in the other Laender, we shall concentrate our attention on Prussian field administration, for it was there that the Nazi reforms appeared in their starkest form.

In Prussia as in the Reich, Papen's government in 1932 set the precedents that Hitler later expanded. After seizing control of the Prussian government in July 1932, Papen attempted to reorganize Prussian field administration so that it would prove politically reliable, i.e. conservative. The Braun government during its twelve years in office had slowly created a relatively large corps of loyal civil servants. A sizable number of the Prussian field officials had affiliated themselves with one of the republican parties. Realizing this, Papen dismissed many of the key field officials suspected of republican loyalties. Papen discharged the Provincial Governors of four of Prussia's twelve provinces, the police chiefs of Prussia's principal cities, and seven of Prussia's thirty-four District Officers.[45] In addition, Papen revived a county reform plan which the Braun government had once considered but shelved. On August 1, 1932, Papen suddenly announced that 111 of Prussia's 352 counties were dissolved and combined into 53 larger ones. In the course of this reorganization, Papen dismissed 61 Landraete who had been appointed by Braun's republican government; five-sixths of the dismissed Landraete had served in the politically more liberal areas of Prussia west of the Elbe River.[46]

By these acts, Papen set a precedent for the wholesale dismissal of field officials and the widespread reorganization of Prussia's field administration. When Hitler came to power in 1933, his government vigorously continued the politically motivated reorganization of Prussia's field administration.

Structural reforms first occupied Nazi attention. The Nazi regime focused its energies on destroying legislative and judicial restraints which the Second Reich and Weimar Republic had imposed on Landraete. Popularly elected county councils could hinder the execution of Nazi policies, especially by refusing to approve local appropriations. The Nazis viewed such councils as

45. Severing, *Mein Lebensweg,* 2, 359–60. The cities where police chiefs were replaced included Berlin, Koenigsberg, Cologne, and Magdeburg. Ibid.

46. Ibid.; Behrend, "Die Besetzung der Landratsstellen in Ostpreussen, Brandenburg, Pommern und der Grenzmark von 1919 bis 1933," p. 140.

relics of the despised Weimar system of unstable democracy. The councils also violated the Nazi principle of dynamic leadership by a single Fuehrer. The Nazi regime consequently first manipulated county council membership to protect itself from undue interference. The government ordered the dissolution of all councils and then reapportioned council seats according to the local results of the March 5 Reichstag election.[47] In many areas this reapportionment gave the Nazis a majority or a dominant position in the council. However, in July 1933, the Nazi regime took the final step and abolished the councils by transferring all their functions to the county committee.[48]

The Nazi government also assured itself of control over the county committees. The Landrat and the party's county leader (*Kreisleiter*) absorbed the council's former power to name the members of the county committee.[49] The Nazis stripped the committee of more than the independence of its members for the Prussian government subsequently transferred many of the county committee's functions to the Landrat. The most important loss was the power to approve police regulations. After December 1933, the Landrat issued all police regulations without seeking the approval of his county committee.[50] Before the first year of National Socialist rule had ended, the Landraete had escaped all local restraints of a legislative nature.

Administrative courts constituted another external check on the Landrat. The administrative court system, therefore, became a second target for the Nazi government's reorganization of field administration. The reforms that made the county committees subservient to the Landraete automatically affected them in their role as administrative courts, for they became a rubber stamp for the Landrat; dissenters simply were not appointed by him. The regime further restricted the scope of administrative justice by

47. Decree of Feb. 4, 1933, GS, 21; Law of March 31, 1933, RGBl, *1*, 153, paragraph 12.

48. Law of July 17, 1933, GS, 257.

49. Theodor A. Fleisch, *Der Landkreis und die kreisangehoerigen Gemeinden* (Halle/Saale, Presse und Wirtschaft Verlagsgesellschaft, 1933), pp. 16 ff.; Gottfried Neesse, *Partei und Staat* (Hamburg, Hanseatische Verlagsanstalt, 1936), p. 70.

50. Law of Dec. 15, 1933, GS, 479.

excluding county committees from participation in administrative appeals (*Beschlussverfahren*) which the committee had previously heard.[51] Finally, in 1939 the Nazis eliminated the administrative court system entirely under the pretext of simplifying administrative procedures for the duration of the war. The Reich government authorized the Landrat to decide all cases alone; appeals went to the District Officer rather than to the district committee which had previously served as an appellate tribunal. Moreover, the District Officer could only accept appeals in extraordinary circumstances; normally the Landrat's decision was final.[52] These measures completely swept away the system of judicial restraints on Prussian field officials which had existed for half a century. Henceforth, the Landrat was legally responsible only to his administrative superior, the District Officer. Quasijudicial administrative tribunals no longer restricted his scope of action.[53]

The Landrat's office remained the center of field operations for the Land and Reich ministries during the Third Reich. As a consequence of the leveling of legislative and judicial restraints, the Landrat's authority in county affairs increased greatly. In addition, his office assumed many fuctions that townships formerly had performed such as constructing public housing, establishing zoning regulations, and administering price controls.[54] World War II lent added significance to some traditional county functions, notably the administration of the selective service laws and the distribution of family allotments to soldiers' dependents.[55] As the county council and county committee had ceased to function, the Landrat alone controlled the execution of all these programs in addition to the continuing local government functions of the county.

51. Ibid.

52. Decree of the Fuehrer, Aug. 28, 1939, RGBl, *1*, 1535; Decree of Sept. 26, 1939, RGBl, *1*, 1981; Decree of Nov. 6, 1939, RGBl, *1*, 2168. A legal discussion of these measures is given by Alfons Rehkopp, *Staats- und Verwaltungskunde* (Berlin, Gersbach und Sohn Verlag, 1944), pp. 225–26.

53. Ironically, the Nazis established a Reich Administrative Court in 1941, fulfilling a promise in the Weimar Constitution which the Weimar regime had neglected. However, the Reich court had no important functions as a result of the 1939 decrees cited above. Cf. Rehkopp, pp. 225 ff.

54. Wagener, *Die Staedte im Landkreis*, pp. 130–34.

55. *Jahrbuch fuer Kommunalwissenschaft* (1940–41), pp. 1–54.

The Nazis did not eliminate legislative and judicial controls in order to leave the Landrat free to act according to his own discretion; they excluded external participation in the administrative process in order to bring the Landrat under the exclusive control of the ministries and the party. In addition to personnel controls (which will be discussed separately below), the government increased the District Officer's authority to supervise the Landrat's activities. The District Officer issued more frequent and more detailed instructions to Landraete than ever before.[56]

Another check on the Landrat's expanded authority resulted from an increase in the number and jurisdiction of specialized agencies that operated at the county level. The Nazi regime once more diminished the Landrat's authority over specialized field agents after the Papen government had bolstered it in 1932. A new decree soon after the Nazis took office emphasized that the Landrat was not pre-eminent; he only possessed the right to be informed and to give advice.[57] Indeed during World War II, the Reich authorized its functional ministries to bypass the Landrat's office altogether when directing the activities of their specialized field agents.[58] Such independent local operations involved numerous agencies; in 1941, forty-five specialized field agencies operated at the district and county levels.[59]

The activity of specialized field agents curbed the scope of the Landrat's powers; they especially prevented him from concentrating control over all administrative functions in his office. However, we should not exaggerate the novelty of this development. Specialized agencies always had operated at the county level. Their continued activity simply set an upper limit to the Landrat's authority; they did not reduce his authority below Weimar standards.

56. Sommerfeld, *Das Amt des preussischen Regierungspraesidenten*, pp. 16 ff.; Rehkopp, p. 213.

57. *Duesseldorf Staatsarchiv*, Decree of March 25, 1933, Rep. LA Muelheim/Rhein 436.

58. Wagener, pp. 212–13; John H. Herz, "German Administration under the Nazi Regime," *American Political Science Review, 40* (1946), 693 ff.

59. Wilhelm Stuckart, "Zentralgewalt, Dezentralisation und Verwaltungseinheit" in Stuckart, ed., *Festgabe fuer Heinrich Himmler* (Darmstadt, L. C. Wittich Verlag, 1941), p. 20. Stuckart was State-Secretary of the Reich and Prussian Ministry of Interior. See also Rehkopp, pp. 207–08.

Large-scale Personnel Changes Large-scale personnel changes constituted the final hierarchical control instrument upon which the Nazis placed heavy reliance to assure a responsive field administration. The Nazis molded their personnel policy in response to their deep-rooted hatred of the Weimar Republic and its alleged malpractices. The Nazis had long accused the Weimar regime of neglecting to appoint career oriented, university trained civil servants and preferring untrained, incompetent party workers. In addition, the Nazis alleged that a high proportion of Jews had infiltrated the public service. In order to dismiss all such officials, the Nazi regime enacted a special civil service law in June 1933. It provided for the dismissal of three classes of officials: 1) civil servants whose political affiliations showed lack of allegiance to the Nazi regime; 2) officials appointed after November 9, 1918, who did not possess the formal requirements for entry into the professional civil service; and 3) all "non-Aryan" civil servants except those in office before 1914 or those who served in the army during World War I. Moreover, any civil servant could be transferred to a lower position or dismissed for the good of the service if his agency were abolished.[60] The law required a review of the dossiers of all of Prussia's 1,663 higher civil servants. The result was that 12.5 per cent of these officials were dismissed because they were allegedly disloyal, non-Aryan, or lacked professional training; an additional 15.5 per cent lost their positions or were downgraded because of administrative reorganizations. In the other Laender, only 4.5 per cent of all higher civil servants lost their positions because of disqualification; another 5 per cent were dismissed or transferred to lower posts as a result of reorganizations.[61] The Nazis euphemistically entitled the law under which

60. Law of June 23, 1933, RGBl, *1*, 389. On its execution, see Marx, "Civil Service in Germany," in White, *Civil Service Abroad*, pp. 161 ff.; Hans Bernd Gisevius, *To the Bitter End*, trans. by Richard and Clara Winston (Boston, Houghton Mifflin, 1947), p. 89; Oskar Georg Fischbach, *Das Reichsgesetz zur Widerherstellung des Berufsbeamtentums* (Berlin and Leipzig, Walter de Gruyter, 1933).

61. Schuetze, "Beamtenpolitik im Dritten Reich," in Hans Pfundtner, ed., *Dr. Wilhelm Frick und sein Ministerium* (Munich, Zentralverlag der NSDAP, 1937), p. 51. Franz Neumann, *Behemoth* (2d ed. New York, Oxford University Press, 1944), p. 380, cites Schuetze but gives different figures. This apparently is the result of an inadvertent misreading of the original by Neumann.

this purge proceeded, "An Act To Restore the Professional Civil Service"; in fact, it violated all the vested privileges of the career civil service which the Weimar constitution had guaranteed.

Dismissal of compromised civil servants comprised but half of the Nazi personnel policy; the regime paid even more careful attention to its appointments to fill key field positions. Minister President Goering reserved to himself the right to appoint all field officials down to the post of Landrat. Subordinate positions were filled by functional ministries or by the field agencies themselves.[62] Immediately after taking office, Goering initiated a purge of the field administration which led to the replacement of almost every leading official in the Prussian field service by Nazi party members. All Provincial Governors were dismissed; six of the new Provincial Governors were also party Gauleiter; four of the remainder were pre-1933 party members.[63] Eleven of Prussia's twelve Deputy Provincial Governors were discharged. The government replaced all but three of the thirty-four District Officers; after this purge, thirty-one of the District Officers were allegedly party members, nineteen of them holding cards before 1933. At the county level, the government appointed new Landraete in 75 per cent of Prussia's counties.[64] The purge was accomplished with little formal opposition, for the Nazis had abolished all representative bodies and no longer needed local approval of their candidates for District Officers and Landraete. As Table 5 shows, the party was not quite as thorough in its purges outside Prussia,

62. Decree of July 17, 1933, GS, 266.

63. Schuetze, p. 55; *Nationalsozialistisches Jahrbuch* (1934), pp. 117 ff., lists the following Regional Governorships as held by Gauleiter: East Prussia (Koch), Brandenburg (Kube), Grenzmark-Posen-West Prussia (Kube), Upper Silesia and Lower Silesia (Bruckner), and Schleswig-Holstein (Lohse).

64. Schuetze, p. 55, states that thirty-one District Officers were party members. On checking their biographies in *Das Deutsche Fuehrerlexikon* (Berlin, Verlagsanstalt Otto Stollberg, 1934), an official NSDAP publication, one finds that only four of the twenty-three whose biographies are given claimed party membership. As there was no reason to hide party membership in this volume, it seems unlikely that Schuetze's claims are true. Landraete unfortunately were not included in the *Fuehrerlexikon* to permit a similar check. As Schuetze's data are the only ones presently available and as his position as personnel officer of the Reich Ministry of Interior gave him access to personnel files, we cite his statements with this cautionary note.

TABLE 5

The Effect of Nazi Purges on the Field Service up to 1937

A. Percentage of Field Officials Replaced (Figures in Parentheses Indicate Total Number of Cases for Each Office)

Office	Prussia	All other Laender
Provincial Governor	100 (12)	—
Deputy Provincial Governor	92 (12)	—
District Officer	91 (34)	71[a] (17)
Deputy District Officer	100 (34)	57 (14)
Landrat	75 (361)	51 (346)

B. Percentage of Field Officials Who Were Regular Party Members and Old Guard (Pre-1933) Party Members in 1937 (Figures in Parentheses Indicate Total Number of Cases for Each Office)

Office	Prussia			All other Laender		
	Not party member	Regular party member	Old Guard party member	Not party member	Regular party member	Old Guard party member
Provincial Governor	8 (12)	—[b]	92	—	—	—
Deputy Provincial Governor	8 (12)	92	—[c]	—	—	—
District Officer	9 (34)	35	56	47 (17)	7	46
Deputy District Officer	38 (34)	47	15	57 (14)	43	0
Landrat	5 (361)	47	48	42 (346)	49	9

[a] In addition, 23 per cent of the posts were vacant.
[b] Schuetze gives no indication whether the single Regional Governor who was not an Old Guard party member was also not a party member at all.
[c] No data given.
Source: Schuetze, pp. 55 f.

for in some Laender numerous Nazis had already held office before
1933.

The purge of key field personnel contrasted sharply with the
Weimar personnel policies. As noted in the previous chapter, the
Weimar regime undertook only marginal changes in key personnel
during its first years in office and then gradually attempted to
develop a loyal civil service by appointing democratically oriented
officials to fill vacancies that occurred through normal attrition.
The Nazi regime removed more Landraete during its first five
years in office than the Weimar Republic had in thirteen. The
Nazis committed precisely the offense for which they heaped so
much abuse on the Weimar regime: they packed the civil service
with partisans rather than professionals.

This review of the administrative changes initiated by the Nazis
reveals their intense concern for obtaining a responsive field administration. The Nazi regime completely restructured the channels of communications through which central mandates were
transmitted to field agents and altered the web of hierarchical
controls by which field agents were supervised in the execution of
central policies. The Reich abrogated Land autonomy and established direct contacts with Land field agencies. Both in law and in
fact, Land field agencies became Reich offices. The Reich directly
controlled all appointments to field offices. In Prussia, it merged
the Land's ministries with its own central offices while in the other
Laender it sent its own agents to become Land ministers. To complete the subjugation of the Laender, the Reich revoked their
right to collect taxes and made them dependent on annually
fluctuating grants-in-aid. By these measures the Nazi regime sought
to overcome the responsiveness barriers that Germany's federal system interposed between Reich ministries and Land field agencies.

The Third Reich also sought to destroy all barriers to responsive field administration in the Laender, as our discussion of Prussia illustrates. The Nazi regime tried to increase the effectiveness
of hierarchical controls by destroying external restraints that
might have impeded the execution of central mandates. The county councils were disbanded and their legislative functions transferred to the Landrat; county committees ceased to function
either as a legislative check on the Landrat or as an administrative
court. Having pushed aside all traditional external controls, the

Nazi regime increased the District Officer's supervision over the Landrat. The district office closely supervised the execution of central mandates by the Landrat's office. Moreover, specialized agencies that operated under direct ministerial control performed their county functions with little supervision or coordination by the Landrat. Like the regime's abrogation of Land autonomy, these changes were intended to streamline command channels and promote field responsiveness.

The Nazi regime also feared civil service disloyalty. After years of accusing the Weimar Republic of violating civil service neutrality, the Nazis were convinced that the bureaucracy was saturated with officials committed to democratic government who would sabotage the administration of Nazi programs. Consequently, the Nazis sharpened central personnel controls. The regime brought all civil servants under direct Reich control. The Reich amended civil service laws to allow dismissal for political unreliability. These provisions set the stage for the first widespread civil service purge in 200 years of Prussian history.

Despite all these measures Nazi fears of unresponsive field administration were not allayed. The National Socialists never believed that a bureaucratic corps could execute Nazi mandates with sufficient vigor and enthusiasm. Conventional controls served to prevent disloyal administration but they could not promote zeal and fanaticism. The party considered itself as the only leavening agent which could activate routine-smothered administrators by direct contact. Therefore, from its first days in power, the Nazi regime supplemented the reforms we have discussed with the development of unconventional, external controls.

THE DEVELOPMENT OF EXTERNAL CONTROLS

The Nazi regime developed three kinds of external checks on its field agents to promote zealous as well as loyal field administration. These were: 1) infiltration of party officials into key field positions; 2) supervision of field agencies by party units; and 3) usurpation of governmental functions by party agencies. The regime intended these controls to supplement the hierarchical restraints described above. Each of the external controls placed field administrators in close contact with party officials; they enabled the Nazi regime to prod field officials to act with more vigor. However, they also tangled command channels and provoked conflicts between the public and party bureaucracies. Infiltration by party officials and supervision of field agencies by party units were most evident at the Landrat's office; we shall, therefore, focus our attention on the organization and operation of the Landrat's office to examine the functions of these external checks. Then we shall turn our attention to police organization in the Third Reich to investigate how usurpation of governmental activities by party agencies operated as a check on the field administration.

Party Infiltration and Supervision of Field Agencies The Nazi party possessed an extensive and well-organized regional organization. For party purposes, the NSDAP divided Germany into thirty-five regions (*Gaue*) during the Third Reich.[65] A Gauleiter was the chief party official in each region. These regions had originally matched the electoral districts of the Weimar Republic; like those election districts, the party Gaue often did not coincide with administrative districts. Each party region was further divided into counties (*Kreise*) which mostly corresponded to the administrative county areas (*Landkreise* and *Stadtkreise*) used by the Laender. A Kreisleiter was the chief of the party's county office. Town units (*Ortsgruppen*) operated under the Kreisleiter's supervision.

From the very beginning of the Nazi era, the party used its regional organization as a check on the field administration. As we have already seen, the party's regional leaders (Gauleiter) often served as Reich Governors or as Prussian Provincial Governors. Many Gauleiter, however, held only their party post because no administrative district coincided with their party region. At the county level the situation was different as almost all the party's Kreis areas coincided with the administrative boundaries of the counties.

65. The thirty-five *Gaue* included all areas within the 1937 boundaries of Germany. After 1937, so-called *Reichsgaue* were established in annexed areas; these Reichsgaue simultaneously served as party regions and as administrative districts. Our discussion is restricted to administration in Germany proper where no Reichsgaue existed. See Artur Norbeck, *Die Formen der Zusammenarbeit von Partei und Staat*, pp. 29–30; A. V. Boerner, "Towards Reichsreform— the Reichsgaue," *American Political Science Review, 33* (1939), 853 ff.

In most counties, the party appointed proven Nazis as Landraete. During the first years of the regime, however, the party had difficulty finding persons who were both qualified and loyal for Landrat positions. Consequently, in some counties the government appointed the party's Kreisleiter to be Landrat. In others, the SA—the party's para-military organization—sent special commissars to supervise county administration at first hand. In most counties, the party also planted members of its county staff in key positions in the Landrat's office.[66] Some of these practices gained official sanction as the Third Reich matured; others were abandoned.

The activity of SA commissars was limited to a handful of counties; they disappeared completely after the purge of the SA on June 30, 1934.[67] Appointment of the Kreisleiter to the post of Landrat, however, was a more widespread practice. It appeared to offer a double guarantee of field responsiveness to the Nazi regime in Berlin. In his party post the Kreisleiter received orders from the party hierarchy; as Landrat, he executed commands from the Nazi-controlled central bureaucracy. As Kreisleiter, he directed the party's organizations; as Landrat, he supervised the execution of all public functions in the county. Such dual office-holding allowed the party to implant their most loyal and zealous officials in the government's field agencies; it also gave local party units direct access to government information and an opportunity to provide comprehensive guidance to most governmental field operations.

No data are available to indicate the precise number of Kreisleiter appointed to Landrat posts during the first years of the Nazi regime. However, the 1935 party census indicates a maximum of 78 such personal unions, for 10.7 per cent of all Kreisleiter were civil servants though not necessarily Landraete.[68] The propor-

---

66. Schuetze, p. 55, described the regime's personnel policies in 1937 as follows: "When no trained officials were available, we were forced to abandon . . . [our] principle and appoint men without professional training who through many years of activity in the party had developed special qualifications for the post of Landrat."

67. Fleisch, p. 17.

68. Reichsorganisationsleiter der NSDAP, *Partei Statistik* (Munich, Franz Eher Verlag, 1935), 2, 322–26, 350.

tion of Kreisleiter who were Landraete varied considerably from Gau to Gau. In Silesia, 63.5 per cent of the Kreisleiter were Landraete; in Schleswig-Holstein, only 25 per cent were. In other regions such as Hanover and Hesse, dual office-holding was rare.[69]

Although dual office-holding occurred rather infrequently in the Reich as a whole, the party soon became uneasy about the practice. The party found that its Kreisleiters, who had been zealous party leaders and had recklessly followed party commands, became meek bureaucrats after a few months in their governmental office.[70] The party feared that such bureaucratization of its leadership elite would sap the vigor of the movement.[71] As a consequence, the Nazi party issued instructions in 1937 forbidding the Kreisleiter to serve simultaneously as Landrat.[72] The practice of holding both offices, however, lingered on in scattered areas of the Reich as late as 1942. In that year 24 Kreisleiter still held Landrat posts; half of these cases occurred in one party region, East Prussia under Gauleiter Koch.[73]

Even when the Landrat and Kreisleiter posts remained separate, the Kreisleiter supervised the Landrat in many matters. The Kreisleiter had to be consulted on all appointments and promotions in the Landrat's office. In 1937, the Reich Civil Service Code required clearance of personnel actions through party channels.[74] The

69. Carl Dernedde, "Die Praxis der Aemtervebindungen in der Verfassung und Verwaltung des Reichs," *Zeitschrift fuer die gesammte Staatswissenschaft*, 93 (1938), 555 ff.

70. For instance, the Gauleiter of Weser-Ems wrote in an undated document: "The result [of personal unions between party and state offices] has always been an advantage for the state and a disadvantage for the party." U.S. National Archives, "Captured German Documents," microfilm T–81, reel 7, frames 14515 ff. See also *Partei Statistik*, 2, 155.

71. Friedrich W. Lampe, *Die Amtstraeger der Partei* (Stuttgart, W. Kohlhammer Verlag, 1941), p. 109; Neesse, p. 70; Rehkopp, p. 104.

72. Lampe, p. 108.

73. Based on compilation by author of names of all *Kreisleiter* as listed in *Addressenwerk der Dienstellen der NSDAP, 1942* (3d ed. Berlin, Die Deutsche Tag Verlag, 1942), and names of all German Landraete as listed in *Taschenbuch fuer Verwaltungsbeamte 1942* (Berlin, Carl Heymanns Verlag, 1942).

74. Reich Civil Service Code, paragraphs 24–25. See also commentary on the law by Georg Fischbach, *Deutsches Beamtengesetz* (Berlin, Carl Heymanns Verlag, 1940), *1*, 411 ff.

Kreisleiter also won an influential position in the administration of the Landrat's office through the Local Government Act of 1935 which reorganized town governments throughout Germany on a uniform pattern.[75] Under the provisions of this law, the county retained its role as supervisor of town governments; the Landrat, however, had to share his tutelary powers with a Party Delegate (*Beauftragter der NSDAP*) who specialized in local government problems in the party's Kreis office. The Party Delegate—a subordinate of the Kreisleiter—supervised town governments in political affairs. Often the Landrat was forced to appoint the same man to direct the town supervision section of the Landrat's office. The Kreisleiter's subordinate thus exercised the Landrat's tutelary powers.[76] In Wuerttemberg, the Party Delegate also participated in county committee meetings (as long as they still were held) and exercised a veto over its decisions.[77]

Strife often marred relations between the Landraete and Kreisleiter. German administrative literature during the Third Reich reflects these tensions; it exhorts the party and the bureaucracy to respect each others' jurisdictional boundaries. The party's function was to lead; the bureaucracy's role lay in administration.[78] However, the distinction between leadership and administration remained too vague to prevent conflicts. Clashes with the Kreisleiter inevitably arose when the Landrat sought to protect the powers of his office, for the party absorbed some of the county's functions. Welfare work, for instance, became a principal activity for local party organizations who often took over county orphanages or welfare homes.[79] The party also took a keen interest in limiting religious observances and sought to convince the Landrat that he should discourage or prohibit church processions and par-

---

75. *Deutsche Gemeindeordnung*, RGBl, *1*, 49.

76. Statements by Ministerialdirektor a.D. Wormit, Bonn, April 28, 1959, Landrat a.D. Leuthner, Neustadt an der Weinstrasse, April 15, 1959, and Landrat Salzmann, Trier, April 27, 1959, personal interviews. See also Dernedde, pp. 555 ff.

77. Norbeck, pp. 30–31.

78. See, for example, Otto Koellreutter, *Deutsches Verfassungsrecht* (Berlin, Junker und Duennhaupt Verlag, 1935), pp. 150 ff.; Lampe, pp. 109 ff.; Neesse, pp. 70 ff.

79. Wagener, p. 137.

ticipation in religious services by county officials.[80] During the war, the Kreisleiter increased their interference with administrative matters. For instance, a Kreisleiter in Hesse recommended in the weekly morale report to his Gauleiter that he, as Kreisleiter, be given full executive power in order to overcome the Landrat's bureaucratic inertia.[81] In 1944, party intervention in county administration became serious enough to warrant a clarifying circular from Ernst Kaltenbrunner, chief of the security police (*Ordnungspolizei*), and Wilhelm Stuckart, State Secretary of the Reich and Prussian Ministry of Interior. They specifically prohibited the performance of county government functions by party organizations, party interference with individual administrative decisions, and intentional disregard for the Landrat in executing civil defense measures. They wrote to their subordinates: "The maxim: 'Only one can lead' is the motto to be applied to town and county government."[82] Curiously, leadership in this instance was assigned to the bureaucracy.

Another source of tension between Landraete and Kreisleiter was the Landrat's resentment of the Kreisleiter as an outsider who lacked the university training the Landrat had acquired. Moreover, like most career civil servants, Landraete came from quite different social backgrounds than party leaders. While no biographical data for Landraete are available, one can extrapolate from existing biographical information on District Officers, their career superiors, and compare it with information on party administrators.[83] As Table 6 shows, more civil servants than party officials came from high-status families (landowners, military, and civil service), had finished a university education, and had begun

80. Hofer, pp. 119–66. Pressure against the church was perhaps most resisted in the Rhineland; statements by Landrat Salzmann and Landrat Unkrich, Neustadt an der Weinstrasse, April 14, 1959, personal interviews.

81. Archiv, Institut fuer Zeitgeschichte, Munich, Rep. NSDAP, MA 53, 25-a/14.

82. Ibid., Rep. NG 2656.

83. There is good reason to believe that career Landraete did not differ significantly from the District Officers in the characteristics listed in Table 6. Almost all District Officers reached their position after service as Landraete; both posts were normally filled with career civil servants who had completed a university education. Moreover, such career officials usually entered the civil service at an early age and thus they enjoyed regular employment.

TABLE 6

Selected Biographical Data of District Officers
and Party Administrators, 1934
(Expressed as Percentage)

	District officers (N=34)[a]	Party administrators (N=151)[b]
Occupation of Father		
Landowner	8.8	2.0
Military	8.8	5.3
Civil Service	26.4	7.9
Professions	0.0	11.9
Business	5.9	9.9
Artisan	0.0	6.0
Peasant	8.8	7.3
Other	0.0	6.7
Unknown	41.3	43.0
Total	100.0	100.0
Education		
University	61.8	25.2
Other	38.2	74.1
Unknown	0.0	0.7
Total	100.0	100.0
Primary Life Work		
Civil Service	67.7	13.2
Profession	0.0	17.2
Business	0.0	23.2
Nazi Party Official	0.0	15.9
Military	2.9	14.6
Other	0.0	13.4
Unknown	29.4	2.0
Total	100.0	100.0
Age at First Career Job		
Below 35	67.7	64.3
35–50	0.0	12.2
51–65	0.0	4.6
Unknown	32.3	17.9
Total	100.0	100.0

Sources:

[a]Compiled from *Fuehrerlexikon,* using all District Officers listed.

[b]Lerner, pp. 7, 17, 21, and 44. Lerner also drew his data from the *Fuehrerlexikon* so that data of the two columns are comparable.

their life's career work at an earlier age (despite their long education). Lerner characterizes the party administrator as a marginal
social type;[84] in contrast, the District Officers were typically solid
—one might say, stolid—citizens. It appears reasonable to assume
that Landraete exhibited similar social characteristics, for almost
all District Officers began their careers as Landraete. It is therefore quite likely that such career officials resented the sudden rise
of marginal elements of German society to positions of leadership
over them. Indeed, time in party work eventually counted toward
civil service seniority for those party members who entered the
civil service.[85] Thus party workers who had served prison sen-
tences during the Weimar Republic and had been in official positions a few years in 1936 were placed at the head of promotion
lists in front of career officials who had served ten years in government positions.[86]

It is impossible to estimate the frequency of such conflicts between the Landrat and Kreisleiter without intensive investigation
of surviving archives. The frequency of conflict, however, seems to
have varied greatly throughout Germany.[87] When a Kreisleiter
was disinterested in administrative affairs, few clashes occurred.
Conflicts also remained infrequent when a Landrat was eager to
defer to the Kreisleiter because he agreed with Nazi policies or
because he was fearful of the Kreisleiter's power. But occasionally
a Kreisleiter was fanatical or deeply interested in administrative
affairs and was opposed by an equally firm Landrat. In such circumstances, fell-fledged administrative battles raged over the most
minor matters, with the bureaucracy arrayed on one side and the
party hierarchy aligned on the other.

Surviving evidence makes it clear that conflicts between the
Landrat and Kreisleiter rarely threatened a complete administrative breakdown. The existence of such conflicts rather illustrates

---

84. Lerner, et al., *The Nazi Elite*, pp. 51–52.
85. RFBl (1936), p. 105; ibid. (1940), pp. 252–53; ibid. (1941), p. 88.
86. Examples of such conflicts are recorded in the NSDAP documents, U.S.
National Archives, "Captured German Documents," microfilm T–81, reel 63,
frame 71194, and reel 176, frame 318474.
87. The following is based on statements by Landrat Unkrich, Landrat
Salzmann, Ministerialdirektor a.D. Wormit, and Landrat a.D. Leuthner, personal interviews. All served as Landraete during the Third Reich.

the continual pressure that the party county organization exerted on the Landrat to obtain a more vigorous administration of Nazi policies. The Kreisleiter's supervision of the Landrat's office often became a real factor in administrative decision-making at the county level. Without a government position and sometimes without government sanction, the Kreisleiter gave the party a powerful instrument to check bureaucratic action at the local level.

Competition and Usurpation—The Police   Infiltration of key positions in field agencies and control of the administration by party organs comprised two of the supplements to tighter conventional controls that the Third Reich developed. The third external control consisted of party competition with government agencies for the performance of public functions and the usurpation of some governmental activities by party organs. Heinrich Himmler especially relied on this technique in reorganizing Germany's police forces. It was used to a lesser degree with other administrative functions, as, for example, with welfare activities at the county level.

Himmler developed competition and usurpation only as a supplement to all the other hierarchical and external control devices already noted. Therefore, our discussion of police organization must describe these other control instruments as they functioned in the police organization as well, in order that we may understand the emergence of competition and usurpation in the context in which Himmler developed them.

The police occupy a sensitive position in any political system. Together with the army, the police is the principal instrument of force that a government possesses. When a revolutionary regime seizes power, it must win control over these two coercive instruments lest an opponent use them to overthrow the regime. In 1919, the revolutionary government that eventually formed the Weimar Republic reorganized both the army and police from the ground up. As noted in the preceding chapter, political circumstances forced the Reich to accept Land control over the Security Police. The Reich issued only skeletal regulations except during political crises when it sought to direct police action against subversive elements. Without Land cooperation, however, the Reich remained completely impotent to direct police operations.

After winning control over the Reich government in 1933, Hitler did not allow the police forces to remain decentralized. The Nazi regime at once began to concentrate control over the police in Reich agencies. In addition, the Nazis merged the police with their own para-military units. The Nazi party possessed two armed groups that performed quasipolice functions: the SA (*Sturm-abteilung,* commonly "Storm Troopers") and the SS (*Schutzstaffel,* commonly "Black Shirts"). The SA, under Captain Roehm, was the larger organization in 1933; it focused its activities on breaking up rallies of political opponents; the SS, under Himmler's leadership, guarded Hitler, other high-ranking party officials, and party meetings. The SA fell into oblivion after the purge of June 30, 1934, in which Himmler's SS murdered Roehm and decimated the SA leadership.

The political police were the Nazi regime's first target for centralization and nazification. The political police of the Laender had served during the Weimar period as an intelligence service for Land governments and as an instrument through which evidence on subversive activities could be collected to justify the banning of opposition newspapers and the dissolution of subversive political organizations. In no Land did the political police possess an extensive field organization. It relied on field reports from police chiefs of the larger cities and from Landraete.[88] The Reich had no political police of its own.

The Nazis desired a more effective secret police, for they had a paranoid fear of Communist and Socialist plots that might overthrow their regime. Nazi ideology compelled the regime to label large portions of the German population—Communists, Socialists, Jews, liberals, Masons, etc.—as active or potential opponents to their regime. Uprooting this opposition by the most expedient means available became the function of the political police.

When the regime was three months old, the Prussian Prime Minister, Hermann Goering, set aside a special section within the Prussian Ministry of Interior for the Secret State Police (*Geheime Staatspolizei,* commonly *Gestapo*).[89] To assure continued personal control, he transferred the Gestapo to his own office in November

88. See Bernhard Weiss, *Polizei und Politik* (Berlin, Gersbach und Sohn Verlag, 1928), pp. 27 ff.
89. Law of April 26, 1933, GS, 122.

1933, and established it as an independent central office under his direct supervision.[90] Goering's jurisdiction, however, remained limited to Prussia. Outside Prussia, Goering's rival, Heinrich Himmler, toured through Germany's Land capitals, winning appointment from each Land government as "commander of the political police." At the end of his grand tour in January 1934, Himmler had won control over the political police in all the Laender except Prussia.[91] For operational purposes, Himmler combined the Gestapo with the SS Security Service (*Sicherheitsdienst*) which was also under his command.[92] In April 1934, Himmler finally completed his conquest of the political police when Goering reluctantly appointed him as his deputy in charge of the Prussian Gestapo.[93] In this manner, Himmler concentrated control over the Gestapo in his own hands and combined it with the party's intelligence service. Within fourteen months, the political police had become both centralized and nazified.

Centralization and nazification of the general police organization proceeded with equal speed. Papen's coup d'état in 1932 had already neutralized the Prussian police force—Germany's largest—over which the Nazis won control when Hindenburg appointed Hitler as Reich Chancellor. When the Reich deposed the governments of the other Laender in March 1933 and installed Reich Commissars, it won indirect control of the remaining Land police forces. Thus, during its first two months in power, the Nazi regime won *de facto* control over all police forces in Germany.

In February 1934, the Reich formally assumed jurisdiction over the Land police under the provisions of the Reich Reorganization Law of January 30, 1934.[94] The law and the executive ordinances

---

90. Law of Nov. 30, 1933, GS, 413. The rest of the Ministry of Interior was transferred on that date to the Reich and fell under the jurisdiction of the Reich Minister of Interior, Frick.

91. Hans Buchheim, "Die organisatorische Entwicklung der politischen Polizei in Deutschland in den Jahren 1933–34," in *Gutachten des Instituts fuer Zeitgeschichte* (Munich, Selbstverlag des Instituts fuer Zeitgeschichte, 1958), pp. 294–307; Hans Buchheim, "Die SS in der Verfassung des dritten Reiches," *Vierteljahrshefte fuer Zeitgeschichte, 3* (1955), 133; Gisevius, *To the Bitter End*, pp. 181 ff., gives a vivid account.

92. Buchheim, "Die organisatorische Entwicklung . . .," pp. 294–307.

93. *Schulthess' Geschichtskalender 1934*, p. 109.

94. Executive Decree of Feb. 2, 1934, RGBl, *1*, 81.

that followed it vested broad supervisory powers in the Reich Minister of Interior, Wilhelm Frick, but left the organizational structure untouched. Frick made only occasional use of his new powers, for he planned an extensive reorganization of the Land police on a uniform basis in order to make centralized control more effective.[95] Frick, however, lacked the necessary influence to win Hitler's acceptance of his reform plans. These circumstances forced Frick to adopt partial measures which centralized certain functions while allowing fundamental regional variations in the organization of the police to remain. Frick's reforms required the Land police to seek his approval for any basic changes in their organization or personnel procedure as well as for appointments to key positions.[96] He also concentrated top-level control of the Prussian police in his own hands. In November 1934, when the Reich and Prussian Ministries of Interior were combined, he transferred the police section of the Prussian Ministry of Interior from its office on *Koenigsplatz* to his own office on *Unter den Linden*.[97] All other divisions of the two ministries, even though both were headed by Frick, remained separately housed in their former offices.

These were piecemeal reforms. Their effect was to concentrate top-level direction of police operations in the Reich section of the combined Reich and Prussian Ministry of Interior. However, the Land ministries of interior continued to stand between the Reich and the local police agencies. Moreover, variations in the organization of the Land police forces remained standing as under the Weimar Republic.

When Himmler deposed Frick in the Ministry of Interior, the Reich took more vigorous action to uniformize and nazify the regular police forces. Himmler won appointment as chief of the German police in June 1936, despite the opposition of Frick and the entire staff of the Reich Ministry of Interior.[98] Himmler re-

95. Hans-Joachim Neufeldt, Juergen Huck, and Georg Tessin, *Zur Geschichte der Ordnungspolizei 1936–1945*. Schriften des Bundesarchivs, Heft 3 (Koblenz, Als Manuscript gedruckt, 1957), part I, pp. 8 ff.

96. Decree of Feb. 5, 1934, cited in Neufeldt, Huck, and Tessin, p. 8.

97. Neufeldt, Huck, and Tessin, p. 8.

98. Ibid., pp. 11–17, gives an account of the struggle between Frick and Himmler as reflected in surviving documents in the Bundesarchiv in Koblenz.

mained nominally subordinate to Frick, but, in fact, he functioned free from Frick's control.[99] His title indicates Himmler's peculiar hierarchical position; he became "Reich Leader of the SS and Chief of the German Police in the Reich Ministry of Interior." Himmler combined party and governmental positions; his office was "in" not "under" the Ministry of Interior. Himmler won jurisdiction over the ministry's entire police section and some functions of other divisions as well. He retained the chief of the ministry's police section, the former SA organizer Daluege, and named him chief of the Office for the Security Police (*Ordnungspolizei*). This office won jurisdiction over the regular police, what formerly had been the *Schutzpolizei*, Gendarmerie, and municipal police.[100] Himmler transferred the detective forces (*Kriminalpolizei*), the sections responsible for surveillance of the press, for regulation of firearms, and for issuance of identification cards, and the general organization section to his own office on *Prinz Albrecht Strasse*. These sections were assigned to Himmler's adjutant, Heydrich, who also headed the Gestapo and the SS Intelligence Service (the SD). Heydrich's section became known as the Central Office for Security Police (*Hauptamt Sicherheitspolizei*).[101]

Himmler at once used his new authority to concentrate direction of all German police forces in his office. In July 1936, he extended his control to the police of the smaller municipalities who until then had remained under Land control.[102] In September 1936, the Office for Ordnungspolizei dispatched inspectors to the Provincial Governors in Prussia and to the Land Ministries of Interior or Reich Governors in the other Laender.[103] These inspectors checked the organization and training of the Ordnungspolizei and made sure that Himmler's directives were being executed. Some of the cities to which Himmler sent inspectors also

99. Buchheim, "Die SS in der Verfassung des dritten Reiches," pp. 134–38.

100. Neufeldt, Huck, and Tessin, pp. 20–21; Werner Best, *Die deutsche Polizei* (Darmstadt, L. C. Wittich Verlag, 1940), pp. 57–58.

101. Neufeldt, Huck, and Tessin, pp. 22–23; Best, p. 62; Gerald Reitlinger, *The SS: Alibi of a Nation* (London, William Heinemann, 1956), p. 138.

102. Circular Decree, RFSS&CdDP of July 22, 1936, II, E 5117/36, reprinted in Kurt Bader, *Aufbau und Gliederung der Ordnungspolizei* (Berlin, Verlag fuer Recht und Verwaltung, 1943), pp. 13–19.

103. IMT, German edition, vol. 42, Document SS(A)-87, pp. 657 ff.; Neufeldt, Huck, and Tessin, part II, pp. 19–20.

happened to be district headquarters for the army; the police inspectors located there had the additional duty of coordinating civil defense plans with the army commanders, a function which the provincial governors had previously performed.[104] In November 1937, Himmler's office sent out another set of field officials to army district headquarters; these were called "Regional SS and Police Leaders."[105] As their title indicates, these officials commanded both the SS and police forces in their area. The police inspectors became directly subordinate to the regional police leaders and relayed the leader's instructions to the district police units.[106] These initial reforms gave Himmler far greater control over local police operations than Frick had possessed. For the first time, the Reich's central police office had a direct channel of communication and information with local police forces.

In the following years, Himmler greatly increased central control over the Land police by a series of fiscal measures. In March 1937, he transferred all but the police units' administrative personnel to the Reich budget thus winning complete budgetary control over the tables of organization, pay, and equipment of all police forces in Germany.[107] In 1940, administrative officials also came under the budgetary control of Himmler's central office.[108] Transfer of police budgets from the Laender to the Reich police office held special significance in increasing Himmler's single-handed control of Germany's police forces. With nineteen Land police budgets, staff controls had been unwieldy; with a single budget, they became possible. Moreover, Himmler's police budget escaped control by the Reich Finance Ministry, for police budgets remained open-ended just like the army's.[109] Himmler thus achieved an extraordinary degree of concentrated control by transferring police finances from the Laender to his own accounts.

Like Frick, Himmler failed to enact a single, comprehensive

---

104. Neufeldt, Huck, and Tessin, part II, p. 20.

105. Ibid.; Best, p. 43; IMT, pp. 659–60.

106. Best, p. 43.

107. Law of March 19, 1937, RGBl, *1*, 325; Neufeldt, Huck, and Tessin, part I, pp. 19–20.

108. Law of March 28, 1940, RGBl, *1*, 613.

109. IMT, Krosigk Dokument Buch, III, Document No. 15, paragraphs 5–8, located in Archiv, Institut fuer Zeitgeschichte, Munich.

reorganization of Germany's police forces. Regional differences in hierarchical structure continued and led to considerable confusion. In Prussia, for instance, the ordinary police administrators, such as the Landrat and the District Officer, had no Gestapo functions. The Gestapo possessed its own district and regional offices and sent liaison officials to work with municipal police and the Gendarmerie.[110] The SD (*Sicherheitsdienst*), a party organ, also participated in Gestapo work.[111] Consequently it frequently occurred that a local party leader knew of a projected police action long before the Landrat.[112] However, in Bavaria the political police were merged with the regular police administration. The Bavarian Landrat served as the Gestapo's local agent and, for instance, participated in Gestapo interrogations.[113] As the Landrat remained responsible for the general political security of his county, participation in Gestapo work was a distinct advantage for him as it kept him informed of Gestapo intentions. If the Landrat was a party stalwart, he could initiate programs to counteract subversive tendencies. If the Landrat was cool to some party programs, he could sometimes forestall Gestapo actions and protect his own programs.

Himmler continued to rely partially on administrative officials not selected by him and not subject to his hierarchical controls. Consequently, the party developed external controls designed to circumvent this weakness as well as to strengthen the Nazi position in the police itself. On the one hand, Himmler placed high-ranking party officials in key police posts and filled the ranks of the police with old-time party members. On the other hand, some police functions were transferred completely out of the jurisdiction of the police and entrusted to party organizations.

Key positions in the police quickly fell to SA and SS men. Daluege, the chief of the Prussian and later of the Reich Ordnungspolizei, was one of the founders of the Berlin SA;[114] Heydrich,

110. Best, pp. 53 ff.

111. Ibid., p. 56.

112. Statements by Landrat a.D. Leuthner, Landrat Unkrich, Landrat Salzmann, and Ministerialdirektor a.D. Wormit, personal interviews.

113. U.S. National Archives, "Captured German Documents," microfilm T–81, reel 184, frames 333603 ff.

114. *Wer Ist's, 10* (1935), 268.

chief of the security police, gained all his experience from SS service.[115] Of the 51 officials who served in Himmler's central police office from 1937 until 1945, at least seven (14 per cent) were career Nazis.[116] The rank-and-file was even more thoroughly infiltrated by party workers. The Nazis discharged 17.7 per cent of all police officers and 7.3 per cent of the enlisted men.[117] As the Nazis planned to transfer many of the barracked police units to the army, they enlisted almost 100,000 SA men for the Prussian police corps in the fall of 1933.[118] Thereafter, recruitment became somewhat more normalized. In 1936, however, Himmler apportioned 10 per cent of the police force's vacancies to "old party fighters" who were still unemployed.[119] The most important indicator of party infiltration of the police was Himmler's revocation of the prohibition against police membership in the SS in January 1937.[120] Eventually, almost all police officers and some enlisted men held an SS rank in addition to their police rating. Even the police uniforms were remodeled in 1937 to resemble the party's uniforms; at the same time, the Hitler greeting replaced the military salute for the police.[121]

By the time World War II broke out the police had become thoroughly nazified. During the war, many police units were transferred to occupied areas to guard frontiers, fight guerillas, and police rear-echelon areas. To replace them, Himmler ordered the formation of a rural guard (*Landwacht*) and municipal guard (*Stadtwacht*). Party members manned these units on a voluntary

115. Ibid., p. 672.

116. Neufeldt, Huck, and Tessin, part I, pp. 106–15.

117. Horst-Adalbert Koch, "Zur Organisationsgeschichte der deutschen Polizei 1927–1939," *Feldgrau, 6* (1957), 88. Reitlinger, p. 39, asserts that many of the Gestapo members were already Nazi party members before 1933 and active in Land political police. The source Reitlinger cites (IMT, *21,* 165) does not support this contention. The author could find no other evidence to sustain the allegation.

118. Koch, p. 88.

119. Circular Decree, RFSS&CdDP of April 28, 1936, RMBliV, p. 585.

120. Circular Decree, RFSS&CdDP of March 4, 1938, RMBliV, p. 390; Neussuess-Hunkel, *Die SS* (Hanover, Norddeutsche Verlagsanstalt O. Goedel, 1956), pp. 44–45.

121. Neussuess-Hunkel, pp. 44–45; Circular Decree, RFSS&CdDP of Oct. 5, 1937, RMBliV, p. 1640b; Circular Decree, RFSS&CdDP of March 4, 1938, RMBliV, p. 390.

basis.[122] Such volunteer organizations brought even more rank-and-file party members into the police corps.

In 1944, Himmler finally won control over the last major police unit not already under his direction: the Finance Ministry's border patrol (*Grenzschutz*). Himmler's persistent pressure on the Finance Ministry to win control over this police force had already caused it to conform to Nazi policies in every regard in order to avoid provoking conflicts which would justify its transfer to Himmler's office.[123] In June 1944, the bomb plot against Hitler provided the justification for its transfer. An SS officer assumed direction over the border police although no time remained to absorb it completely in Himmler's police-SS complex.[124]

Party usurpation of police functions supplemented party infiltration of key positions and of the rank-and-file of the police. During its first weeks in power in 1933, the party relied on the SA and SS to uproot opposition elements. A gruesome competition between the SA, SS, and Gestapo developed while the regular police often stood idly by.[125] However, the Roehm Putsch on June 30, 1934, by which Himmler decimated the SA leadership, pushed the SA into relative oblivion. Thereafter, only the SS took an active role in police work. It specialized in sensitive assignments with which the regular police could not be trusted. Guarding concentration camps became an exclusive SS function although prison duty is normally a function of the police.[126] The secret police (Gestapo) became indistinguishably merged with the security police (SD) of the SS; both in Berlin and in the field, the SD played a major role in guarding Germany's internal security.[127] During the war, other party organizations joined the police in more minor duties. For example, the NSKK (the party's motor pool) and the NSRK (the party's veterans' organization) functioned as auxiliary civil defense groups.[128]

122. Koch, p. 112; Neufeldt, Huck, and Tessin, part I, pp. 28 ff.

123. Statement, Reichsfinanzminister a.D. Krosigk, personal interview.

124. Ibid.

125. Gisevius, German edition, pp. 129 ff.

126. See Eugen Kogon, *Der SS-Staat* (Munich, Verlag Karl Alber, 1946).

127. Buchheim, "Die SS in Verfassung des dritten Reiches," pp. 134 ff.

128. B. H. Lankenau, *Polizei im Einsatz waehrend des Krieges* (Bremen, H. M. Hausheld, 1957), pp. 62 ff.

Party usurpation of public functions was a last-resort control which the regime invoked only in extreme cases. Normally the civil service vigorously resisted the party's encroachments of its jurisdiction. Moreover, the party itself was not sure to what degree it ought to absorb administrative tasks as it wanted to avoid bureaucratization. Finally, as we shall see below, application of these external controls entailed a high cost, for they undermined the bureaucracy's channels of communication and promoted confusion.

COORDINATION PROBLEMS

The external controls that the Nazis developed were designed to promote a zealous as well as a responsive field administration. They were to supplement the ordinary hierarchical checks which —as we saw—were applied with renewed vigor. Together, hierarchical controls and external restraints were to produce a zealous, reliable, and responsive field administration.

The results, however, fell far short of the regime's goal. Field agencies remained unresponsive to central instructions in numerous instances. The principal cause of the continued lack of responsiveness lay in the haphazard nature of Nazi administrative reforms. Law after law increased centralization. Some increased the authority of government agencies; others increased the power of party units. It appears as if little discretion remained with field agents if one examines the legal provisions under which they operated. But numerous flaws persisted. As a result of the administrative reorganizations, dozens of conflicting instructions rained on Germany's field agents. The Nazi regime made inadequate— often no—provisions for coordination of the bureaucracy's and party's central offices both of which directed the Landraete and District Officers. In fact, therefore, field agents often possessed enormous discretion, for they decided which set of instructions to obey; in many cases, they simply procrastinated while they awaited clarification.[129] The difficulties of coordinating the efforts of the

129. Statements by Landrat Unkrich, Landrat Salzmann, and Ministerialdirektor a.D. Wormit, personal interviews.

police, bureaucracy, party, and the army were epitomized in Germany's civil defense preparations.

Civil defense against air raids presented German administration with many novel problems. Warnings of air raids had to be broadcast, blackouts enforced, and, after the raids, the rubble had to be cleared. In 1939, the Reich appointed the party Gauleiter as regional civil defense commissioners (*Reichsverteidigungskommissare*) to coordinate the work of all agencies in civil defense operations. The commissioner's functions included all wartime economic controls as well.[130] The appointment of Gauleiter for civil defense functions proved to be a typical mistake for the Nazi regime. It was typical, for the Nazis usually preferred to grant new functions to party rather than administrative officials. It was a mistake because it hopelessly complicated civil defense operations. The regions over which the Gauleiter had jurisdiction failed to coincide with the regular administrative areas (provinces, districts, and counties) according to which the police were organized. The party regions also differed from army and air force regional districts.[131] Yet civil defense operations required the use of police forces as well as army equipment; they also needed the air force to sound alerts. The profusion of overlapping areas caused endless confusion during the first major air raids on German cities.[132] In 1942, the government reshuffled the army districts so that they coincided with party regions. In addition inspectors of the Ordnungspolizei were shifted to party regional headquarters.[133] The party regions, however, never matched the air force's regions or the general administrative districts. Throughout the war, confusion continued in the civil defense organization as a result of the failure to organize administrative agencies on a more uniform areal basis.

Organizational bottlenecks were only one cause for the lack of

130. Brecht, *Federalism and Regionalism in Germany*, p. 124; see also Wilhelm Stuckart, *Fuehrung und Verwaltung im Krieg* (Berlin, Industrieverlag Spaeth und Linde, 1941).

131. Brecht, pp. 125 ff.

132. Lankenau, pp. 36, 41–42, and 55–56.

133. Document PS 3235, Archiv, Institut fuer Zeitgeschichte, Munich; Brecht, p. 127. The inspectors were also given a new title at this time: "Commanders of the Ordnungspolizei" which reflected new command duties in civil defense functions. Neufeldt, Huck, and Tessin, part II, pp. 20 ff.

coordination. The Nazi failure to establish a completely uniform and unified administrative organization had deep roots in the Nazi style of governing. Both Hitler and Himmler preferred competition among their subordinates to complete coordination and uniform organization. Both feared that subordinates would use undivided power for their own purposes rather than according to Hitler's (or Himmler's) instructions.[134] Despite the Nazi ideological commitment to centralization and unification of power, Nazi leaders in practice preferred to maintain their power by encouraging internal divisions and incomplete unifications. The development of administration during the Third Reich offers a unique illustration of the endeavor to centralize according to the dictates of ideology in order to achieve full implementation of a revolutionary regime's goals. Yet the regime resisted complete centralization and unification lest it give power to opposition elements within its own camp. The Nazi regime undoubtedly achieved a higher degree of administrative concentration than any other regime in Germany. It utilized hierarchical controls to their utmost; it invented external controls to bolster its grip on the administration. Despite all these measures, field administrators often remained unresponsive to the demands of the central government.

134. Reitlinger, p. 219, develops this theme more fully.

6. THE SECOND EXPERIMENT WITH DEMOCRACY:
FIELD ADMINISTRATION IN THE GERMAN FEDERAL REPUBLIC

When Hitler committed suicide on April 30, 1945, he symbolized the fate of the Nazi Third Reich. The Allies had conclusively defeated Germany. Admiral Doenitz tried to organize a new government in the first days of May 1945, but his government both failed to win Allied recognition and lacked an operating administrative machine to support itself. In fact, governmental operations had ceased to function in those isolated pockets still free from Allied troops before the surrender on May 8. The Reich had disintegrated, and the Laender and counties were no longer capable of governing themselves after twelve years of dependence on central direction. Moreover, many government officials fled in fear of punitive action by the Allies for their role in the Nazi regime. On May 8, 1945, German government came to a complete halt.

It appeared as if the Allies would begin their occupation with an almost clean slate. Bombs and artillery duels had leveled most of Germany's cities. Streams of refugees from the East and scores of homeless Germans milled through the rubble-strewn cities; the social fabric of German life had been ripped apart. Economic activities had come to a standstill, and the government ceased to function. Yet, the destruction of existing institutions did not leave the Allies a free hand to begin their occupation. Certain economic and political imperatives, the policy goals of the Allied governments, and the preconceptions about Germany and about democratic government that the occupation forces brought with them molded the development of postwar Germany.

The pressing nature of immediate needs forced the occupying powers to make several basic decisions immediately after beginning their occupation. Humanitarian motives impelled the Western Allies to allow the Germans a minimal standard of living. The task of rebuilding their own countries forced the British, French, and Russians to make Germany self-sufficient at a subsistence standard as quickly as possible. The security of the Allied armies also made a minimal standard of social and political stability desirable. The distribution of food, regulation of prices, resumption of industrial production, commerce, and trade, the prevention of disease, the housing of refugees, and thousands of other tasks required public regulation by governmental agencies. None of the Allies possessed a sufficient number of trained personnel to accomplish these imperative, minimal tasks by themselves; all required the assistance of German officials.[1]

Even though the Allies possessed the power to reconstruct German government from the ground up on any model they desired, the urgency of the task made it convenient to resort to governmental institutions with which the Germans were already familiar. Even before the surrender, military government units used counties and towns as the framework for occupation rule; later the Allies re-erected district offices and Land governments. These measures constituted some of the most basic decisions that the Allies made in their task of reconstructing German government. For the most part, they chose familiar German institutions under the compulsion of pressing needs without much consideration of the consequences or the alternatives available.[2]

Subsequent decisions about the nature of postwar German government relied more heavily on considered policy positions. The

1. Lucius D. Clay, *Decision in Germany* (Garden City, N.Y., Doubleday, 1950), pp. 15–16; Harold Zink, *American Military Government in Germany* (New York, Macmillan, 1947), pp. 79 ff.

2. Clay, p. 55; Zink, pp. 90 ff.; Harold Zink, *The United States in Germany* (Princeton, N.J., D. Van Nostrand, 1957), pp. 39–40 and 170 ff.

Big Three tried to reach agreement on broad issues among themselves; in addition, each of the Allied governments prepared more detailed instructions for the use of its own occupation forces. Inter-Allied policy always remained vague; its most definite statement came at the Potsdam Conference in August 1945. Like all policy documents on Germany issued immediately after the war, the Potsdam Agreement primarily emphasized punitive and restrictive measures which the Allies deemed necessary. However, the agreement also looked forward to the eventual re-establishment of German government. The guiding principles for its re-erection were:[3]

> The administration of affairs in Germany should be directed towards the decentralization of the political structure and the development of local responsibility. To this end:—
> (i) local self-government shall be restored throughout Germany on democratic principles and in particular through elective councils as rapidly as consistent with military security and the purposes of military occupation;
> (ii) all democratic political parties with rights of assembly and of public discussion shall be allowed and encouraged throughout Germany;
> (iii) representative and elective principles shall be introduced into regional, provincial, and state *(Land)* administration as rapidly as may be justified by the successful application of these principles in local self-government;
> (iv) for the time being no central German government shall be established. Notwithstanding this, however, certain essential central German administrative departments, headed by state secretaries, shall be established, particularly in the fields of finance, transport, communications, foreign trade and industry. Such departments will act under the direction of the Control Council.

These provisions formed the framework for the re-establishment of German government in the Western zones. Despite the agreement's provisions for the formation of central German administrative departments, the Allies never organized them. The French

3. Report of the Tripartite Conference of Berlin (Potsdam), Aug. 2, 1945, reprinted in Beate Ruhm von Oppen, *Documents on Germany under Occupation 1945–54* (London, Oxford University Press, 1955), p. 44.

(who were not represented at Potsdam) vetoed all proposals in the Control Council to establish any organs that might lead to a new central German government.[4] The Allied Control Council did become a reality; it was a joint, four-power agency for governing postwar Germany. Basic policy differences between Russia and the Western powers, however, undermined the Control Council's efforts to reach agreements. It enacted only a few restrictive measures directed against the revival of nazism; it reached no agreements on more far-reaching issues such as goals for German economic reconstruction, steps to break down zonal boundaries, or measures to reunify Germany.[5]

Each of the Allied powers occupied part of Germany and could enact its own policies within that zone.[6] The Russians administered all Germany between the Elbe River and the Oder-Neisse line except Berlin which acquired a special status. German territories east of the Oder-Neisse line were transferred to Poland. The Big Three allocated all of Germany west of the Elbe River to the Western Allies. The Americans administered Bavaria, small parts of Baden and Wuerttemberg which became the Land Wuerttemberg-Baden, and most of the former Land Hesse and the Prussian province Hesse-Nassau which were combined into a new Land Hesse. The Americans also won jurisdiction over the North Sea port of Bremen which later became the Land Bremen. The French occupied the Bavarian Palatinate and part of Prussia's Rhineland province which were combined to become the Land Rhineland-Palatinate. The French also controlled segments of Baden, Wuerttemberg, and the Prussian district of Hohenzollern; these became the Laender South Baden and Wuerttemberg-Hohenzollern.[7] Finally, France occupied the Saar.[8] The British received jurisdiction

---

4. Clay, p. 40.

5. Ibid., pp. 107 ff. and 154 ff.

6. For the background and details of the zonal divisions of Germany see the excellent study by John F. Golay, *The Founding of the Federal Republic of Germany* (Chicago, University of Chicago Press, 1958), pp. 38–39.

7. In 1950, the Germans combined the French zone Laender South Baden and Wuerttemberg-Hohenzollern with the American zone Land Wuerttemberg-Baden to form a new Land called Baden-Wuerttemberg.

8. In 1959, the Saar was returned to Germany and attained the status of a Land.

over all of northwestern Germany which comprised parts of three Prussian provinces and several of Germany's smaller Laender. England formed four new Laender out of its territory: North-Rhine-Westphalia, from parts of the Prussian provinces Rhineland and Westphalia; Lower Saxony, from the Prussian province Hanover and the former Laender Brunswick and Oldenburg; Schleswig-Holstein, from the Prussian province of the same name; and the traditional Hanseatic city-state, Hamburg. The Allies drew the boundaries of the new Laender principally for military and logistical reasons; their political import or administrative convenience received scant attention.[9] However, the erection of the new Laender automatically signified the disappearance of Prussia from the map; a Control Council law in February 1947 confirmed this event.[10]

The Western Allies administered their zones independently without any formal agreement on goals or methods. Yet certain broad aims were common to all of them. All three Western powers wanted to prevent the revival of a chauvinistic, aggressive Germany. As a preventive measure, they hoped to establish a decentralized government in Germany that delegated many of its functions to autonomous agencies. The government was to be democratic and provide multiple opportunities for popular participation in the making and execution of laws. The new German government's powers were to be restricted not only by peace treaty provisions reminiscent of Versailles but also by popularly elected legislatures that were to be responsive to currents of public opinion and effectively able to restrain the executive. Finally, German bureaucrats were to be checked by an independent judiciary composed of civil and criminal courts and supplemented by specialized administrative tribunals.[11]

Each of the occupation powers emphasized different portions of this program in reconstructing German government in its zone. Each also introduced reforms reflecting the way things were done

9. Golay, pp. 38–39; Edward H. Litchfield, ed., *Governing Postwar Germany* (Ithaca, N.Y., Cornell University Press, 1953), p. 21.

10. Control Council Law No. 46, Feb. 25, 1947, reprinted in Oppen, p. 210.

11. W. Friedmann, *The Allied Military Government of Germany* (London, Stevens and Sons, 1947), pp. 27 ff.; Golay, p. 5.

back home. The French, despite their fear of a centralized national government in Germany, established Land regimes that were relatively highly centralized. The Laender in the French zone granted little autonomy to their localities; all field officials, including the Landraete and local police officials, remained solely responsible to the Land governments.[12] The British tried to establish a highly professional, nonpolitical administration with many functions delegated to local, autonomous bodies. Counties and cities performed a wide range of functions that were left to Land officials in the French zone. The British also tried to introduce a number of the peculiarities of British local government into German administration. The chief local administrator in England is the town clerk while the mayor is a political figurehead. In Germany both these functions had previously been combined in the *Oberbuergermeister* (or *Buergermeister*) in the cities and in the Landraete in the counties. The British tried to separate politics from administration by assigning political and representational duties to elected Buergermeister and Landraete but giving administrative duties to appointed *Oberstadtdirektoren* and *Oberkreisdirektoren*. Police administration was also decentralized and anglicized. Special police committees (*Polizeiausschuesse*) were established in the larger cities and at the district offices. The police committees were composed of representatives of town and county governments; they selected police chiefs who managed the police forces in the Laender of the British zone. It is clear that the British ranked decentralization and the re-establishment of an effective administration as their primary goals. Democratization came later, as evidenced by the fact that the British staged local and Land elections almost a year later than the Americans.[13]

The Americans emphasized democratization and decentralization; efficient administration was for the moment dispensable. As

---

12. Roger H. Wells, "Local Government," in Litchfield, pp. 72–73.

13. Friedmann, pp. 84 ff. British innovations in local administration are described from a German viewpoint by Walter Cantner, "Verfassungsrecht der Landkreise," in Hans Peters, ed., *Handbuch der kommunalen Wissenschaft und Praxis* (Berlin, Springer Verlag, 1956), *1*, 448; police reforms are described by Pioch, *Das Polizeirecht einschliesslich der Polizeiorganisation*, pp. 81 ff., and Bill Drews and Gerhard Wacke, *Allgemeines Polizeirecht* (6th ed. Berlin, Carl Heymanns Verlag, 1952), pp. 238–39.

a result, the Americans held town and county elections in January 1946, and established elected Land governments in December 1946. The Americans also decentralized the police in their zone by forcing all but the smallest towns to form their own police forces. Only the Gendarmerie remained an organ of the Land governments; moreover, Gendarmerie operations were restricted to villages and rural areas.[14]

As we shall see in the following pages, Allied changes in the structure of government had a lasting impact on German administrative developments. However, the Allied attempt to purge the civil service of Nazi elements attained far less success. The Allies linked denazification of the civil service to the general denazification program which sought to isolate and punish all adherents of the Nazi regime. Consequently, when the general denazification came to a virtual halt in 1948, the civil service purge also ended.[15] While the military governments in the Western zones had removed 53,000 officials from their posts, only 1,004 of these civil servants were declared permanently ineligible for office. The remainder could reapply for government positions and often won key appointments.[16] The Allies had little choice in this matter. A strict denazification policy would have permanently disqualified almost all civil servants as well as most individuals who had the training necessary to hold high-level administrative positions. As the hatred of the war years mellowed and as the cold war rivalry with Russia intensified, the Western Allies increasingly felt it necessary to establish as strong a government in West Germany as possible. Consequently they had to rely on civil servants tainted with Nazi associations if they were to use the civil service at all. This decision was ratified by the Bonn government in 1951 when

14. U.S. Department of State, *Germany 1947–1949, The Story in Documents* (Washington, Government Printing Office, 1950); Clay, pp. 84 ff.; Zink, *The United States in Germany*, pp. 169 ff.; Richard Hiscocks, *Democracy in Western Germany* (London, Oxford University Press, 1957), p. 38; Drews and Wacke, pp. 233 ff.; Pioch, pp. 127 ff.

15. John H. Herz, "The Fiasco of Denazification in Germany," *Political Science Quarterly, 63* (1948), 569 ff.; John Gimble, "American Denazification and German Local Politics," *American Political Science Review, 54* (1960), pp. 83 ff.

16. Arnold Brecht, "Personnel Management," in Litchfield, p. 267.

it ruled that all civil servants not judged "major offenders" could regain their positions or be retired on a full pension.[17]

The Allies executed the denazification program and all their other measures independently in their separate occupation zones. It soon became evident, however, that occupation of Germany in airtight zones was a folly; the western zones were patently too small and economically too unbalanced to become self-sufficient. The United States also did not share French fears of a central German government if its powers were sufficiently restrained by a federal system of checks and by independent legislative and judicial bodies.[18] The State Department formulated the American position in 1947 as follows.[19]

> The United States favors a united Germany with a federal structure. It does not oppose a central government for Germany. . . . It would prefer an ultimate central regime of federal character, that is, of defined and limited powers with residual powers reserved for the Laender governments. It would approve such a degree of federalistic autonomy as may be the outgrowth of indigenous German sentiment.

Consequently, the United States took the initiative and created a bizonal government with the British zone in 1947; at that time, the French still objected to a central regime. The Berlin Blockade during the winter of 1947–48, however, convinced the French that a regional government embracing all three Western zones was imperative.[20] France, therefore, joined England and the United States in authorizing the Germans to form a central government for Western Germany.

In July 1948, England, France, and the United States invited the Germans to draft a constitution. The Big Three specified cer-

17. Basic Law, Article 131; Law of May 11, 1951, BGBl, *1*, 307. However, Herz notes that most civil servants are loyal to the West German regime; they have accommodated themselves to the existing situation. John H. Herz, "Political Views of the West German Civil Service," in Hans Speier et al., *West German Leadership and Foreign Policy* (Evanston, Ill., Row, Peterson, 1957), pp. 110–11.

18. Golay, pp. 6 ff.

19. U.S. Department of State, *Occupation of Germany, Policy and Progress* (Washington, Government Printing Office, 1947), p. 49.

20. Golay, pp. 6–13.

tain conditions insisting especially on a more decentralized national government than the Germans originally desired.[21] However, the Germans themselves drafted the constitution in lengthy negotiations over the course of a year. The Germans insisted on calling their document a "Basic Law" (*Grundgesetz*) rather than "constitution" (*Verfassung*) to indicate the provisional nature of their government pending reunification of West Germany with the Russian-occupied Eastern zone. The document, however, has all the earmarks of a constitution.[22] After the German Laender ratified the Basic Law in May 1949, Germany regained full control over legislation and administration. The Allies retained responsibility only for foreign affairs and reserved for themselves the right to participate in denazification and economic development, as well as the prerogative to intervene in any matter " if they consider that to do so is essential to security or to preserve democratic government in Germany or in pursuance of international obligations of . . . [the allied] Governments."[23]

The government that the Bonn constitution established and that emerged from the occupation era in the Laender attempts to promote stable political development and efficient administration in a democratic setting. The administrative institutions of contemporary German government are characteristically German; they lean heavily on traditions established during the Second Reich and the Weimar Republic. But many innovations introduced by the occupation forces have taken root. In the following pages, we shall consider how the tasks of field administration are performed in a Germany whose goals contrast sharply with those of the Third Reich. Administration by autonomous agencies with democratic restraints has replaced uniformity and maximum central direction as the goal of German field administration. Yet, the federal and Land governments still desire a responsive field administration which will execute centrally formulated policies. The techniques that the West German government has evolved to at-

21. Ibid., pp. 14 ff. Golay gives the best available account of the negotiations which led to the establishment of the Bonn Republic.

22. We shall use the terms "Basic Law" and "constitution" synonymously in this study.

23. Occupation Statute of April 8, 1949, reprinted in Oppen, *Documents on Germany,* p. 376.

tain field responsiveness without destroying the autonomy of field agencies or the effectiveness of democratic restraints will be the focus of the following pages. We shall turn our attention first to federal administration and then to field administration in the Laender.

THE FEDERAL GOVERNMENT AND FIELD ADMINISTRATION

The German Federal Republic's value commitments and the barriers to administrative responsiveness that it confronts are quite different from those of any previous German government. The Bonn regime has committed itself to the pursuit of democratic ideals and stands on the principle that government ought to be restrained from arbitrary action and be responsible to the electorate. It officially views federalism as one of the foundations on which German democracy can best be built.

West Germany's commitment to federalism is particularly important to our study of field administration because federalism in Germany has traditionally entailed a division of powers which assigns most administrative functions to the Laender and most legislative authority to the national government.[24] While the Allies were the most insistent advocates of a federal structure, Adenauer's Christian Democrats adopted the plank as their own in 1948. It is true that centralist tendencies have since grown stronger within the Christian Democratic party, for it enjoys wielding power from Bonn and is occasionally irked by resistance from the Laender. But federalism is still part of the Christian Democratic program; it is reinforced by the Bavarian wing of the party which is, as always, strongly federalistic.[25] The Socialists, on the other hand, have accepted the federal system much more graciously than one would have expected from their vehement protest in 1949. They have failed four times to capture control over

24. A good recent exposition of German federalism can be found in Peter Merkl, "Executive-Legislative Federalism in West Germany," *American Political Science Review*, 53 (1959), 732–41.

25. Golay, pp. 41 ff. Indeed, Bavaria was the only Land to reject the Bonn constitution because the Bavarians thought it established too strong a central government. Bavaria accepted it only after it had been ratified by the other Laender. See U.S. Department of State, *Germany 1947–49*, p. 282.

the Bonn government. But in the Laender—in Bremen, Hamburg, Hesse, Lower Saxony, North-Rhine-Westphalia, and Bavaria— they have occasionally held majorities or led a coalition government.[26] Federalism, thus, has given the Socialists opportunities to govern, to develop minor policies, and to control administration. This reality has weakened their principled opposition to a federal system.[27]

The fact that the Bonn Republic does not face the fierce opposition that plagued the Weimar regime is as important to the development of administrative controls as the general acceptance of the federal system. The Bonn Republic has not experienced the equivalent of Kahr's reactionary regime in Bavaria or the Communist government of Saxony. The one has disappeared as a significant, independent political force; the other exists in the Russian zone where it does not directly threaten the internal security of the Bonn regime. Land governments in the German Federal Republic have been loyal to the Bonn regime. The barriers the Bonn regime has had to overcome consist of partisan differences with Land governments and problems of communication with field agencies which have no direct hierarchical ties with the federal government. The federal government consequently has developed controls tailored to meet such communication barriers and partisan obstacles to responsive field administration. Before examining them in detail, however, we must briefly look at the structure of the West German federal government.

The Bonn constitution prescribes the traditional German federal division of powers. The ten Laender control most administrative agencies; the federal government legislates in all fields except education and cultural affairs.[28] A two-chamber parliament exercises the federal government's legislative powers. The lower house (*Bundestag*) is elected by popular vote; the upper house (*Bundes-*

26. The composition of Land governments from 1945 until 1953 is given in Max Gustav Lange et al., *Parteien in der Bundesrepublik* (Stuttgart, Ring Verlag, 1955), pp. 521 ff.

27. Golay, pp. 41 ff.; Lange, p. 263.

28. Basic Law, Articles 73–75. While most police functions lie outside the scope of federal legislation, criminal investigation and the prevention of subversive activities are within federal jurisdiction. The criminal code is also a federal law.

rat) consists of representatives of the Land governments. The Bundesrat is the guardian of states' rights; it possesses a suspensive veto *(Einspruchsrecht)* which may be overridden by the Bundestag on all legislation and an absolute veto *(Zustimmungsrecht)* over any legislation that affects the balance of power between the federal government and the Laender.[29] The Bundesrat must also approve many of the federal government's administrative measures that impinge on Land agencies. The Chancellor is the German Prime Minister; he and his cabinet are responsible to the Bundestag alone.[30] Each cabinet member directs one of the federal government's ministries; together with the Chancellor, the cabinet composes the executive organ of the federal government. The Bonn Republic also has a Federal President *(Bundespraesident)* who performs only ceremonial functions except during cabinet crises when he may play a major role in appointing a new Chancellor, dissolving the Bundestag, or enacting emergency legislation without Bundestag approval.[31]

The Bonn constitution excludes the federal government from most administrative functions. The Laender are to execute federal laws as a matter of their own concern *(als eigene Angelegeheit)* except where the constitution specifically provides otherwise. The constitution allows direct federal administration only for: 1) execution of foreign policy, 2) collection of taxes, 3) administration of the border police and defense forces, 4) management of the post office, and rail and water transportation, 5) investigation of criminal and subversive activities, 6) administration of some social insurance programs, and 7) execution of new functions when there is an "urgent necessity" for federal administration.[32]

The federal government has established its own field agencies in only one sphere of domestic administration: that of unemployment insurance. In addition, the federal government has evolved

29. Ibid., Articles 77–78.

30. Ibid., Articles 63 and 67–68.

31. Ibid., Articles 54 ff. The Federal President is indirectly elected by an assembly consisting of members of the Bundestag and members of Land legislatures—Article 54. Since the constitution has been in effect, no opportunity has arisen for the President to make use of his emergency powers. He has not even had the opportunity to name a new Chancellor.

32. Ibid., Articles 83, 86–87, and 87b.

joint federal-Land agencies for the collection of taxes. No field agencies have been established for new functions. The Laender administer all other domestic federal programs as matters of their own concern subject to federal supervision. This supervision operates through the Bundesrat, through informal conferences between federal and Land officials, through a highly specialized administrative court system, and through political channels that transcend the constitutional bounds of the federal government. We shall first examine the federal unemployment agencies and the joint federal-Land tax offices; then we shall scrutinize the techniques the federal government has developed to supervise Land administration of federal programs.

The federal government administers the unemployment insurance program through a fully autonomous central agency—the Unemployment Insurance Authority—which possesses its own field organization. The Authority is a successor to the original Reich Authority established by the Weimar regime in 1927 but transferred to the Reich Ministry of Labor during the Third Reich. The Authority once more possesses full administrative autonomy and is not directly responsible to any federal ministry. A board of elected employer and employee representatives chaired by the Authority's president determines its administrative policies. The Federal Ministry of Labor cannot intervene in budgetary, personnel, or administrative questions. The ministry may only rule on the legality of the Authority's actions.[33] Physical remoteness symbolizes the Authority's autonomy; its headquarters are located in Nuremberg, 250 miles away from Bonn, the federal capital.

The Federal Ministry of Labor, however, possesses indirect controls over the Authority. The Authority must administer the unemployment insurance law according to regulations issued by the ministry which interpret the basic statute. These interpretations have become a massive set of prescriptions regulating all major policy questions in considerable detail.[34] Moreover, the federal government appoints the president of the Authority and his

33. Employment Service and Unemployment Insurance Act (AVAVG) of July 16, 1927, as amended on April 3, 1957, BGBl, *1*, 322, paragraph 34.

34. See, for example, Heinrich Krebs, *Kommentar zu AVAVG* (Munich, C. H. Beck'sche Verlagsbuchhandlung, 1957).

deputies. Although these officials possess tenure and are not removable for political reasons, they are subject to normal civil service discipline.[35]

The Authority's field offices have been reorganized to take the new Land boundaries into account. The Authority has twelve regional offices (*Landesarbeitsaemter*) and 208 local offices (*Arbeitsaemter*).[36] In contrast to the situation during the Weimar Republic, the Authority's regional areas match the Land boundaries. Each Land has one regional office except Bavaria and Rhineland-Palatinate, each of which possess two. The districts for local offices, however, cut across city and county lines to encompass the economic bounds of labor markets; the Authority's 208 local offices serve West Germany's 566 cities and counties. The regional and local offices are under the general policy and administrative control of the Federal Authority. The advisory board of the Federal Authority appoints the directors of the local offices; the federal cabinet itself appoints the chiefs of the regional offices after recommendations have been made by the Federal Authority's advisory board.[37] However, advisory councils—composed of representatives of employers, workers, and the cities and counties—at the local and regional level have relatively greater authority than during the Weimar period. Notably, the councils, rather than the civil service directors, enact the annual administrative budget.[38]

National administration of social insurance programs through autonomous agencies is now a familiar practice in Germany. The Unemployment Insurance Authority's organizational structure in the main follows the pattern that the Reich Authority established during the Weimar Republic. Even some defects of the 1927 organization have been repeated. Although the new regional boundaries facilitate cooperation with Land governments, arrangements

35. Unemployment Insurance Act, paragraphs 25–28.
36. *Die Bundesrepublik 1958/59* (Berlin, Carl Heymanns Verlag, 1958), pp. 160 ff. The *Arbeitsaemter* are referred to as local unemployment insurance offices in the subsequent text. It should be noted that they operate an employment service in addition to their function in disbursing unemployment insurance. These two functions, linked in the original 1927 law, have remained joined in all subsequent reorganizations.
37. Unemployment Insurance Act, paragraph 27.
38. Ibid., paragraph 30.

remain rudimentary for coordination of local unemployment insurance offices with other field agents. The local districts of the unemployment insurance offices still overlap the general administrative districts. The Landrat is only one of many representatives on the local office's advisory board despite the fact that he directs the general welfare programs of the Laender. If unemployment once more becomes a chronic problem, the Landrat and county government will again be caught in the squeeze they experienced in 1929–32. The counties with their inadequate resources will have to care for thousands of unemployed who have exhausted their insurance benefits. Despite the heavy immigration of refugees from the Eastern zone, unemployment has not been a chronic problem for the Bonn Republic; therefore, no significant conflicts between unemployment insurance offices and the Land's field agencies have yet arisen.[39]

Although the Unemployment Insurance Authority is a federal agency, it remains fairly autonomous. The federal government possesses only broad policy controls but cannot interfere with administrative details. The federal government, however, acquired another, perhaps more effective control, in 1953 when it established a system of social courts (*Sozialgerichte*). The system consists of local, regional, and national courts specializing in social insurance litigation. The Land and local courts are composed of professional and lay judges whom the Laender appoint. The Laender name lay judges for four years from lists prepared by trade unions and employer associations; professional judges are appointed for life like all other judges.[40] The Federal Social Court also consists of professional judges with life tenure and lay judges who serve four years; both are appointed in the same manner as Land judges but by the federal government.[41] The federal court hears appeals from Land court decisions, disputes between the Laender, and

39. Although we have only spoken of the Landrat, the same coordination problem exists between municipal officials and the local unemployment insurance offices. Cities also have only one representative each on the council of the local unemployment insurance office. As cities carry the same welfare responsibilities as the counties, their situation in a depression would be as acute as the counties'.

40. Social Court Act of Sept. 3, 1953, BGBl, *1*, 1239, paragraphs 11, 13–14, 32, and 35–36.

41. Ibid., paragraphs 38 and 45 ff.

disputes between the federal government and the Laender as long as the cases do not involve questions of constitutional interpretation.[42]

The social courts offer the federal government a substantial guarantee that the laws and regulations it enacts will be executed in a uniform fashion. The federal court's decisions are binding on all lower courts and on all administrative agencies as well. Germans find it relatively easy to appeal to the courts if they feel their insurance agency, for instance, the local unemployment insurance office, has decided their case unjustly. Usually no costs can be assessed against the complainant; if he hires a lawyer, the maximum fee for representation before a local social court is 100 Deutsche Mark ($25).[43] These provisions make the courts accessible to all; they also make it likely that many cases of noncompliance with the social insurance laws will be brought before them. The social courts thus serve to promote the uniform execution of the Unemployment Insurance Act as well as of the other social insurance laws. The federal government, of course, has no policy control over such courts. Although social courts may not declare a law unconstitutional, they may interpret it in a manner considered undesirable by the federal government. In that case, the federal government would have to reassert its viewpoint through corrective legislation. Such difficulties rarely arise; they are a risk the federal government incurs for relying on judicial rather than hierarchical controls to promote responsive administration.

The field organization of the Unemployment Insurance Authority, thus, does not afford the federal government frequent opportunities to direct the activities of the local offices. As the field offices are responsible to an autonomous federal central agency, the federal government's controls are limited to indirect measures. The Federal Ministry of Labor determines most basic policies, helps appoint some of the key field personnel, and depends on a specialized administrative court system to assure uniform execution of its policy decisions.

The federal government chose a quite different organizational structure to control the collection of federal taxes. Allied insistence

42. The courts may not rule on constitutional issues; the Federal Constitutional Court possesses exclusive jurisdiction over such cases.

43. Social Court Act, paragraphs 183 and 196.

that the Laender possess independent tax sources led to the development of joint federal-Land tax collection agencies.

Before approving the West German constitution, the Allies demanded that it provide for a decentralized tax system that would give the Laender their own source of revenue. The Allies wanted the Laender to possess a solid financial base that would guarantee their autonomy; financially independent Laender were to provide the foundation for a viable federal system. When an early draft of the constitution veered away from this principle, the Allied military governors sharply reminded the Germans of it with the following detailed instructions:[44]

> The powers of the federal government in the field of public finance shall be limited to the disposal of monies, including the raising of revenue for purposes for which it is responsible. . . . The federal government may set rates and legislate on the general principles of assessment with regard to other taxes for which the uniformity is essential, *the collection and utilization of such taxes being left to the individual states.*

After extensive negotiations, the Germans conceded this point; they carefully enumerated which tax revenues would flow to the federal government and which to the Laender. The federal government received all indirect taxes while the Laender obtained all direct taxes. In addition, the Laender had to contribute one-third (now 35 per cent) of the income tax to the federal government. Federal agencies were to manage government monopolies and collect customs, use taxes, the turnover tax, and transportation taxes; all other taxes were to be collected by Land agencies.[45]

Had these constitutional provisions been carried out to the letter, West Germany would have possessed two competing field organizations for collecting taxes: one for the *Bund* and one for the Laender. To avoid such costly duplication, the federal govern-

44. Military Governors' Aide Memoire to the Parliamentary Council, Nov. 22, 1948, reprinted in Golay, *The Founding of the Federal Republic*, p. 264. Italics added.

45. Basic Law, Articles 105–06. Golay, pp. 74–86, especially pp. 76–77, gives an excellent account of the Allied-German negotiations and the discussion among the Germans on the distribution of tax powers.

ment chose to delegate the collection of its internal revenues to Land agencies. But the federal government specified the structure of the Laender's internal revenue offices in order to assure itself of some control over collection procedures. Moreover, the federal government specified that regional offices (the *Oberfinanzdirektionen*) were to be joint federal-Land agencies.[46] Each Land now possesses one or two such regional offices. The Regional Director (*Oberfinanzpraesident*) is jointly appointed by the federal and Land governments. On Land matters he is responsible to the Land government; on federal matters he is responsible to the federal government.[47] One division of the regional office supervises the federal government's customs offices (*Zollaemter*); federal officials staff this division as well as the customs offices scattered throughout Germany. These officials are directly responsible to the Federal Ministry of Finance in Bonn. A second division of the regional office supervises the Land's local tax offices (*Finanzaemter*); Land civil servants staff this division and the local tax offices. A small group of federal officials—attached to the Regional Director's office—supervises the collection of the federal turnover and transportation taxes by the Land's local tax offices.[48] The Regional Director provides "household" services for all these divisions, but he exercises policy supervision only over Land taxes. He must refer all queries regarding federal levies to the Federal Finance Ministry.[49]

The joint regional tax offices are functioning to the mutual satisfaction of both Bund and Laender despite the awkward appearance of their organization. Yet as late as 1953, the joint office arrangement had many vehement critics. The Bundestag failed by only 53 votes to pass a constitutional amendment requiring federal collection of all taxes even though Adenauer's Christian Democrats opposed the amendment and though it faced certain

---

46. Finance Administration Act of Sept. 6, 1950, BGBl, *1*, 448, paragraph 5; Litchfield, ed., *Governing Postwar Germany*, pp. 341 ff.

47. Verordnung, Nov. 23, 1950, BFBl, pp. 642 ff.

48. Finance Administration Act, paragraphs 6–9.

49. Ibid., paragraph 7. On functions of the Regional Director, the author has drawn heavily on statements by Regierungsdirektor Hirschmann, *Oberfinanzdirektion*, Munich, July 3, 1959, and Regierungsrat Kaiser, North-Rhine-Westphalia Finance Ministry, Duesseldorf, March 17, 1959, personal interviews.

defeat in the Bundesrat.[50] The arguments that critics directed against the joint regional offices were mostly speculative, colored with reminiscences of the seemingly simpler procedures of the Reich Finance Administration which collected taxes without Land participation from 1919 until 1945.[51] After a decade of the present arrangement's existence, however, none of the officials whom the author interviewed found insuperable faults in the operation of the joint tax-collecting structure. In their judgment, the collections have proceeded at an orderly and efficient pace.[52] German officials attribute this success to the nature of the taxes collected, to federal audits of tax returns, to the background of the personnel who staff the Land and federal finance ministries and field offices, and to the existence of a nationwide system of tax courts.

The taxes earmarked for the federal government were particularly well chosen for collection by Land agents, for they possess "self-executing" guarantees of careful collection by the Laender. The turnover and transportation taxes are the principal levies involved. Assessment of both taxes depends on the taxpayer's report of his gross business volume. These estimates also form the basis for assessing the income tax levies from which the Laender derive most of their revenue.[53] Careful assessment of gross business revenues, therefore, benefits the Laender as much as the federal government. Once the assessments have been made, collection of the federal tax is a relatively simple operation. If the Laender had to perform burdensome additional operations to collect federal taxes, they would have an incentive to neglect them. However, as the accurate estimation of gross revenues is essential to the maximization of their own income tax yields, the Laender in

50. The vote was 214 in favor, 146 against the amendment; a two-thirds majority was required. *Bundestag Verhandlungen*, 1. Wahlperiode, *16*, 12872 ff.; ibid., *17*, 13609; ibid., Appendix vol. *23*, document no. 4300.

51. Ibid., *16*, 12872 ff.

52. Statements by Ministerialrat Dr. Gielen and Ministerialrat Dr. Hauser, Federal Finance Ministry, Bonn, March 19, 1959; Regierungsrat Kaiser and Regierungsdirektor Hirschmann, personal interviews.

53. Between 1950 and 1953, the Laender received 70–80 per cent of their revenues from the personal and corporate income tax. *Statistisches Jahrbuch fuer die Bundesrepublik 1955*, p. 400.

fact are not lax in these operations. From tax assessments prepared by and for the Land governments, the federal Ministry of Finance can itself check the accuracy of the tax collections with relative ease.

The federal government also tries to promote uniform collection of federal taxes by issuing detailed instructions on assessment procedures and binding interpretations of tax laws.[54] The federal tax group in the regional office seeks to assure application of these regulations by inspecting the records of local tax offices, by ruling on appeals that taxpayers file, and by meeting with the directors of the local offices several times a year to instruct them on federal regulations and to hear any difficulties they are encountering.[55] The most effective enforcement procedure, however, consists of annual audits of the tax accounts of particularly large business concerns which operate in several Laender. The Federal Finance Ministry maintains a group of experts in Bonn to conduct these audits. Each year, the Bonn ministry and the Land finance ministries agree to audit jointly the returns of a number of the largest taxpayers. The federal government benefits from Land cooperation as the Laender keep all the records. The Laender also profit, for the federal auditors possess expert knowledge of large taxpayers' operations in other Laender. The auditors often help the Laender detect tax evasions. Any increase in assessments coming from such audits brings the Bund higher receipts from the turnover and transportation taxes while the Laender usually receive higher revenues from the income tax.[56]

A third factor that contributes to the success of joint Bund-Land tax collections is the fact that most of the personnel of the federal and Land tax agencies are former officials of the Reich Tax Administration which existed before 1945.[57] Few have developed particularistic loyalties to a Land; many are still in the habit of cooperating with each other as former colleagues of the same

---

54. See, for example, BFBl, 1949–50, p. 3.

55. Statement by Regierungsdirektor Hirschmann, personal interview.

56. Second Finance Administration Act of May 15, 1952, BGBl, *1*, 293 ff. Statement by Ministerialrat Dr. Hauser, personal interview. Hauser was chief of the organization section of the Federal Finance Ministry in 1959.

57. Statement by Ministerialrat Dr. Gielen, personal interview. Gielen was chief of the personnel section of the Federal Finance Ministry in 1959.

agency. This common background has apparently minimized antagonisms that often arise between representatives of different government agencies. It has engendered cooperation rather than conflict.

Finally, tax courts provide a specialized administrative court system which aids in assuring a uniform interpretation of tax laws throughout the country. Almost all tax laws are enacted by the Bundestag; tax courts adjudicate all claims that arise from them. The Laender appoint the judges for the lower tax courts but the Federal Tax Court (*Bundesfinanzhof*) in Munich is staffed by federal appointees. Like the Federal Social Court, the Tax Court hears appeals from lower courts and adjudicates nonconstitutional disputes between the Laender or between a Land and the federal government.[58] Its rulings bind all tax-collecting agents. It, therefore, acts as a powerful stimulant to uniform tax collection.

It is quite possible that the joint Bund-Land tax collection arrangements will not continue to work so smoothly in the future. Land officials will eventually lose their bonds of affinity with federal officials and develop loyalties to their own administrative agencies. The federal ministry—which drafts the tax laws for all Germany—may become too isolated from practical administrative problems, for it has no way of training young officials in field operations as long as all field offices are staffed by Land civil servants. Yet, the tax collection system is far more favorable for the Bonn government than it was for the national government of the Second Reich. The federal government does not rely on Land contributions; it does not depend on impotent inspectors who could only report to the Bundesrat any irregularities they found, leaving the Bundesrat to negotiate a settlement. The federal government now enacts all tax legislation, possesses its own taxes, and can rely on efficient Land collection of federal taxes because it is in the Laender's own interest to do so. Joint tax collections are reinforced by a common interest in the maximization of revenues.

No other joint administrative agencies exist in West Germany.

---

58. Ottmar Buchler, "Finanzgerichtsbarkeit," *Staatslexikon* (Freiburg, Verlag Herder, 1959), *3;* Otto Bachof, "Special Administrative Tribunals," *International Review of Administrative Sciences, 25* (1959), 184–92.

The Bund delegates all other domestic programs to the Laender who execute them as "matters of their own concern." However, the Bonn constitution and the practices that have evolved from it give the federal government a multiplicity of channels by which it may supervise Land administration of federal programs. Direct federal supervision is available through the Bundesrat; informal contacts with Land officials also give federal civil servants an opportunity to guide Land administration. The general administrative courts (*Verwaltungsgerichte*) promote a uniform execution of federal laws. Finally, the federal government attempts to influence Land administration through extraconstitutional political channels.

The Bundesrat is the principal organ through which the federal government can supervise Land administration directly. With Bundesrat consent, the federal government may specify the field organization and administrative procedures of Land agencies that execute federal laws; in this way the federal government may also enact administrative regulations that interpret federal legislation. The Bund may in addition dispatch inspectors to a Land's central agencies; with Land or Bundesrat approval, the federal government may send these inspectors to the Land's field offices as well.[59]

The Bundesrat represents the Laender; it was established to safeguard Land autonomy from encroachment by the federal government. Unlike the Bundesrat of the Second Reich, the Bonn organ is not dominated by a single Land like Prussia. As Table 7 shows, the largest Land, North-Rhine-Westphalia, has only five of the forty-one votes while the smallest Land, Bremen, has three. The votes of each Land are cast as a bloc according to the directions of the Land Minister President or cabinet.[60] In order to gain Bundesrat approval of its administrative measures, the federal government must, therefore, win the approval of at least five Laender.

The federal government has not succeeded in dominating the

---

59. Basic Law, Articles 84–85; Hans Schaefer, *Der Bundesrat* (Cologne, Carl Heymanns Verlag, 1955), passim.

60. Theodor Eschenburg, *Staat und Gesellschaft in Deutschland* (3d ed. Stuttgart, Curt E. Schwab, 1956), pp. 631–32; Karlheinz Neunreither, "Politics and Bureaucracy in the West German Bundesrat," *American Political Science Review*, 53 (1959), 724–25. The Land legislatures may not directly instruct a Land's delegation how to vote in the Bundesrat.

TABLE 7

*Distribution of Population, Area, and Bundesrat Votes
Among the Laender of the German Federal Republic, 1956
(Expressed as Percentage)*

Land	Population[a]	Area[a]	Bundesrat votes[b]	
North-Rhine-Westphalia	27.9	13.0	12.2	(5)
Bavaria	17.1	27.8	12.2	(5)
Baden-Wuerttemberg	13.3	14.1	12.2	(5)
Lower Saxony	12.2	18.7	12.2	(5)
Hesse	8.6	8.3	9.8	(4)
Rhineland-Palatinate	6.2	7.8	9.8	(4)
Schleswig-Holstein	4.2	6.3	9.8	(4)
Hamburg	3.3	0.3	7.3	(3)
Saarland	1.9	1.0	7.3	(3)
Bremen	1.2	0.2	7.3	(3)
Berlin	4.1	2.5	—*	
Total	100.0	100.0	100.0	(41)

* Berlin is not a full-fledged Land and has no votes in the Bundesrat or Bundestag.
Sources:
[a]*Grassold's Ortslexikon fuer die Bundesrepublik Deutschland, Nachtrag* (2d ed. Regensburg, Verlag A. Grassold, 1957).
[b]Samuel H. Beer et al., *Patterns of Government, The Major Political Systems of Europe* (New York, Random House, 1958), p. 364. Number in parentheses indicates actual number of votes possessed by each Land.

Bundesrat through party controls as it does the Bundestag.[61] The Bundesrat has never voted consistently according to party blocs. Laender controlled by the Socialists vote almost as often for government proposals as against them.[62] Indeed, a German observer, Karlheinz Neunreither, found that only two Bundesrat votes out of sixteen in 1956 and one out of thirteen in 1955 were decided by outspoken party alignments.[63] The Laender apparently relegate partisan viewpoints to a secondary position in deciding how to

61. Neunreither, p. 723; Karlheinz Neunreither, *Der Bundesrat zwischen Politik und Verwaltung* (Heidelberg, Quelle und Meyer, 1959), pp. 107 ff.; Arnold J. Heidenheimer, "Federalism and the Party System: The Case of West Germany," *American Political Science Review*, 52 (1958), 809–28.
62. Neunreither, *Der Bundesrat*, pp. 109–10.
63. Ibid., pp. 110–11. See also Hiscocks, pp. 147–49.

cast their Bundesrat votes. Although Neunreither's study does not specify how strong a factor the protection of Land rights is, the composition of the Bundesrat makes it reasonable to assume that this consideration plays a major role in determining Bundesrat decisions. The federal government, therefore, must formulate its administrative proposals in such a way that they will not arouse the principled opposition of the Laender. In practice this means that the Bundesrat only approves the federal government's proposals on the condition that it bow to Land objections.[64]

Despite this obstacle, the federal government has won the right to specify the organization and procedures of numerous Land field agencies and to issue detailed instructions to Land field officials in a number of significant areas. An important example is the administration of compensatory payments (*Lastenausgleich*) to Germans who lost their homes and businesses in World War II. Federal law specifies the organization of local offices dispensing this aid; in addition the central federal agency for this program has issued a mountain of detailed instructions on its administration.[65] Similarly detailed regulations apply to the administration of payments to veterans and their survivors (*Versorgungshilfe*), to the construction of highways, and to the operation of housing programs. If a Land refuses to comply with federal regulations, the Bund possesses the right to apply sanctions with the approval of the Bundesrat; the Bund may also appeal to the Federal Constitutional Court for a judgment against a Land.[66]

The federal ministries have also cultivated informal contacts and conferences with Land officials outside the framework of the Bundesrat. Conferences on federal legislative proposals frequently occur between federal and Land officials. Indeed bills rarely reach the Bundesrat without having been the subject of intensive consultation and negotiation between the federal and Land ministries.[67] Federal and Land officials also consult frequently on the

---

64. Neunreither, *Der Bundesrat,* p. 89.

65. *Lastenausgleichgesetz* of March 7, 1952, BGBl, *1,* 446. See, for example, the 960-page commentary by Rudolph Harmening, *Kommentar zur Lastenausgleichgesetz* (Munich, C. H. Beck'sche Verlagsbuchhandlung, 1958).

66. Basic Law, Articles 37 and 84; Herman von Mangoldt, *Das Bonner Grundgesetz* (Berlin, Verlag Franz Vahlen, 1953), pp. 219–22.

67. Neunreither, "Politics and Bureaucracy," pp. 716–17.

distribution of federal grants-in-aid to the Laender.[68] Such informal contacts give the federal ministries additional opportunities to guide Land administration of federal programs.

The administrative court system offers another indirect assurance for the federal government that its programs will be enforced and executed uniformly throughout West Germany. In addition to the social courts and tax courts which we have already discussed, Germany possesses a labor court system (*Arbeitsgerichte*) to adjudicate disputes rising from labor laws and a general administrative court system to settle claims arising from other administrative programs. The Laender staff the Land and local administrative courts, but the federal government names the judges for the Federal Administrative Court which sits in Berlin.[69] In contrast to the administrative courts of the Second Reich and Weimar Republic, today's courts are completely independent of administrative agencies. As with other independent judicial bodies, the Federal Administrative Court does not give the Bund an opportunity to exercise policy control over the Laender, but it assures the Bonn regime uniform interpretation of federal laws and regulations. If the courts interpret federal laws and regulations in a way which the federal government considers undesirable, the Bund may adopt corrective legislation.[70] Admittedly, this is awkward and often time-consuming. However, when the courts interpret federal regulations, they normally rely on the intent of the ministry which issued them.[71] In most cases the court is an effective supplement to Bundesrat controls.

An even less direct control of Land administration by the federal government hinges on its intervention in Land politics. Chancellor Adenauer has tried several times to help the Christian

---

68. *Bundesverfassungsgericht Entscheidungen, 1*, 299 ff.

69. Bachof, "Special Administrative Tribunals," pp. 184–92; Otto Bachof, "German Administrative Law," *International and Comparative Law Quarterly*, 2 (1953), 368–82; Otto Forsthoff, *Lehrbuch des Verwaltungsrechts* (7th ed. Munich, C. H. Beck'sche Verlagsbuchhandlung, 1958), *1*, 493–95; Carl H. Ule, "German Administrative Jurisdiction," *International Review of Administrative Sciences*, 25 (1959), 173–83.

70. Like the social courts and tax courts, the administrative courts may not declare a law unconstitutional; only the Federal Constitutional Court has that power.

71. Forsthoff, *1*, 493–95.

Democrats and their allies win Land elections with the expectation that Land governments dominated by the Chancellor's party would be more responsive to the Bonn government's demands. Federal intervention in Land elections would promote party control of the Bundesrat as well as the Bundestag. Moreover, Land governments indebted to the Chancellor for their victory might be more likely to respond to federal policies, for bureaucratic pressures could be reinforced by appeals to party discipline. Yet as Neunreither points out, even Christian Democratic Land governments are not always servile to the demands of Adenauer's government.[72] Moreover, the growing federalization of Land elections has other causes besides the desire to control Bundesrat votes. Land politicians have found it difficult to raise exciting issues on which to base their election campaigns. The Land legislatures handle so little legislation—most of which simply serves to execute Bund laws—that few issues besides the question of church versus state schools can be found. In addition, many of the most vigorous and best known politicians now serve at the federal level. Land parties find it attractive to attempt to ride on Adenauer's or Erhard's coattails rather than depend solely on their own appeal. Adenauer's picture, for instance, ornamented most of the Land election posters in 1958–59; his rallies were the highlights of Land election campaigns.[73]

Adenauer's attempts to dominate Land elections have not been uniformly successful. In two recent elections, his actions backfired and led to the formation of unfriendly Land governments in North-Rhine-Westphalia and Lower Saxony.[74] However, even with unsuccessful campaigns, federalization of Land politics offers the federal government an alternative—perhaps marginal—control over Land policies and administration. The threat to intervene in Land elections can appear dangerous to Land governments and may persuade some of them to concede to Bonn's demands. This control instrument is one that was never before available to

---

72. Neunreither, *Der Bundesrat*, pp. 109–10.

73. Ibid., pp. 115 ff. It is interesting to note that the Social Democrats have no national figures of comparable importance as they have not held any cabinet positions. Their leadership stems from Laender where they control the government—for example Brandt from Berlin.

74. Heidenheimer, pp. 818–24.

a democratic national government in Germany. During the Weimar Republic, no party was strong enough on the national scene to intervene in Land elections successfully. Moreover, local patriotism had deeper roots in the 1920s than in the 1950s, for all the Laender had long histories as sovereign states. Today's Laender, with the exception of Bavaria, are postwar creations that scarcely antedate the Bonn government's existence.

The federal government, thus, relies on a battery of indirect controls to supervise field administration of federal programs by Land agencies. The Bund possesses far fewer powers than the Nazi Reich government; the Bonn regime does not even have the centralized Finance Administration which exerted such powerful financial pressures on the Laender during the Weimar Republic. Instead, the federal government relies almost entirely on Land administrative agencies to execute federal programs. Bonn tries to keep these Land agencies responsive to federal policies through regulations approved by the Bundesrat, informal conferences with Land officials, the unifying force of centralized administrative courts, and the marginal pressures exerted through extraconstitutional political channels. Despite the fact that West German federalism has stripped the national government of its field administration, federal programs appear to be executed loyally by Land governments. No Land government doubts the legitimacy of the Bonn regime; no class distinctions hinder cooperation between Land and Bund officials; even partisan differences between some Laender and the federal government impose no insuperable barrier to loyal administration of federal programs. The supervisory powers that the federal government possesses are designed to maintain the federal division of power in Germany which allocates administration to the Laender. They appear to have afforded the federal government adequate guarantees of effective field administration within the federal framework.

FIELD ADMINISTRATION IN THE LAENDER

The Bonn constitution has prescribed a return to the system of administrative federalism which characterized the Second Reich. The Laender administer almost all federal programs as well as their own. They control most field agencies which exist in Germany. But the structure of field administration in the Bonn Republic is quite different from that of any previous regime. Whereas the chief all-purpose field agencies of the Laender—the counties—had always been subject to direct ministerial control, they are today autonomous. Moreover, variations among the several Laender are more significant today than ever before, for no single Land has inherited Prussia's dominant position. In the following discussion we shall, therefore, examine the structure of field administration and the techniques used to maintain responsive administration in all the Laender possessing field agencies. We will exclude Hamburg and Bremen because they are essentially metropolitan governments with no extended field areas; we shall also not include the Saarland, Germany's newest Land, for France had not yet relinquished all its controls to German officials while research for this study was underway.[75]

Although all central and field agencies of the Laender had ceased to function at the end of World War II, field administration in Germany quickly reassumed its old forms during the occupation.[76] Each of the occupying powers divided his zone into two or more new Laender. In each Land the Allies established central ministries and field agencies in the traditional Prussian administrative pattern. Only the provincial level of government was abandoned as no Land remained large enough to be divided into provinces. District offices, counties, and townships as well as the larger cities once more serve as all-purpose field agencies.

Although the Western Allies chose traditional German institutions for the framework of field administration during the occupation, the military governors introduced many practices novel to German administration because such procedures appeared to have nurtured democratic government in England, France, or the United States. The English, for instance, installed town and county clerks in local government; together with the Americans,

75. The Laender that remain are North-Rhine-Westphalia, Bavaria, Lower Saxony, Baden-Wuerttemberg, Schleswig-Holstein, Hesse, and Rhineland-Palatinate.

76. In addition to the sources cited in note 2 of this chapter, see Heinrich Triebert, "Die Landkreise unter der Herrschaft der Bestazungsmaechte," in Verein fuer Geschichte der deutschen Landkreise, *Die Landkreise in der Bundesrepublik Deutschland* (Stuttgart, W. Kohlhammer Verlag, 1955), pp. 14 ff.

they insisted on elections for choosing key field officials. The French introduced their own form of town government though they left German counties untouched. Moreover, the English and Americans tried to change the context in which the field administration operated by granting a large measure of autonomy to local field offices.

It is true that local self-government had constituted an increasingly more important element in the German administrative tradition between 1808 and 1933. But the German Laender had always maintained ministerially controlled field agencies at the side of the local government organs; the Land units, rather than local governments, administered most national and Land programs. In Prussia, for instance, the Landrat's office was a ministerially controlled agency; the autonomous county agencies—the county council and county committee—performed only minor functions which the Landrat helped execute. Even in the larger cities, the police and numerous specialized agencies remained subject to the direct control of the District Officer and the Ministry of Interior rather than to the locally elected city government.

The British and Americans drastically altered this distribution of powers between the Land government and its subordinate agencies. The occupation regimes granted the Landrat's office autonomy, making it primarily responsible to the local county council and county committee rather than to a Land ministry. Today, the Landrat's office still executes most federal and Land programs, but it is not under the direct control of a Land ministry. Cities have won a comparable degree of autonomy. The extension of autonomy to local field offices is based on the grant of generous home-rule powers; local autonomy includes authority for local units to select their own personnel without—or with only minimal —Land supervision.

All the Laender, except Rhineland-Palatinate, have granted their counties and towns (*Gemeinden*) the power to function autonomously. For example, the County Organization Act of Lower Saxony provides:[77] "The counties are associations of towns and

77. *"Die Landkreise sind Gemeinderverbaende und Gebietskorperschaften die ihre Angelegenheiten im Rahmen der Gesetze durch ihre Organe in eigener Verantwortung verwalten."* LKO of March 31, 1958, GVBl, p. 17, paragraph 1. Parallel provisions of other Laender are: Schleswig-Holstein LKO of Feb. 27,

areal agencies which autonomously administer their functions as provided by law through their own agencies." The law authorizes the counties to perform all functions which towns are unable to assume because of their small size or financial weakness.[78] The counties, rather than a designated Land field official, administer all Land programs which the Land delegates to them.[79]

Moreover, the Laender no longer appoint the Landrat[80] except in Rhineland-Palatinate. The French had occupied Rhineland-Palatinate and did not alter county government because the Landrat resembled the Prefect so familiar to French officials. But even in this Land, the central government must defer to local opinion when appointing the Landrat. The county council must approve the Ministry of Interior's nominee to the post before the Landrat can formally take office. If the council withholds its approval, the Minister of Interior must appoint another candidate.[81] Such conflicts between the county council and Minister of Interior are rare but not unknown. In 1958, for instance, Kaiserslautern rejected the ministry's appointee because it had transferred a popular Landrat away. As a result of the rejection, the Minister of Interior was forced to propose a second candidate whom the county council accepted after a long delay made it clear that the former Landrat would not return.[82]

1950, GVBl, p. 49, paragraph 1; Hesse LKO of Feb. 25, 1950, GVBl, p. 37, paragraph 1; North-Rhine-Westphalia LKO of July 21, 1953, GBl, *1*, 305, paragraphs 1–2; Baden-Wuerttemberg LKO of Oct. 10, 1955, GBl, p. 207, paragraph 1; Bavarian LKO of Feb. 16, 1952, GVBl, p. 39, paragraph 1.

78. Lower Saxony LKO, paragraph 2.

79. Ibid., paragraph 3; Schleswig-Holstein LKO, paragraph 1; Hesse LKO, paragraph 3; North-Rhine-Westphalia LKO, paragraph 2; Baden-Wuerttemberg LKO, paragraph 1; Bavarian LKO, paragraph 1. Rhineland-Palatinate, in contrast, assigns this function to the Landrat's office: LKO of Oct. 5, 1954, paragraph 2.

80. In North-Rhine-Westphalia and Lower Saxony, the Landrat's functions are performed by an *Oberkreisdirektor* (OKD); the Landrat has only representational duties. In the following text, when we refer to the Landrat in general, we mean the OKD in these two Laender unless specifically noted otherwise.

81. Rhineland-Palatinate LKO, paragraph 23.

82. Statements by Dr. Dehe, Geschaeftsfuehrer Landkreistag Rhineland-Palatinate, Mainz, April 14, 1959; Landrat Salzmann (Trier); Landrat Lingen, Oberwesterwald, March 23, 1959; and Kreisinspektor Schreiber, Bingen, April 14, 1959, personal interviews.

In the other Laender the central government possesses only a limited influence or none at all in selecting the Landraete. The county councils select the Landrat in all Laender except Bavaria where he is elected by direct popular vote. In several Laender the Ministry of Interior retains limited influence on the selection. In Baden-Wuerttemberg, the county committee and Ministry of Interior agree on a list of three candidates acceptable to both. The county council then selects one of the three.[83] In Schleswig-Holstein and North-Rhine-Westphalia, the Minister of Interior must ratify the county council's choice before the Landrat (OKD) is formally appointed.[84] In the remaining three Laender—Hesse, Lower Saxony, and Bavaria—the Land government has no authority to intervene in the election of the Landrat (OKD). However, in Hesse the District Officer (who is a Land official) sometimes confers informally with the county council before it makes its choice.[85]

The Laender that emerged from the French and British occupation zones set stringent qualifications for candidates for Landrat positions in the County Organization Acts. In Rhineland-Palatinate, Lower Saxony, and North-Rhine-Westphalia the law states that a candidate must normally have the qualifications of a higher civil servant; these qualifications entail a university education in law, an apprenticeship with a government agency, and the successful passing of a state examination.[86] In Schleswig-Holstein the county may select a Landrat without these qualifications only if it hires another official who possesses the rank of a higher civil servant.[87] The remaining three Laender, which were under American occupation,[88] impose only vague qualifications. Baden-Wuerttemberg simply requires a candidate to be in full possession

83. Baden-Wuerttemberg LKO, paragraph 23.

84. Schleswig-Holstein LKO, paragraph 49; North-Rhine-Westphalia LKO, paragraph 38.

85. Statement by Landrat Stieler, Fulda, April 15, 1959, personal interview.

86. Rhineland-Palatinate LKO, paragraph 23; Lower Saxony LKO, paragraph 55; North-Rhine-Westphalia LKO, paragraph 38.

87. Schleswig-Holstein LKO, paragraph 49.

88. Only a portion of Baden-Wuerttemberg was under American occupation. When the new Land was formed, however, it adopted a number of practices of the American zone Laender.

of his civic rights and over thirty years old. Hesse demands that a Landrat have the confidence of the population and the necessary qualifications for the post. Bavaria asks that a candidate have shown ability for public administration through active participation over a number of years in the work of building a democratic state.[89]

Such a variety of election procedures and qualifications never before existed for the Landrat's post in Germany. The effect, however, has not been as diverse as the legal provisions suggest. Despite the lack of rigorous qualifications and the exclusion of Land participation in the selection of Landraete in many Laender, more than half of the Landrat posts are again occupied by professionally trained civil servants who came directly from posts in government agencies. As Table 8 shows, Landraete with professional civil service training are still the largest group even in Laender where no formal requirements for such training exists. In every Land, the tendency is to elect Landraete with professional training.[90] It is the Laender who gain from this preference for professional civil servants. As the new Landraete often come from Land positions, they are familiar with Land policies and administrative procedures. Moreover, the Laender are assured of Landraete who are trained in the law and can interpret the legal provisions that apply to county administration.

The counties have sought to solidify their autonomous position by organizing voluntary county leagues (*Landkreisverbaende*) to lobby before the Land legislatures and in the Land ministries. County councillors in all the Laender form a sizable group in the

89. Baden-Wuerttemberg LKO, paragraph 33; Hesse LKO, paragraph 39; Bavarian LKO, paragraph 31.

90. The tendency to select civil servants as Landraete even where these qualifications are not demanded by the LKO largely stems from the influence of the county leagues (*Landkreisverbaende*). The county leagues are voluntary associations of the counties of each Land; their function is to lobby at the Land legislature and in the ministries and to give the counties expert advice on common problems. The permanent officials of the leagues are invariably former civil servants. The author interviewed these officials in every Land except Schleswig-Holstein. To a man they felt that professional civil servants should occupy Landrat posts. Moreover, they admitted that they used their influence with the counties to promote this policy.

TABLE 8

The Landraete and Oberkreisdirektoren in West German Laender, 1958

Laender	Selection procedures[a]				Qualifications[b]		Percentage who have:[c]				Percentage whose last previous position was:[c]					
	Named by land	Named by county with participation of Land ministry	Named by county alone	Elected by people	Professional civil service	No precise qualifications	Civil service training	Other university training	No university training	Total	In Land agency	In county or city service	In business	In professions	In politics	Total
Rhineland-Palatinate	X				X		61.1	—	38.9	100 (36)	75.0	11.1	—	13.9	—	100 (36)
Baden-Wuerttemberg		X				X	42.5	16.5	41.0	100 (63)	66.6	7.6	19.2	6.6	—	100 (63)
North-Rhine-Westphalia		X			X		77.2	1.8	21.0	100 (57)	36.8	47.2	7.2	8.8	—	100 (57)
Lower Saxony		X			X		81.6	6.7	11.7	100 (60)*	50.0	25.9	12.9	9.3	0.9	100 (54)*
Schleswig-Holstein		X				X	82.4	11.8	5.8	100 (17)	23.5	49.0	17.7	11.8	—	100 (17)
Hesse			X			X	70.0	—	30.0	100 (22)*	38.9	25.0	33.3	2.8	—	100 (36)*
Bavaria				X		X	42.5	16.5	41.0	100 (139)*	46.0	7.2	30.5	16.3	—	100 (141)*

* Differences in the totals reflect the unknown category.

Sources:

[a] Compiled from the various Landkreisordnungen as cited above.

[b] Ibid.

[c] Data collected by the author through interviews with the directors of the county leagues of each Land. In Bavaria, the county league placed at the author's disposal a questionnaire the league had circulated among its Landraete. In the other Laender the author depended on the league director's personal knowledge of the Landraete's backgrounds. As the directors often were influential in the Landrat's appointment and met with him frequently, they could answer the questions on

Land legislatures.[91] In Schleswig-Holstein, Bavaria, Baden-Wuert-temberg, and Hesse, the Landraete themselves may serve in the legislature. In each case only a handful of Landraete actually hold seats in the Landtage, but these few often wield great influence on administrative matters as they are expert on county affairs and frequently hold key committee seats.[92] County league officials unanimously rate the practice of Landraete serving in the Landtage as an indispensable aid in the defense of county autonomy.

Although the Landrat's office—the all-purpose local field office —has become autonomous, Land governments have not lost all control over county administration of Land and federal programs. The Laender have substituted indirect supervision for the direct hierarchical controls they once possessed. The principal control mechanisms that the Laender now use are: 1) reserving policy decisions to Land agencies, especially the district offices; 2) establishing standards for staffing county offices; 3) staffing bureaus of the Landrat's office with Land civil servants; 4) increasing the county's dependence on Land grants-in-aid; and 5) assigning functions to specialized field units that remain under direct ministerial control. In addition, the general administrative court system assures the Laender uniform interpretation of their policy directives.

The Laender rely most heavily on the district offices to supervise county administration. The Allies re-established district offices in the Laender soon after the occupation began; all Laender except Schleswig-Holstein have since retained them as their principal regional field offices.[93] West Germany's district offices are larger and have a wider jurisdiction than ever before. Although the internal organization of the district offices differs in detail from Land to Land, none have fewer than four divisions ranging over general administrative, economic, agricultural, religious, and educational

91. In Lower Saxony, for instance, there were 70. Statement by Dr. Geffers, Geschaeftsfuehrer, County League of Lower Saxony, Hanover, Aug. 6, 1959, personal interview.

92. Statements by Geschaeftsfuehrer Dr. Koch, Bavarian County League, Munich, June 20, 1959; Geschaeftsfuehrer Dr. Schlempp, Hessian County League, Wiesbaden, April 15, 1959; Geschaeftsfuehrer Dr. Frick, Baden-Wuerttemberg County League, Stuttgart, Aug. 10, 1959, personal interviews.

93. In Schleswig-Holstein all functions which the District Offices perform in other Laender are performed by the Ministry of Interior. The Land is too small to justify separate regional offices.

matters.[94] The District Officer is exclusively a Land official; no
representative organ must approve his appointment as the provincial legislatures did during the Weimar Republic. The civil
servants on his staff are also Land officials. The district office receives instructions both from the Land Ministry of Interior and
from functional ministries; in most cases, central directives are
passed on to the local field officials—the Landraete, municipal
officials, or special field agents.[95] The district office thus serves as
a funnel for all policy directives that flow to the local field offices
from the Land ministries. However, when the ministries wish to
withhold some policy-making functions from an autonomous
agency, they assign the matter to the district office. For instance,
counties and cities must normally seek the District Officer's approval of costly construction projects, for the issuance of bonds to
cover indebtedness, and for police measures which are likely to
have more than local significance.[96] Many Land programs also
allow citizens to appeal county and city decisions to District Officers before taking the case to an administrative court. In all these
capacities, the District Officer serves as a check on the performance
of delegated Land duties by Landraete and municipal field
officials.

Additional powers give the District Officers a more detailed
check on county administration. In every Land except North-
Rhine-Westphalia, the Landrat must submit to the district office
a list of county positions and the names of the officials who fill
them. The District Officer approves the personnel plan only if he
finds that: 1) the county is employing enough officials to perform
the functions that the Land has delegated to it; 2) the officials
assigned to Land functions possess the requisite civil service rank,

94. *Die Bundesrepublik 1958/59*, passim.

95. Statements, Professor Erich Becker, Speyer, April 13, 1959, and Professor Hans Peters, Cologne, Jan. 15, 1959, personal interviews. No secondary
literature on the district offices exists; nor are they dealt with in special laws
as the counties are. They operate exclusively on the basis of Land administrative regulations. A legislative report for Baden-Wuerttemberg gives some interesting information. See *Gutachten des Sachverstaendigenausschusses zur
Ausarbeitung von Vorschlaegen zur Vereinfachung, Verbesserung, und Verbil-
ligung der Verwaltung*, 2. Landtag von Baden-Wuerttemberg, *Landtag Verhandlungen*, Beilage 1450, Jan. 22, 1958.

96. *Gutachten des Sachverstaendigenausschusses*, pp. 2094 ff.

training, and experience; and 3) the county officials are being paid according to a scale established by Land law.[97] Some Laender interpret these requirements broadly and grant the Landraete considerable latitude in staffing their offices.[98] In other Laender, for example, Rhineland-Palatinate, the Ministry of Interior has drawn up a detailed master plan which specifies the number and rank of all positions in the Landrat's office for counties of various sizes.[99] Such a master plan severely limits the Landrat's flexibility in staffing his office. It also restricts promotion opportunities for county officials, for the master plan specifies the maximum ranks for the various positions. The Laender, however, strongly favor such restrictions as they limit personnel costs which must be met by grants-in-aid to the counties. Such supervision also prevents the counties from offering higher salaries than the Land and thus bidding civil servants away from Land agencies. Above all, these restrictions assure the Land that each county has an adequate number of trained personnel assigned to perform Land and federal functions.

In Rhineland-Palatinate, Baden-Wuerttemberg, Bavaria, and Hesse, the District Officer directly controls part of the Landrat's staff by assigning Land civil servants to work in the county office to help the Landrat in the execution of Land functions.[100] Such Land officials work under the Landrat's direction but are transferred and promoted solely by the District Officer. Their presence

97. Statements, Geschaeftsfuehrer Frick, Baden-Wuerttemberg County League, Geschaeftsfuehrer Koch, Bavarian County League, Geschaeftsfuehrer Dr. Schlempp, Hessian County League, Geschaeftsfuehrer Geffers, Lower Saxony County League, and Geschaeftsfuehrer Dr. Dehe, Rhineland-Palatinate County League, personal interviews.

98. Such latitude is typical of Baden-Wuerttemberg. Statements by Landrat Steinbrenner, Heidelberg, July 7, 1959, Landrat Seebich, Goeppingen, June 29, 1959, and Landrat Geiger, Tuttlingen, July 6, 1959, personal interviews.

99. Circular Decree of March 10, 1959, *Ministerialblatt*, Rhineland-Palatinate, pp. 573 ff.

100. Bavarian LKO, paragraphs 37–38; Rhineland-Palatinate LKO, paragraph 2; Baden-Wuerttemberg LKO, paragraph 37; Hesse LKO, paragraph 56. Schleswig-Holstein only assigns Land officials to the counties during the civil servants' apprenticeship period for training purposes. Statement by Kreisburodirektor Frick, Oldenburg, Aug. 10, 1959, personal interview. The other Laender do not assign any Land officials to the Landrat's office.

gives the Land direct influence in the administration of Land programs at the county level. Most Landraete welcome their assistance, for these officials are often well-trained civil servants; moreover, they are paid by the Land so that the county receives free help from them. Yet almost all Landraete with whom the author spoke complained of their lack of influence over the transfer of such Land officials. They lost good officials just when they became familiar with the problems of county administration; on the other hand, relatively incompetent officials occasionally remained in the county despite all efforts of the Landrat to have them transferred.

Assignment of Land personnel to the Landrat's office has another advantage for the Laender. Where Land officials serve in the Landrat's office, they often staff a separate division which is wholly devoted to the performance of Land tasks. The Landrat remains nominal chief of the division; however, a Land civil servant usually directs the day-to-day activities.[101] Such separate administration of Land functions by Land officials affords the District Officer numerous opportunities for detailed supervision of county operations. In contrast, county officials perform both Land and county functions in those Laender where no Land officials are assigned to the Landrat's office. Such amalgamation of related Land and county functions often leads to more efficient performance, for it allows organization according to function rather than according to whether the program is Land or locally sponsored. However, it does not allow the Laender to exercise a direct supervision over the administration of Land policies.

The Laender also exert considerable budgetary control over the counties. It is true that the district office does not as a rule possess authority to disapprove county budgets. However, the counties depend on Land grants-in-aid for much of their income. West German counties receive almost half their revenues from such

101. The author found separate divisions for Land functions in counties in Rhineland-Palatinate, Bavaria, Baden-Wuerttemberg, and Hesse. In all these Laender, the LKO allows Landraete to use Land officials for county programs but in practice they do not do so for fear of losing them through transfer. In Baden-Wuerttemberg, the counties must ask the District Officer's permission before assigning Land officials to county functions; the permission is rarely granted.

grants. At one extreme, Bavarian counties depend on Land grants for 63.9 per cent of their income; at the other, counties in North-Rhine-Westphalia receive only 37.9 per cent of their income from this source.[102] The remainder of the counties' income comes from minor taxes and from assessments (*Umlagen*) against towns within the county. The counties' dependence on Land grants makes it relatively easy for the Land to control county activities by exerting financial pressure on them. Although some grants flow to the counties on the basis of statutory formulas, others are distributed according to the District Officer's judgment of the county's need. If the District Officer feels the county can execute a program with smaller grants by effecting economies, he possesses the authority to reduce the county's grants.[103] The threat of losing part of its Land funds is ordinarily enough to induce a county to agree to minor reforms in its administration of Land programs.

Finally, the Laender have retained control over the execution of many field operations by withdrawing functions from the jurisdiction of the autonomous Landrat and assigning them to specialized field agents operating at the county level under the control of the district office. A number of technical functions have traditionally been administered in this fashion. The public health doctor, the public veterinarian, and the school superintendent (*Schulrat*) are the principal officials who have always performed their function in the county free from the Landrat's direct control. In all Laender except North-Rhine-Westphalia, they are still formally separated from the Landrat's office. In addition, most Laender have assigned to specialists functions that formerly were performed by the Landrat. In most Laender, specialized field agencies administer the Land's building codes, assess property for real estate taxes (*Katasteraemter*), and execute the federal labor code (*Gewerbeaufsichtsaemter*).[104] In Bavaria, the Land even maintains a separate county agency to distribute compensation

102. Albert Nouvortne, "Betrachtungen zur Einnahmseite des Landkreishaushalts," in *Die Landkreise in der Bundesrepublik Deutschland*, p. 215.

103. Erich Becker, "Die Selbstverwaltung als verfassungsrechtliche Grundlage der kommunalen Ordnung in Bund und Laendern," in Peters, ed., *Handbuch der kommunalen Wissenschaft, 1*, 173 ff.

104. Walter Cantner, "Verfassungsrecht der Landkreise," in Peters, ed., *1*, 424.

for war damages (*Lastenausgleich*) whereas the other Laender have delegated this function to the counties.[105]

The most important function which many Laender have withdrawn from the Landrat is control over the county police force. The Allied occupation governments bear primary responsibility for initiating this change. The Allies considered central control of police forces to be inimical to democratization. The military governments, therefore, tried to decentralize control over the police and exclude the Landrat from the exercise of general police powers.[106]

In the American zone (what is now Hesse, Bavaria, and part of Baden-Wuerttemberg) the occupation government disbanded the centrally organized Land police and ordered each town to establish its own police force. Only the Gendarmerie was retained to patrol rural areas. In addition, the police lost all administrative functions such as enforcing construction codes and keeping residential registration records. A new office, usually called *Ordnungsamt,* in the city or town administration exercised such functions. The Landrat was virtually excluded from police operations.[107]

The British did more violence to traditional German institutions in their zone (what is now Schleswig-Holstein, Lower Saxony, and North-Rhine-Westphalia). In addition to stripping the police of all administrative functions, they separated control of the police not only from the Landrat and Land central ministries but also from local government units—the counties, cities, and towns. The British established separate police committees at the district level to control the police forces. Each larger city and each district office possessed such a committee; town and county councillors but not the mayor or Landrat sat on the committee and elected a police chief. The committee and its police chief controlled all local police forces.[108]

105. Ewald Wientgen, "Die Landkreise als Verwaltungstraeger des Lastenausgleichs," in *Die Landkreise in der Bundesrepublik Deutschland,* pp. 102 ff.

106. Robert Kempner, "Police Administration," in Litchfield, ed., *Governing Postwar Germany,* p. 407.

107. Ibid., p. 412; Drews and Wacke, *Allgemeines Polizeirecht,* pp. 233 ff.; Pioch, *Das Polizeirecht,* pp. 127 ff.

108. Kempner in Litchfield, ed., p. 413; Drews and Wacke, pp. 238–39; Pioch, pp. 81–82. The French, in contrast, declined to reorganize the police in their zone. Drews and Wacke, p. 244.

The reforms introduced by the Allies only partially survived postoccupation German revisions. The degree to which they survived, however, is inversely related to the autonomy of the Landrat's office. Only those Laender where the Minister of Interior retained some influence on the selection of the Landrat have allowed the Landrat's office to regain control over the police. This has occurred in North-Rhine-Westphalia and Rhineland-Palatinate; in Baden-Wuerttemberg, vigorous efforts are being made to return the police to the Landrat's control.[109] In North-Rhine-Westphalia the police committees have lost all their functions; the *Oberkreisdirektor* now serves as chief of the county police.[110] In Rhineland-Palatinate, the police like the Landrat remain under the direction of the Ministry of Interior. The ministry assigns to each county a police chief who serves as the Landrat's subordinate. In other Laender—where the Land governments have little or no influence on the selection of the Landraete—the police forces have remained separate from the Landrat's office even though they have once more fallen under the control of the Ministry of Interior. In Bavaria, for instance, all towns over 5,000 population are authorized to maintain their own police. In fact, by July 1959 only fourteen towns retained their own police; the others found the performance of this function too expensive.[111] When the towns surrendered their police functions, the Land government assumed the responsibility. However, the Land police are not integrated with the Landrat's office in Bavaria. They constitute a special office at the county level. When the Landrat requests police assistance, they must do his bidding, but the police are not under his organizational control. The number of policemen in the county, the placement of police posts, all matters of recruitment, equipment, and training are the responsibility of the county and

109. See *Gutachten des Sachverstaendigenausschusses*, pp. 2101–02.

110. Law of Aug. 11, 1953, GVBl, p. 330, paragraph 6, reprinted in Hans Schneider, *Polizeirecht* (Munich, C. H. Beck'sche Verlagsbuchhandlung, 1957), pp. 407 ff. The police committees still exist but have only advisory functions.

111. Statement by Regierungsdirektor Martin, Munich, July 23, 1958, personal interview. Martin was at that time chief of the police section of the Bavarian Ministry of Interior. See also G. Greiner, "Probleme der Polizeiorganisation in Bayern," *Die Neue Polizei, 10* (1956), 135–38, 157–58, and 168–70.

district police chiefs rather than of the Landrat.[112] The same organizational pattern is followed in Hesse, Lower Saxony, Schleswig-Holstein, and, until now, Baden-Wuerttemberg.[113] These Laender have bypassed the autonomous Landrat's office and retained direct control over the police.

Finally, the general administrative court system has supplemented the controls we have described by assuring Laender uniform interpretation of statutory and other legal prescriptions. The occupation governments completely severed the administrative courts from the Landrat's office, the county committee, and the district office. Administrative courts now operate in areas usually covering several counties as well as at the Land and federal level. These courts are staffed by professional judges who have no ties with the Land's administrative system and by laymen who serve for a short term. The courts act as a check on the legality of administrative actions and promote uniform execution of the law. In this latter function, they assist the Land's central ministries in keeping the field officials responsive to the Land's legal prescriptions.[114]

Policy control by the district office, approval of county personnel plans, county dependence on Land grants-in-aid, the withdrawal of numerous functions from the autonomous Landrat, and the influence of administrative courts jointly protect the Laender's interest in field administration and promote field responsiveness to central demands. While the over-all effectiveness of these indirect control techniques has been satisfactory, the grant of autonomy to the Landrat's office and the proliferation of specialized field

112. Statements by Landrat Stulberger, Wasserburg/Inn, July 20, 1959, Landrat Held, Freising, July 13, 1959, and Landrat Haschke, Burglengenfeld, July 14, 1959, personal interviews.

113. See Schneider, passim. The case of Schleswig-Holstein is an anomaly as the Landrat there is not less autonomous than his counterpart in North-Rhine-Westphalia. Schleswig-Holstein's small area, however, allows the Ministry of Interior to direct police operations without intermediate field agencies. See Bass, " Gedanken ueber die Organisation der Polizei in Schleswig-Holstein," in *Die Polizei in Schleswig-Holstein 1945–55* (Kiel, Innenministerium des Landes Schleswig-Holstein, 1955), pp. 33–37.

114. Bachof, "German Administrative Law," pp. 368–82; Forsthoff, *1*, 493–95.

agencies have introduced irritating coordination problems for West Germany's field agents.[115]

Several Laender authorize the Landrat to promote coordination among the many specialized field agents operating at the county level. The Baden-Wuerttemberg County Organization Act, for instance, states:[116]

> The special field agencies active in the county and the Landrat shall cooperate in the interest of the general welfare.
>
> The Landrat is responsible for cooperation between the agencies referred to above; he is to be informed of incidents and proposed actions which are of general significance for the county.

North-Rhine-Westphalia and Hesse have similar statutory provisions.[117] However, little is apparently achieved by such prescriptions. The Landraete whom the author interviewed in North-Rhine-Westphalia, Hesse, and Baden-Wuerttemburg were uniformly surprised by his interest in these provisions and hastened to refresh their memory by reference to the law. They had never used the provisions to support any specific coordinative action. Coordination, however, has not been entirely neglected.

A major inducement to coordination exists when both the Landrat and the county's specialist agencies gain from a joint effort. A typical example is an agreement between the Land public health doctor and the Landrat in a county in Baden-Wuerttemberg.[118] The county provides transportation for the doctor from its car pool as the Land has refused his requests for adequate transportation allowances. In return, the doctor promptly examines applicants for county welfare payments. In Bavaria, both the Land and county employ social workers to check applicants for the separate Land and county welfare programs. In one county, the Landrat negotiated a local agreement by which the two

115. A German view of coordination problems is given by Anton Schmid, "Einheit der Verwaltung auf der Kreisebene," *Die oeffentliche Verwaltung* (December 1954), pp. 719 ff.

116. Baden-Wuerttemberg LKO, paragraph 48.

117. North-Rhine-Westphalia LKO, paragraph 48.4; Hesse LKO, paragraph 55.

118. Statement, Landrat Geiger, personal interview.

Land and two county social workers divided the county into four areas; each worker checked all cases (Land and county) in her area.[119] In another county, such an agreement could not be reached.[120] The Land social workers there can only see Land cases and the county social workers are restricted to county cases. Both must cover the entire county, losing much time and incurring considerable travel expenses. The difference between the two counties apparently lay in the personalities of the Landraete and the social workers. The Ministry of Interior in Munich had no objections to a cooperative agreement, but also did nothing to promote one.

The Landrat's status assists him in promoting coordination at the county level. He still holds the most important and prestigious position in the county. He is highly paid, usually drawing the pay of an *Oberregierungsrat* in the Land civil service—more than any other field agent in the county. In addition, the Landrat can make some use of his political position as an elected official and his constant contact with local party officials in the county council and county committee. He can offer his good offices to Land specialists when they need the cooperation of political leaders or town officials. Such cases occur frequently, for the specialists often need the assistance of town mayors who sit on the county council. The town mayor is a locally elected official who mostly possesses only a limited experience in administrative matters; he often refers such questions to the Landrat. When a specialist demands information from a mayor, the mayor is likely to come to the Landrat for advice. If the specialists inform the Landrat of their proposals first, the Landrat is more likely to give the mayor proper advice.[121]

The Landrat's ability to promote coordination depends more on his personal attributes today than ever before. A Landrat with no administrative training may find that specialists try to overwhelm him with technical details; alternatively they may negoti-

---

119. Statement, Landrat Haschke, personal interview.

120. Statement, Landrat Stulberger, personal interview.

121. The Landrat's role as a political broker was emphasized by several of the Landraete whom the author interviewed. Statements by Landrat Geiger, Landrat Lingen, Landrat Steinbrenner, personal interviews. Also Oberkreisdirektor Grimm, Fallingsbostel, Aug. 6, 1959, personal interview.

ate directly with subordinate officials of the Landrat's office. In these cases, much depends on the relationship between the Landrat and his senior officials who possess the training he lacks. This is a dimension which was rarely important in earlier periods of German history, for Landraete were almost always professional civil servants. Sometimes, the Landrat's personal position is enhanced by his holding a seat in the Landtag or Bundestag.[122] A Bundestag seat confers greater prestige but a Landtag seat can have very practical consequences. The local specialists—who must judge more by the appearance of power than by its actual exercise at the Land capital—are likely to defer to such a Landrat.

TABLE 9

*Terms of Office and Actual Tenure of Landraete
and Oberkreisdirektoren (Expressed as Percentage), 1958*

Laender	Term of office*	LR-OKD Appointed before 1948	LR-OKD Appointed between 1949–53	LR-OKD Appointed between 1954–58	Total†
Rhineland-Palatinate	Indef	38.8	35.9	33.2	100 (39)
North-Rhine-Westphalia	12 Yrs	38.6	28.1	33.2	100 (57)
Baden-Wuerttemberg	8–12	44.3	27.9	27.8	100 (62)
Lower Saxony	6–12	43.4	30.0	26.4	100 (60)
Hesse	6–12	35.9	38.2	25.9	100 (39)
Schleswig-Holstein	6–12	17.1	29.4	53.5	100 (17)
Bavaria	6	32.2	28.6	39.2	100 (143)
West Germany		35.6	28.8	35.6	100 (425)

* All but those who have not served in a public office before are selected for twelve years.
† Numbers in parentheses indicate number of counties in each Land.
Sources: *Landkreisordnungen; Der Bundesrepublik 1958/59.*

122. See comments on Landraete in Land legislatures above. All Landraete except those in Rhineland-Palatinate may sit in the Bundestag, for only appointed officials are excluded from its membership. Law of Aug. 4, 1953, BGBl, 1, 777.

Moreover, Landraete gain prestige as well as useful knowledge from their long tenure in office. In North-Rhine-Westphalia, the *Oberkreisdirektoren* are selected for twelve years; in Rhineland-Palatinate, the Landrat is appointed for an indefinite term; in all the other Laender, he is elected for a term varying between six and twelve years. As Table 9 shows, over one-third of the Landraete in office in 1958 have already served thirteen or more years. The Landraete's long tenure in the midst of the change from occupation rule to West German sovereignty undoubtedly gives many Landraete a special position of prestige in their counties. As the organizational structure in the near future is likely to remain more stable than it has during the postwar years of transition, we may expect the average tenure of Landraete to increase still more.

Yet, no matter how well endowed a Landrat is with political prestige, professional knowledge, and local expertise resulting from long tenure, he has difficulty promoting effective coordination between his own office and the specialized field offices of the Land's ministries. Effective coordination would require subordination of the Landrat to the central ministries or subordination of the central ministries' field officials to the Landrat. The former would destroy the county's autonomous position which many Germans feel to be the foundation of a sound democratic regime. The latter would rob the Land ministries of one of their most effective controls over field administration. Inadequate coordination, therefore, is an unavoidable cost of mixing autonomous and ministerially controlled agencies at the same level.

CONCLUSIONS

It is evident that the democratic context in which the local agencies of the Laender today must function has had a significant impact on the structure of field administration. With the exception of Rhineland-Palatinate, the county offices have become autonomous; the Laender have lost their authority to direct county activities through hierarchical channels. County and city autonomy, however, has raised new barriers to responsive field administration. The Laender's principal problem in West Germany is to overcome awkward communication channels; moreover, the Laender

have to counter loyalty barriers resulting from field agents' identification with partisan and local groups that tend to subordinate
their sense of obligation to the central government.

The Laender have developed novel controls to overcome these
barriers. Some of the control mechanisms parallel those that the
federal government has evolved. Like the federal government, the
Laender rely on informal contacts and on administrative courts
to promote uniform and responsive field administration. Other
controls are quite different. The Laender have retained some
marginal controls of a hierarchical nature: they supervise the staffing of the field agencies, and they exercise a great deal of influence
on local budgets through grants-in-aid which they distribute.
Those Laender that have lost most of their influence over the
appointment of the Landrat have established specialized field
agencies that operate at the county and city level under direct
ministerial control. However, such proliferation of specialized field
agencies makes local coordination extremely difficult. Lack of
coordination is the cost of exacting field responsiveness through
a proliferation of specialized, ministerially controlled field units.

At both the Land and federal levels, West Germany has developed an entirely new set of controls to overcome the unique
responsiveness barriers that the Federal Republic has encountered.
These control mechanisms have been designed not only to be
compatible with the federal institutions of the Republic but also
to be suitable to the democratic ideology to which West Germany
is now committed. For the first time in her history, Germany is
encouraging local control of administrative agencies. The indirect
controls that Germany's federal and Land ministries have developed succeed to a large—even if not complete—extent in promoting responsive and effective administration without sacrificing
the autonomy of the Laender or of their local field agencies.

7. THE QUEST FOR RESPONSIVENESS

Many paths lead to responsive administration; the German experience illustrates some of the most important ones. During the Second Reich Germany attained a sufficiently responsive administrative machine with very few direct controls. The confluence of interests and values among all participants in the political process almost automatically produced responsiveness. Those who dissented from the conservative consensus were simply excluded from the political arena. In contrast to such low-pressure techniques, the Third Reich found it more congenial to place great emphasis on direct hierarchical controls. Direct controls, however, were not sufficient to obtain the degree of responsiveness that the regime desired; only when hierarchical pressures were coupled with external controls did the Nazi government succeed in getting loyal administration. Between these two extremes stand Germany's two democratic regimes: the Weimar government which relied on only slightly more stringent hierarchical controls than did the Empire, and the Bonn Republic which mixes hierarchical with political controls to secure loyal administration. In retrospect, each German regime commanded a loyal enough administration so that not once in the last century did a breakdown of the administrative process lead to the collapse of a regime.

Yet the ninety years we have surveyed were turbulent ones for Germany. The political turmoil in which German officials operated much of the time stimulated the development of many of the most common barriers to responsive field administration.

Disloyalty to the central regime manifested itself in numerous ways. At the extreme, disloyalty bordered on treason when some civil servants considered the Weimar government to be usurpers of the legitimate rule of the Kaiser and treacherous representatives of socialistic ideology. Far more common but less serious was the disloyalty of some Landraete during the Second Reich. They accepted the Reich and Prussian monarchy as legitimate institutions but sometimes disagreed with specific mandates which these governments expected them to execute, for they had developed local ties and identifications. Such Landraete hesitated to execute unpopular mandates; they occasionally tried to assuage local groups by modifying such edicts in the administration of central policies.

Communication barriers to responsive administration constitute a second almost universal obstacle to responsive administration; in Germany every sort of communication barrier arose. Awkward hierarchical structures impeded the flow of orders from Berlin to the field and of information from the localities to Berlin. During the Weimar Republic, when international and economic crises shifted the political center of gravity from the Laender to the Reich, the Reich rarely established sufficient new agencies to carry out its responsibilities nor developed adequate channels to expedite communications between Land agencies and the Reich. Less frequently, differences in language and frame of reference led to misunderstandings between Berlin and field agencies, even though communication channels posed no barriers. During the Third Reich, for instance, the language of command used by Nazi politicians was not always understood by administrators. At the same time, the Nazis misperceived the work of administrators because officials did not always speak or write in the brusque, abusive dialect of the party. The bureaucracy's use of civilized language was misunderstood as a lack of zeal and fervor.

Despite the difficulties Germany faced, her regimes overcame most barriers to responsiveness. In part this was due to the control mechanisms we have described; in part it was the consequence of peculiar characteristics of the German administrative system. Germany's civil service corps, the legalistic perspectives of German administrators, the flexibility of Germany's federal system, and the development of nonhierarchical controls bear special responsibility for Germany's achievement of a responsive administration. Each of these factors justifies a somewhat closer look.

The German Civil Service   The observation originally made of France that governments rise and fall but the bureaucracy remains appears particularly applicable to Germany. Although this century has seen Germany ruled by four regimes whose ideological perspectives and power bases were fundamentally different, the civil service remained stable. The structure of the civil service was altered only once; its personnel changed only slowly.

The German civil service attained its remarkable staying power by striking deep roots in German society. During the Second Reich and before, the civil service was almost entirely composed of Junkers, aristocrats, and upper-class bourgeois elements. Such a social composition had several consequences. It brought into executive positions men whose feudal and commercial backgrounds gave them a policy orientation which coincided with the government's. As long as the government defended the status quo, it could be sure of a loyal bureaucracy on most important policy questions, for the government's goals were consonant with the private interests of its bureaucrats. What was good for the Kaiser was good for the civil service and vice versa.[1]

A more lasting effect of the upper-class nature of the bureaucracy was its prestige in the eyes of the German public. Germans respected civil servants not only because they were powerful and wore the uniform of the State, representing Kaiser and King. Government officials were also respected because they came from high-status families. Such respect for civil servants and the concomitant desirability of a career in the bureaucracy long outlived the Second Reich. World War I discredited the King and Kaiser but not the civil service in the eyes of many Germans, for the new regime granted special guarantees to the civil service which had been recruited by the King's government and loyally served it. Later most Germans lost faith in the Republic because it failed

1. Muncy, *The Junker in the Prussian Administration,* pp. 220–34.

to achieve their nationalistic goals and proved unable to overcome the depression; still later the Nazi Reich was blamed for Germany's disastrous defeat in World War II. Yet the bureaucracy that served each of these regimes remained relatively untainted; it retained its high status and position of respect.

Moreover, the civil service was a career elite; the career element promoted long tenure and stabilized civil service perspectives. High-level positions were invariably filled by officials who had served a long apprenticeship in subordinate posts. The only major exceptions to this rule occurred during the Nazi regime when party veterans received high-level appointments; in contrast to this, the number of "outsiders" appointed during the Weimar Republic remained relatively insignificant.[2] Indeed, most regimes found it extremely difficult to dismiss career officials. The Third Reich ousted more career civil servants than any other regime, yet the conquering Allied armies found innumerable career officials at their posts when they occupied Germany.[3]

The career character of the civil service also stabilized the perspectives of the bureaucracy. Administrative procedure and even policy outlook remained conservative, for little fresh blood entered the administrative structure at the top. New recruits were almost entirely limited to subordinate echelons; by the time they reached policy-making positions, they usually had lost whatever innovating spirit they possessed. The long apprenticeship imposed on civil servants instilled them with the bureaucracy's norms as well as its procedures; it produced meek men.

Another characteristic that made the civil service an extraordinarily useful tool for the various regimes it served was that it was a highly trained elite. To enter the higher civil service, a candidate required a university degree and had to pass several state examinations.[4] The expertise that resulted was perhaps not indispensable, for it is easy to overestimate the need for expertise in administrative matters. But the bureaucrat's training gave him the aura of an expert; in German society, expertise gave one the right to act authoritatively, for Germany has retained to a surpris-

2. See pp. 96–99 and 128–32 above.

3. See Hiscocks, *Democracy in West Germany*, pp. 195 and 203 ff.

4. Morstein Marx, "Civil Service in Germany," in White, ed., *Civil Service Abroad*, pp. 210–12 and 221–25.

ing extent the values of a guild culture. Only those individuals who are trained, tested, and licensed are allowed to practice their vocation. These requirements apply to common occupations like selling and laundering as well as to professions like the law or engineering. Consequently, the training a civil servant received gave him his credentials to appear on the political scene as the expert in administration and policy-making. Everyone else should defer to him—and in fact often did. Administration was the bureaucrat's monopoly. In this way the civil servant gained a preeminent administrative and political status which allowed him to carry out his function with little interference from outsiders.

These characteristics joined to give the German civil servant the perspectives of the bureaucrat whom Weber described—committed to a career in government service, oriented solely to his job, proud of his status in the society, and wed to the authority of the State.[5] Unlike many American bureaucrats,[6] there were few German civil servants who derived most of their satisfaction from the specialized profession which they practiced in their official position (law, medicine, or engineering) or from the clientele they served. As a result, the German bureaucrat depended almost entirely on the governmental hierarchy to gain fulfillment of his desire for prestige, security, and life-purpose. His dependence on the government for these satisfactions made him a relatively pliable instrument for whichever regime held power.

For much of the period we have surveyed, these characteristics of the civil service aided Germany in attaining a responsive field administration. To an amazing extent the civil service identified with whatever regime possessed power and served it ably. Of course, there were some exceptions. Some bureaucrats sought to undermine the Weimar Republic; a few others tried to resist the Nazi regime. But on the whole the bureaucracy served loyally. No regime needed to purge it entirely; all could rely on the personnel controls described earlier to secure loyal administration. Moreover, a weak regime like the Weimar Republic could capitalize on the bureaucracy's prestige and win better compliance from

5. H. H. Gerth and C. Wright Mills, *From Max Weber: Essays in Sociology* (New York, Oxford University Press, 1958), pp. 198–204.

6. Leonard Reissman, "A Study of Role Conceptions in Bureaucracy," *Social Forces,* 27 (1957), 353–59.

the populace than it might have otherwise by using the civil service. The bureaucracy lent all German governments after the Second Reich a measure of legitimacy and respect which made their task of governing somewhat easier.

Legalistic Perspectives of German Administrators Another peculiar characteristic of German officials was their emphasis on jurisprudence and on the legal aspects of their work. All bureaucracies, of course, operate within the context of general rules. In liberal democracies these rules are in the form of laws or regulations derived from law. German administration, however, went much further in its obeisance to legal formulas than most administrative organizations, for its officials were specifically trained in the law. Moreover, administrative law possessed a special political significance in Germany, for it developed as a consequence of the effort to restrain the Prussian autocracy.

The university training received by German administrators concentrated heavily on law. In contrast to the British higher civil servant who is educated in the liberal arts and the American civil servant who is often trained in the arts of administrative procedure, the German official attended law classes at the university and sought specialized training in administrative law. Public administration as an academic discipline did not exist in Germany; the prospective civil servant learned nothing about the uses of budgeting, the intricacies of personnel management, or the art of structuring an administrative agency to obtain clear channels of communication and authority. Instead, he was trained in the legal force of various mandates—laws, ministerial regulations, administrative decrees, etc. He also learned the legal significance of an "administrative act" (*Verwaltungsakt*) and the administrative and judicial procedures by which such acts could be challenged. He was taught the legal limits of bureaucratic authority. Finally, he was indoctrinated into the mystique of the civil service by learning of his special privileges and tenure as a bureaucrat as well as his solemn obligation to serve the government and obey his superiors.[7]

7. Morstein Marx, "Civil Service in Germany," pp. 202–26. For a typical contemporary textbook see Ernst Forsthoff, *Lehrbuch des Verwaltungsrechts* (7th ed. Munich and Berlin, C. H. Beck'sche Verlagsbuchhandlung, 1958).

Administrative law won such a peculiar status in the training of prospective bureaucrats largely because of Germany's historical development. Following the French practice, Germany's monarchs often required legal training for entry into the civil service as early as the 18th century, for administration was couched in legal forms. However, Germany lagged behind most West European nations in abandoning monarchical autocracy. Even the 1848 revolution which profoundly affected the political development of the other continental powers left almost no imprint on Germany's political structure. However, by 1870 the autocratic power of the monarchy had become unacceptable to an ever growing portion of Germany's population. As Germany's economy shifted from an agricultural base to an industrial one, a large and economically influential bourgeoisie developed. In time it demanded political as well as economic power. It especially desired freedom from governmental interference in commercial and industrial affairs. As we saw in our discussion of the Second Reich, these aspirations found their expression in attempts to reform the administrative structure—especially to impose a set of external controls on the administrative bureaucracy. On the one hand, political controls were attempted in the form of locally elected councils; these failed to restrict administrative activity. On the other hand, special administrative courts were established to impose a judicial curb on bureaucratic actions. These courts, although staffed by civil servants, eventually had a profound impact on German administration, for they imposed real limits on bureaucratic action. Each Land possessed a court of last resort which often rendered the final decision on controversial matters and was not subject to political controls.

Much of the intellectual support for these innovations came from university professors of law.[8] The professors also gave clear support to the authority of administrative law in their texts.[9] In their classes, students were taught to circumscribe their adminis-

8. The leader of the movement was Rudolf Gneist; another administrative legalist influential both in academic and political circles was Hugo Preuss.

9. See, for example, Forsthoff, passim; Otto Koelreutter, *Grundfragen des Verwaltungsrechts* (Cologne, C. Heymanns Verlag, 1955), passim; Walter Jellinek, *Verwaltungsrecht* (2d ed. Berlin, Verlag von Julius Springer, 1929), passim; and Meyer and Anschuetz, *Lehrbuch der deutschen Staatsrechts*, passim.

trative actions by legal bounds; they learned to respect administrative tribunals. Administrative law became the bench mark for measuring administrative activities.

The emphasis on administrative law had several further consequences for German administration. It sensitized German officials only to legal problems, for it meant that almost all literature on administration was restricted to its legal aspects. For instance, there are dozens of German books and countless articles on financial law, the civil service code, and administrative courts, but scarcely one on the budgetary process, on personnel management, or on the politics of administrative regulation. While German administrators often played a key role in German politics, they normally viewed their activity as that of legal experts rendering judgment rather than as a politically oriented group advancing a partisan viewpoint. To many bureaucrats, politics connoted an illegitimate activity; administration was good—politics was bad.

The emphasis on legalism also imparted a strong nationalizing tendency to German administrators. National laws won special respect and a receptive response because they emanated from the legal sovereign—the Reich. Moreover, a large and influential segment of the bureaucracy sought to concentrate all administrative functions in the national government. The values they invoked were legal uniformity as well as administrative efficiency. The administrative legalists at universities were often in the vanguard of this movement. While they remained relatively mute during the Second Reich, they became vocal during the Weimar Republic.[10] Schemes to restructure the federal system were a frequent topic for administrative and political dispute. Some plans centered on changing the boundaries of the Laender, dividing Prussia into several smaller Laender, and making the Republic a union of nearly equal states. Others foresaw the complete abolition of Germany's federal system and the transfer of Land functions to the Reich. These schemes were often discussed in administrative law texts; many of the texts reflected their authors' preference for a centralized administrative structure, for viewed from the statute books such a structure would be neater and make the development of a national administrative law possible. Partly because of

10. Brecht, *Federalism and Regionalism in Germany,* pp. 73–113; also see Bracher, *Die Aufloesung der Weimarer Republik,* pp. 559–71.

these predispositions, many administrators flocked to the Nazi banner in 1933 when the Nazis promised to introduce the reforms suggested by the legalists. The destruction of Germany's federal system by the Nazis thus found willing partners among many officials who saw a nationalized structure as the most efficient one for Germany and the one that would stress German nationalism by overcoming the parochialism of the Laender.

The legalistic perspectives of German bureaucrats aided the central governments in still other ways to achieve a high degree of responsiveness in the field administration. It gave all higher civil servants a common perspective and common jargon in which they could communicate. It introduced an element of uniformity in the administrative system even though the legalistic focus of the administrators may also have made them more conservative in their policy preferences and relatively hesitant to accept change. It also produced a high degree of interchangeability in the bureaucratic corps. With similar perspectives among most civil servants regardless of which Land they served, the administrative system attained a degree of flexibility which did much to promote responsiveness to central mandates.

The Adaptiveness of Germany's Federal System   Germany's federal structure—during the three regimes which utilized it—also helped her national governments attain field responsiveness. Federalism enabled these governments to meet new challenges more flexibly and to adapt to new situations more readily. Federalism in Germany meant that the national government avoided the necessity of establishing administrative offices throughout the country; rather, it depended on the Laender to carry out national programs. None of the regimes that operated within the federal structure developed elaborate field organizations of their own. The Weimar Republic came closest, but even it used Land agencies for most purposes.

The federal structure raised problems which sometimes seriously hampered the successful administration of national policies at the local level. Communications often were awkward—the national government could not deal with field agents directly but had to go through the Land ministries. This led to relatively greater isolation of the Reich ministries from the actual operative arena than might have been desirable. It also forced the federal government to rely heavily on the Bundesrat, Reichsrat, and other extra-hierarchical contacts to establish effective communication channels. Insofar as such organs were solely concerned with administrative matters, the system worked reasonably well, but when they became the site of partisan conflicts and Land-Reich rivalries, they stopped functioning as effective coordinators. The system became a handicap when some of the constituent state governments valued their partisan advantage above the interest of the national regime. During the unsettled years following World War I, the Reich was forced into this position when it delegated administrative programs to Land governments that were unalterably opposed to the Reich policy and dominated by politicians of the national opposition party. At least once it caused real political damage when the Reich had to suspend its police actions against subversive elements in order to maintain peace with Bavaria. The Reich's failure to deal sternly with Hitler and his reactionary allies in 1923 did much to embolden the Republic's enemies and in this way contributed to the ultimate dissolution of the Weimar regime.

To classify administrative federalism as a clear weakness in German administrative practice, however, would be misleading. While it sometimes promoted certain barriers to administrative responsiveness, it also served as a device to strengthen the tenuous political links that bound united Germany together. The federal structure indeed is what made the Second Reich possible, for through it the constituent states retained an important role in governing, enabling them to join the Reich without forceful subjugation by Prussia. Throughout the Second Reich, the system of administrative federalism worked extremely effectively because the Reich and Laender were basically in agreement on most policies. Both were conservative and drew their support from conservative elements of the society; they both were relatively nationalistic. The accord of Land governments to Reich policies allowed the Reich to rule with minimal hierarchical controls.

Even during the Weimar Republic when Reich and Land governments often were not in accord with each other, the federal system on the balance probably strengthened the regime. Germany's defeat in World War I had destroyed the national consensus which dominated the Second Reich. No new consensus arose in its place; instead, events fragmented German opinion. On the one hand, radical leftists who viewed the Russian revolution as their model sought to dominate the German revolution and impose a proletariat dictatorship. Arrayed against them were reactionaries who wished to return to the halcyon days of Bismarck or even Frederick the Great. The new Reich government was caught in the middle with much passive backing but with few enthusiastic supporters. Under these circumstances, it is doubtful that greater direct control over administration would have eased the national government's political problems; it might well have exacerbated them. The federal structure—by allowing the Laender to control administrative functions—permitted a flexible administration of national programs and glossed over the extreme differences among Germany's political factions. The ultimate failure of the Republic cannot be traced to its administrative system. External events simply dealt too harshly with a disillusioned and fragmented German populace. Probably any government would have fallen, given Germany's internal fragmentation and the crises generated by the Great Depression.

The adaptability of Germany's federal system had other advantages for the central government as well. It allowed German governments to experiment with new policies without upsetting domestic political alignments. The social insurance schemes promoted by Bismarck succeeded so well because they minimized political opposition through delegation of their execution to the Laender; at the same time, delegation to the Laender allowed sufficient administrative flexibility to take into account local variations in Germany's regions. Likewise, during the Bonn Republic, the federal system has allowed Germany to absorb a great portion of the Allied political reconstruction program. Each Land was subjected to somewhat different reforms. The absence of a strong, national government in postoccupation Germany allowed the Laender to retain some of these reforms as a badge of their independence. Rather than bearing the mark of foreign imposition, many structural innovations have become a symbol of Land autonomy, a rallying point for native parochialism.

Consequently, Germany's federal system often gave the national government a significant measure of political support. It also promoted effective adaptation of national programs to local contingencies. While some communication obstacles arose, these were rarely serious enough to endanger administrative responsiveness.

The Development of External Controls Germany's reliance on administrative federalism forced her regimes to develop a repertory of control techniques that operated outside hierarchical channels. Most frequently other institutions of government were adapted to exert influence over Land administrative agencies. The best example of such adaptation was the use of administrative courts. Administrative courts were established to restrain administrative autocracy in Prussia and elsewhere in Germany. At all except the highest level, they were composed of active administrators and laymen. Until the Bonn Republic, German administrative courts never possessed the complete independence of the regular judiciary nor did they have jurisdiction over all Germany. Yet within Prussia and many other Laender, administrative decisions could be appealed to a High Court whose rulings constituted an effective guarantee of uniform interpretation of statutes by administrative officials in various localities. Under the Bonn Republic a great variety of administrative courts have blossomed, each with a national appeals court ruling for all West Germany. Admittedly such courts cannot be subjected to policy guidance from the national ministries. Yet court rulings rarely have run counter to the ministry's wishes, for ministerial as well as legislative intent have formed the basis of most of their rulings. By imposing uniform interpretations on policy mandates, the administrative courts have performed a valuable service to the central government in assuring relatively responsive administration of central policies.

Political controls constituted a second type of external control over local officials. During the Weimar Republic some politicians had hoped that locally elected county councils would restrain disaffected bureaucrats. However, the councils proved to be unreliable control instruments. Too frequently political enemies of the national regime dominated them; even when the councils were controlled by friendly elements, their localized perspectives often led to conflicts between the councils and national officials. More often than not, locally elected councils stimulated unresponsive administration.

The Bonn Republic, however, has experimented with political controls of a somewhat different nature. Adenauer has used his predominant position in German politics to intervene in Land elections in order to obtain Land governments that would be responsive to his domestic policies. German voters have been so nationally oriented that such intervention has not alienated as many as it might in other countries.[11] While his interference in Land politics has not met with uniform success, it has exerted a not-so-subtle pressure on recalcitrant Land governments, especially those controlled by his own party.

A different sort of political control was applied by Germany's totalitarian regime. It did not rely on other governmental institutions but rather on the Nazi party structure. The party was used in several ways to control administration. Its hierarchy served as an alternative information-command channel to direct administrative actions; party infiltration of the bureaucracy assured the Reich of a relatively submissive and responsive administrative machine; when particularly sensitive tasks had to be performed or when the party felt a special responsibility for certain programs, it simply assigned their execution to party officials, leaving the administrative hierarchy in the cold. Such practices bear a remarkable resemblance to those evolved by the Communist party in the Soviet Union at the same time;[12] they are perhaps endemic to totalitarian regimes.

The characteristics of the civil service, the bureaucracy's legal formalism, the federal structure, and the development of external controls went far to make responsive field administration possible in Germany. Despite the turbulent political events which enveloped Germany during the first part of this century, the administrative structure held together. Only once did it break down entirely—when the Allied armies broke through Germany's last

11. When asked whether the Laender should be abolished in favor of a centralized national government in Bonn, 60 per cent of a random sample of Germans in 1953 answered affirmatively. Erich P. Neumann and Elisabeth Noelle, *Antworten: Politik in Kraftfeld der oeffentlichen Meinung* (Allensbach am Bodensee, Verlag fuer Demoskopie, 1954), p. 156 n. See also Arnold J. Heidenheimer, "Federalism and the Party System: The Case of West Germany," *American Political Science Review*, 52 (1958), 809–28.

12. Fainsod, *Smolensk under Soviet Rule*, pp. 62–92.

defenses in 1945. Even then the skeletal substructure remained viable enough to allow its use by the Allies in their occupation regime.

Although the field administration was not directly responsible for any of the disasters that overtook Germany during the last century, it would be wrong to conclude that the operation of field agencies had no influence on the course of modern German history. On the contrary, the fact that the field administration remained responsive to all its various masters is a fundamental factor in the political calamities which befell Germany in the last fifty years.

It is an axiom that no regime can govern effectively without a responsive field administration. When an existing administrative structure can be made responsive despite political revolutions and fundamental social transformations, a new regime has a far easier task in establishing itself than it would if it had to organize and recruit an entirely new administrative machine. The German field administration proved to be sufficiently pliable in its ideological commitments to serve all its masters. Only minor changes in field structure and personnel were necessary to procure fairly responsive execution of mandates issued under the seal of William II, Emperor of Germany and King of Prussia, as well as the policies decreed by Socialists such as Chancellor Mueller and Minister President Braun. Some of the same field agents later executed orders emanating from the Fuehrer and a decade thereafter obeyed the orders of the democratic government of Chancellor Adenauer. The spineless quality of the German civil service was not responsible for the rapid succession of regimes in Germany, but it cleared the way for new regimes to take control quickly.

The chameleonic quality of German field agents also explains why loyalty barriers could be overcome by German regimes despite the rare use of draconic measures. Only the Nazis were driven to a radical reorganization of the administrative structure and a partial purge of the civil service. Their measures, however, were primarily dictated by Hitler's ideological commitments and by his paranoid fear of subversion. In reality, administrative disloyalty posed no threat to the Third Reich until World War II seemed lost after Stalingrad.

Efforts to attain field responsiveness sometimes had political repercussions and often did not. They usually took place within the framework of the administrative structure and ordinarily had few political consequences. Routine checks on field administrators —such as the requirement that Landraete receive permission to be absent from their county for more than 24 hours—had no political importance and would be forgotten but for the thoroughness of German archivists who preserved files of such requests for three-quarters of a century. However, many measures necessary to procure responsive field administration were effected by political means and had profound political repercussions. The entire Nazi reorganization of the administrative structure was political in nature. It was as much an effort to realize the Nazi ideal of a *Fuehrerstaat*—ambiguous as that was—as an attempt to overcome administrative disloyalty. Efforts by the Weimar Republic had equally strong political repercussions. The attempt to remove disloyal district officers after the Kapp Putsch embroiled the Prussian Minister of Interior in a struggle with Provincial Diets for most of a year. Later the Reich's effort to attain responsive administration in Bavaria took place entirely through political channels; the Reich Chancellor and Minister President of Bavaria negotiated an agreement as if each were heads of equally sovereign states.

Thus the development and application of controls by the central government over field agents must be viewed in the perspective of German politics, society, and culture as well as in the more narrow perspective of administrative organization. Each contributed to the effectiveness of the German way of executing governmental programs.

GERMAN ADMINISTRATION AND THE CONTEMPORARY WORLD

Germany's quest for a responsive field administration also may contain lessons for other countries. A case study such as this one necessarily focuses on many unique elements. The general characteristics, however, need not be ignored. The desire for responsiveness is a universal one whether the government is authoritarian or democratic, whether it pursues a policy of minimal or maximal intervention in economic affairs, whether it is developing or developed. Moreover, many features of Germany's history bear a close resemblance to problems faced by other nations. While Germany in 1871 was not primitive, it had not yet developed the industrial might that made it a feared world power during the 20th century. In 1871 Germany was predominantly rural and agricultural—in short, pre-industrial. During the next forty years, it developed its industrial potential with incredible speed, producing severe social dislocations which reflected themselves in political restlessness and a gradual breakdown of the previously dominant political culture. During those forty years most Germans abandoned village life under near-feudal conditions for city life centered around a factory job. Public welfare programs replaced individual self-reliance and private charity. Eventually Germany's expanding population and increasing economic-military might spilled over into the international arena with demands for a German empire to provide more sufficient resources for the German people. Thus 19th-century Germany displayed many of the characteristics of today's developing nations.

Two defeats in world conflicts restrained Germany's international ambitions. But domestically, the unrest was largely contained by political compromises in which the administrative machine played a major role. The availability of an efficient bureaucracy not only made many domestic policies possible, but the structure of the administrative machine also rendered national policies acceptable.

While the conditions under which German administration developed during the last century bear a remarkable resemblance to those of certain developing countries on the contemporary scene, the German experience certainly cannot be copied blindly. Although Japan apparently managed much imitation quite successfully, contemporary nationalism necessitates a far more eclectic application of foreign experiences. A principal criterion of selection—one substantiated by Germany's development—is that an effective administrative structure must reflect the domestic political balance and support it. This is what made administration such a useful tool in the Second Reich. The bureaucratic structure accurately reflected the political consensus and gave new forces contending in the political arena a chance to exert power. The Prussian reforms of the 1870s specifically sought to absorb the interests of industrialist liberals while the Reich reforms of the same decades sought to take into account the rising proletariat masses of the new urban centers. To a large extent the administrative structure disarmed political opposition and became a solid crutch for the regime. The same principle appears to be applicable to the newly developing countries. Many of them have inherited administrative structures bequeathed them by colonial regimes. Unless those structures reflect the new political balance, it seems unlikely that they can operate with the same success as the German administration.

The special factors operating in Germany that were noted earlier—the existence of an elite civil service corps, emphasis on legal formalism, the practice of administrative federalism, and the use of extrahierarchical controls—are also not entirely peculiar to Germany. Indeed, many of them exist in some of the developing countries as well. India, Ghana, and Nigeria, for instance, embarked on independence with a well-trained, elite civil service that can perform some of the same services the German bureaucracy rendered its country. Moreover, federalism is a structural form available to many of the developing countries. The federal division of powers existing in Germany may be particularly attractive to some of them, for it allows the central regime to keep control over policy-making while the constituent states administer the central mandates. In the face of powerful centrifugal forces, new nations may find that administrative federalism offers an attractive solution to some of their thorniest political problems.

One means of assuring responsiveness appears to be particularly important for other nations. Like Germany, they can seek guarantees of effective administration through controls operating outside the administrative hierarchy. In advising new nations, the perspectives of many experts in public administration may be too narrow; they often emphasize only hierarchical remedies to administrative inefficiency. In addition to hierarchical controls, however, each nation may establish control mechanisms which operate through political or cultural channels. The Second Reich depended on the support of social groupings which it had brought into the administrative sphere; the Third Reich depended on the political support of party organs; the Bonn Republic uses the electoral machinery to control administration. Not each of these means—perhaps none of them—is available in other countries, but it is likely that other extrahierarchical controls are possible. Such external controls may make administrative federalism more effective and allow central governments to secure a responsive administration with minimal political strain.

Finally, the German experience shows that even with a relatively high degree of political instability, it is possible to secure an effective administrative machine. Political instability does not create immediate disturbances in an administrative organization; indeed, the bureaucracy may well continue to function on a business-as-usual basis for quite some time before it feels the impact of a change of regimes or of unsettled political conditions. With controls such as existed in Germany, it appears quite possible to pass through political instability with few adverse effects on administrative responsiveness.

The quest for responsiveness certainly poses no easy challenge. It is one that consumes much of the energies of every regime and tasks the ingenuity of statesmen. However, responsiveness is not an illusive goal. The German experience illustrates some of the paths that lead to it. It is clear that to capture responsiveness not only strictly administrative but also political, economic, and cultural channels must be utilized. In turn, the modern administrator must be bureaucrat and politician and must have roots in his culture and society in order to govern successfully.

GLOSSARY

All translations of German terms are the responsibility of the author. I have not tried to translate literally but rather in a free fashion in order to render German terms meaningful to English readers. The titles of German agencies have been either given the name of their closest American equivalents or translated to indicate the function of the agency. Thus *Landkreis* is translated as "county," *Regierungspraesident* as "District Officer," and *Berufsgenossenschaften* as "Industrial Insurance Corporations."

Amtsvorsteher	police magistrate in Prussia
Arbeitsamt	unemployment office
Arbeitsgericht	labor court
Baukrankenkasse	Construction Health Fund
Beauftragter der NSDAP	Nazi Party Delegate
Befoerderungssteuer	transportation tax
Berufsgenossenschaften	Industrial Insurance Corporations
Beschlussverfahren	nonjudicial appeal
Betriebskrankenkasse	Factory Health Fund
Bezirksausschuss	district committee
Bezirksregierung	district office
Buergermeister	mayor

Buergermeistereien	consolidated townships, township associations
Bund	federal government
Bundesexekution	armed intervention by federal government in Land affairs
Bundesfinanzhof	Federal Tax Court
Bundesrat	federal council
Bundestag	federal legislature
Dienstordnung	operating procedure code for administrative agencies
ehrenamtliche Stellungen	honorary positions
Einspruchsrecht	suspensive veto
Finanzamt	finance office
Gau	party region
Gauleiter	party regional leader
Gemeindekrankenkasse	Municipal Health Fund
Gendarmerie	rural police
Gestapo	secret state police
Gewerbeordnung	Reich Commercial Code
Grenzschutz	border patrol
Grundgesetz	Basic Law, Constitution
Grundsetze	basic regulations
Gutsbezirk	manorial estate
Herrenhaus	House of Lords (Prussia)
Hilfskasse	Auxiliary Health Fund
Hoehere SS und Polizei Fuehrer	regional SS and police leader
Innungskrankenkasse	Guild Health Fund
Kaiser	Emperor
Katasteramt	recorder of deeds, assessor's office
Knappschaftskrankenkasse	Miners' Health Fund
Krankenkasse	health fund
Kreisausschuss	county committee
Kreisartz	public health doctor
Kreisleiter	county leader (of Nazi party)
Kreistag	county council
Kreistierartz	public veterinarian
Kriegsernaehrungsamt	War Food Office
Kriminalpolizei	detective forces of the police state
Land	
Landesarbeitsamt	regional unemployment office
Landeshauptmann	Provincial Executive
Landesversicherungsamt	Land Insurance Office

Landgemeinde	rural village
Landkreis	county
Landkreisverband	county league
Landrat	County Director
Landratsamt	county office
Landtag	Land legislature
Landwacht	rural guard
Lastenausgleich	compensatory payments to Germans for World War II damages
Militaeranwaerter	army veterans
Oberbuergermeister	Lord Mayor
Oberfinanzamt	regional finance office
Oberfinanzdirektion	regional finance office
Oberfinanzpraesident	Regional Finance Director
Oberhandelsgericht	High Court for Commercial Law
Oberpraesident	Provincial Governor (Prussia)
Oberversicherungsamt	District Insurance Office
Oberverwaltungsgericht	Supreme Administrative Court (Prussia)
Ordnungspolizei	security police
Ortskrankenkasse	Local Health Fund
Polizeiausschuss	police committee
Polizeipraesident	police commissioner
Provinzial Landtag	provincial legislature
Raeterepublik	soviet republic
Rechnungshof fuer das Deutsche Reich	Reich General Accounting Office
Regierungspraesident	District Officer
Reichsamt	Reich Office
Reichsanstalt	Reich Authority
Reichsanstalt fuer Arbeitsvermittlung und Arbeitslosenversicherung	Reich Authority for Employment Service and Unemployment Insurance
Reichsbevollmaechtige und Inspektoren fuer Zolle und Steuern	Reich Representatives and Inspectors of Customs and Taxes
Reichsexekution	armed intervention by Reich in Land affairs
Reichsfinanzhof	Reich tax court
Reichsland	Reich province
Reichskriminalpolizeiamt	Reich Investigation Agency

Reichsrat	Reich council
Reichsstatthalter	Reich Governor
Reichstag	national legislature
Reichsversicherungsamt	Reich Insurance Office
Reichsversicherungsordnung	Reich Insurance Code
Reichsverteidigungskommissar	Reich civil defense commissar
Rentenausschuss	pension committee
Schulrat	school superintendent
Schutzpolizei	defense security police
Selbstverwaltung	self-government, lay participation in government
Sicherheitsdienst (SD)	intelligence service of Nazi party
Sicherheitspolizei	security police in republican Prussia
Sozialgericht	social court
Stadtwacht	municipal guard
Stadteordnung	City Charter Law
Umsatzsteuer	turn-over tax
Verfassung	constitution
Verordnung	decree, regulation
Versicherungsanstalt	Insurance Authority
Vertrauensmaenner	trustees
Verwaltungsgericht	administrative court
Verwaltungsrat	Administrative Council
Vorstand	Executive Board
Zollamt	customs office
Zustimmungsrecht	absolute veto

YALE STUDIES IN POLITICAL SCIENCE